AGGRESSION REPLACEMENT TRAINING

A Comprehensive Intervention for Aggressive Youth

Arnold P. Goldstein and Barry Glick

with Scott Reiner, Deborah Zimmerman, and Thomas M. Coultry

Research Press
2612 North Mattis Avenue
Champaign Illinois 61821

D0107691

Advisory Editor, Frederick H. Kanfer

Cover design by Ruth Downes
Composition by Omegatype

ISBN 0-87822-283-9
Library of Congress Catalog Card Number 86-61551

With deepest appreciation to

Les Goldberg and Howard Schwartz for their wise counsel and generous encouragement in helping make the idea of this project a reality

and

Alan Alcon, Warren Albrecht, and Sue Yeres for their energetic assistance in facilitating its actual implementation

Contents

Tables and Figures

Acknowledgments

Aggression Replacement Training is the product of many people in addition to the authors and those to whom this book is dedicated. No intervention is any better than the talents and energy of those who implement it. At the Annsville and MacCormick facilities of the New York State Division for Youth, our Aggression Replacement Training group leaders were special education teachers, counselors, and youth division aides. Their contribution to the development, evaluation, and refinement of this intervention was a very special and very much appreciated contribution to the overall success of the project this book seeks to describe. We are indeed very grateful for their expert and creative assistance.

We also benefited greatly from the generous and skillful help of others associated with the New York State Division for Youth or with Syracuse University and in particular would like to express our gratitude to Lawrence DiStefano, Daniel V. Gold, Paul Fiore, and Carren J. Stika. Their aid was invaluable, and is most thoroughly appreciated.

The Aggression Replacement Training research and development program described in this book was supported by research grants 3110 and 3110A from the New York State Division of Criminal Justice Services to the New York State Division for Youth. Their assistance is very deeply appreciated.

Chapter 1

Juvenile Delinquency:
Incidence and Interventions

Crimes against people or property perpetrated by individuals under age 16, that is, juvenile delinquency, have long been a severe problem in the United States. In recent decades, such criminal behavior has become an especially prominent feature of American society. This chapter will address the incidence of juvenile delinquency and the interventions that have been used with such delinquency. The intervention presented in this book, Aggression Replacement Training, is introduced near the end of the chapter.

INCIDENCE

The 1960s and most of the 1970s were clearly the worst decades for juvenile crime. As Strasburg's (1984) examination of national trends indicates, between 1960 and 1975 juvenile arrests grew by nearly 300 percent, more than twice the adult rate. Furthermore, the greatest growth in arrest rate for juveniles occurred for the most violent crimes—robbery (376 percent), aggravated assault (249 percent), and homicide (211 percent). Although juveniles comprised approximately 20 percent of the population in the United States in 1975, they accounted for 43 percent of the arrests that year for the most serious ("index") crimes according to the Federal Bureau of Investigation's Uniform Crime Report (1975). In 1978, again as reported in the FBI's Uniform Crime Report (1978), the absolute numbers of youngsters under age 18 charged with an offense was approximately 2 million, including those charged with larceny (454,994), burglary (250,649), vandalism (104,265), drug abuse (101,855), robbery (48,088), aggravated assault (41,253), forcible rape (4,517), and murder and manslaughter (1,735). Demographic analysis reveals that approximately three-quarters of the youths charged were males, 700,000 were younger than age 15, and 79,000 were younger than age 10. Feldman, Caplinger, and Woodarski (1983) point out that during the 1960s and into the 1970s the overall rate of violent crime in the United States increased by about 67 percent, but for persons under age 18 the increase in violent crime was 167 percent.

Parallel incidence statistics exist for one of the prime settings for juvenile crime—the school. Goldstein, Apter, and Harootunian (1984) note, for example, that in 1974 in the 84,000 schools across the United States there were 270,000 assaults, 9,000 rapes, and 500 million dollars in damage to school property due to vandalism. Assaults on teachers have grown steadily from 18,000 in 1955 to 41,000 in 1971, 63,000 in 1975, and 110,000 in 1979. These figures depict assaults on teachers only; 73 percent of aggravated assaults occurring in school settings are directed at other students. From 1950 to 1974, furthermore, while the number of students in school grew approximately 100 percent, the cost in damage to school property due to arson increased by almost 1,000 percent.

Since 1978, in schools, in homes, and on the streets, the juvenile crime picture has changed somewhat. For crimes against property (e.g., burglary, larceny, and motor vehicle theft), and to a lesser extent for violent crimes (e.g., murder, rape, robbery, and aggravated assault), a modest decrease in juvenile arrest rates is apparent. We agree with Gurr (1979), Strasburg (1984), and others who attribute this modest downward trend mostly to a decrease in the population under age 18 in the United States as the post-World War II baby-boom generation ages. Unfortunately, therefore, one can draw only meager solace from these declining juvenile arrest rates, especially when they are viewed from the perspective of absolute incidence figures. Arrest rates for some crimes may in a *relative* sense be modestly down, but as Table 1 reveals, the *absolute* number of juvenile arrests for crime against persons or property in recent years remains alarmingly high. Furthermore, there are several reasons to suspect that arrest rates may be a serious underestimation of actual juvenile crime. Williams and Gold (1972), for example, estimate that fewer than 3 percent of juvenile offenses are detected by police, and less than 1 percent are subsequently recorded as official delinquent acts. We have elsewhere held the same to be true with regard to juvenile crime in school settings:

> Inconsistent and imprecise definitions of violence and vandalism, inaccurate or nonexistent record keeping, unwillingness to report acts of aggression, fear of reprisal, wide variance in reporting procedures, and school administrators' concern with appearing inadequate each may lead to markedly underestimated incidence statistics. In fact, it has been estimated that actual levels of school violence and vandalism may be as much as 50 percent higher than generally reported. (Goldstein et al., 1984, p. 9)

Beyond rates and absolute levels that remain a continuing source of concern in American society, what else do juvenile crime incidence figures tell us? Juvenile males are delinquent more than juvenile females in a ratio of 4:1, with females beginning to close the gap in recent years, especially with regard to the number of violent (not property) offenses. This trend toward increased (especially violent) crimes by juvenile females has been evident in a number of European countries also (Pulkkinen & Saastomoinen, 1986). For males, robbery is the most frequent violent crime; for females it is aggravated assault (Strasburg, 1984). For both males and females, in the United States and elsewhere, the average age of arrest for first offense is decreasing. Juvenile arrests are not only occurring for younger and younger children, but this trend is sufficiently pronounced that the peak age for first arrests is now below age 13. Black youth, male or female and at all age levels, are arrested for juvenile delinquency at a rate five times that of white youth. By crime category, the black to white ratios are 3:1 for violent crimes and 11:1 for theft. According to Strasburg (1984), in 1981 black juveniles composed 2.6 percent of the total population and were charged with 19 percent of all robbery arrests. Such statistics, of course, do not speak to such possible artifactual influences upon the arrest rates and criminal behavior of black juveniles as police discretion, social class influences, a cultural history of prejudice and discrimination, and similar confounding variables. Juvenile crime is much more likely to occur (5:1) in urban than rural settings, but perhaps surprisingly does not occur at its highest rates in America's largest cities. Instead, small- to medium-size American cities with populations of 10,000 to 100,000 have the highest juvenile crime rates. Compared to persons over age 16 who commit crimes, juvenile offenders are more likely to act in groups, less likely to use a gun, and equally likely to use a knife or other weapon. The victim of a juvenile offense is seven times more likely to be another juvenile than an adult and is also more likely to be female than male, older than younger, black than white, poor than wealthy. Most commonly, the victim is another juvenile previously known to the offender.

Aside from whatever value knowledge of these diverse correlates of juvenile crime may have for the planning and implementation of prevention or rehabilitative interventions, this information and the incidence rates noted earlier begin to point to the awesome human and financial costs of juvenile delinquency. Delinquency is expensive, very expensive—in pain, unhappiness, unrealized ambition, and money—to its victims, its perpetrators, and to society at large. The goal of creating, implementing, evaluating, and, when appropriate, disseminating successful interventions for the prevention or reduction of juvenile crime should indeed be very high on America's unfinished public agenda.

Table 1.

	1970	1971	1972	1973	1974	1975
Murder and nonnegligent manslaughter	1,346	1,490	1,634	1,497	1,399	1,273
Forcible rape	3,205	3,424	3,842	3,772	3,455	3,093
Robbery	29,289	32,755	34,823	34,374	35,345	41,001
Aggravated assault	20,756	24,633	27,256	26,270	26,230	29,138
Burglary	148,296	160,431	160,376	170,228	181,689	186,481
Larceny	312,066	340,261	336,983	310,452	356,695	379,206
Motor vehicle theft	71,456	69,313	65,255	66,868	59,183	53,802
Arson	5,594	6,180	6,203	6,491	6,318	6,237
Violent crime	54,596	62,302	67,555	65,913	66,499	74,505
Percentage of all violent crime	(22.6)	(22.8)	(22.6)	(22.7)	(22.6)	(24.8)
Property crime	531,818	570,005	562,614	547,548	597,567	619,489
Percentage of all property crime	(51.7)	(50.8)	(50.5)	(50.8)	(50.7)	(48.9)
Total of all crimes	1,660,643	1,796,942	1,793,984	1,717,366	1,683,073	1,740,212
Percentage of all crimes	(25.3)	(25.8)	(25.6)	(26.4)	(27.2)	(27.1)

Note: Data are for youths under age 18. Compiled from Federal Bureau of Investigation *Uniform Crime Reports*, 1970–1984. Washington, DC: U.S. Government Printing Office.

Juvenile Arrests, 1970-1984

1976	1977	1978	1979	1980	1981	1982	1983	1984
1,302	1,670	1,735	1,707	1,742	1,858	1,579	1,345	1,004
3,745	4,257	4,517	4,651	4,346	4,449	4,159	4,388	4,397
36,990	39,259	48,088	41,157	41,997	42,214	36,480	35,219	27,795
32,678	36,182	41,253	39,860	38,135	37,332	34,145	33,730	31,148
209,396	233,904	250,649	227,680	215,387	208,650	172,838	159,192	127,708
399,235	431,747	454,994	444,053	421,082	417,346	371,296	377,435	338,785
58,279	71,648	77,534	70,676	58,798	49,449	39,141	36,497	33,838
7,601	8,235	8,760	9,012	8,161	8,210	6,282	6,457	6,244
74,715	81,368	95,593	87,375	86,220	85,853	76,363	74,682	64,344
(22.0)	(21.0)	(21.4)	(20.1)	(19.3)	(18.5)	(17.2)	(16.8)	(16.8)
666,910	737,299	783,177	751,421	703,428	683,655	589,557	579,581	506,575
(46.1)	(46.2)	(45.5)	(43.5)	(40.2)	(37.4)	(34.5)	(33.9)	(34.9)
1,973,254	2,170,193	2,279,365	2,143,369	2,025,713	2,035,748	1,804,688	1,725,746	1,537,688
(24.9)	(24.0)	(23.3)	(22.5)	(20.9)	(19.8)	(17.9)	(16.8)	(17.2)

5

INTERVENTIONS

Custodialism versus Habilitation

America is getting tough. After a decade of a juvenile justice system which in diverse ways had habilitation* as its ultimate goal and a firm, benevolent parent-like role as its aspired-to mode of operation, "the precepts of 'aid, encouragement, and guidance' are being replaced by the principles of punishment and 'just desserts.' Throughout the land, the rehabilitative ideals of the juvenile court are being reviewed and overshadowed by concern with community protection, punishment, retribution, and, increasingly, secure confinement" (Fagan & Hartstone, 1984, pp. 31-32). In part, it is the political and philosophical climate current in America today that fosters this punitive, custodially oriented view of juvenile corrections. This view, combined with opposition to a habilitation perspective, also grows from imperfections in the juvenile justice system itself—bureaucratic and overburdened court functioning, spiraling costs, denial of youth's constitutional rights, the effects of labeling and stigmatizing, and "prisonization" (the effects of association with other felons), among others. Such concerns, though often overstated, are not without a basis in fact. What we would *not* acknowledge, however, is the main argument utilized by "hard-liners" for moving away from habilitation and toward custodialism in juvenile corrections: that is, the purported failure of habilitation itself. In our view, as we will elaborate, this shift away from habilitation is premature, cost ineffective, and nonprescriptive.

Our prohabilitation stance may surprise many readers, given the apparently consistent negative outcome of a long series of investigations evaluating diverse interventions with juvenile offenders. Study after study reports an apparent failure of habilitation (Bailey, 1966; Gray & Dermody, 1972; Kahn, 1965; Kassenbaum, Ward, & Wilner, 1979; Lipton, Martinson, & Wilks, 1975; Robinson & Smith, 1971; Romig, 1978; Sechrest, White, & Brown, 1979; Wright & Dixon, 1977). Rutter and Giller (1983) summarize the consensus accurately:

---

*We will use the term "habilitation" rather than "rehabilitation" to describe the diverse counseling, psychotherapy, group-oriented, behavior modification, and related intervention programs utilized with juvenile delinquents in the belief that the goal of these programs is to enhance behaviors and attitudes not previously in the repertoires of the juveniles involved. "Rehabilitation" connotes efforts to reinstate earlier learned qualities now in disuse. "Habilitation," in contrast, conveys teaching of that which was never previously learned. The interventions described above typically have as their dual goals the unlearning of antisocial attitudes and behaviors and the new learning of prosocial ones. Thus, our choice of the term habilitation.

Though the relevant literature is immense, most reviews have ended with essentially negative conclusions—"no delinquent prevention strategies can be definitely recommended" (Wright & Dixon, 1977); "with few and isolated exceptions the rehabilitative efforts that have been reported so far have had no appreciable effect on recidivism" (Martinson, 1974); "studies which have produced positive results have been isolated, inconsistent in their evidence, and open to so much methodological criticism that they must remain unconvincing" (Brody, 1978). (Rutter & Giller, 1983, p. 267)

To be sure, delinquency intervention research—as with most intervention research—suffers from very substantial methodological faults. Much of this research involves a lack of appropriate controls, inadequate samples in both size and randomness of selection, poorly conceived and inconsistently implemented interventions, inadequate or inappropriate outcome measures, insufficient attention to minimizing threats to internal or external validity, use of inappropriate statistical analyses, and/or inattention to follow-up measurement—a veritable rogue's gallery of experimental weaknesses. That the relevant research is weak is clear; what is less clear is why a strong conclusion—that habilitation does not work—should follow from weak research. Rather, we would hold the relevant evidence, instead of being interpreted as proof of lack of effectiveness, should more parsimoniously be viewed as indeterminate, generally neither adding to nor detracting from a conclusion of effectiveness or ineffectiveness. As Fagan and Hartstone (1984) observe, accepting the conclusion that nothing works is premature for at least two reasons. First, the evaluation research practices have many weaknesses, and, second, a persistent problem with many studies has been the failure to accurately implement the intended treatment approach. "If the treatment was not operationalized from theory, not delivered as prescribed, or incorrectly measured, even the strongest evaluation design will show 'no impact'" (p. 208). The 1979 Panel on the Rehabilitation of Criminal Offenders (quoted in Fagan and Hartstone, p. 208) concluded that

> research on offender rehabilitation should be pursued more vigorously, more systematically, more imaginatively, and more rigorously. Specifically, treatments should be based upon strong theoretical rationales, perhaps involving total programs rather than weak or piecemeal treatments. In addition, the strength and integrity of all treatments should be monitored and fully documented, along with documentation of the costs of operation of the treatment.

These sentiments strongly reflect our own perspective on altering the attitudes and behaviors of juvenile delinquents. Custodialism as the intervention of choice is, we believe, a poor decision. It is, in its broad, nonprescriptive use, neither humane nor cost effective, nor is it likely to lead to even moderately long-term changes in offender behavior. Custodialism and its reflection in such procedures and views as more punitive sentencing practices, the growing tendency to adjudicate juvenile felons in adult court, and the denigration of habilitative interventions should find fuller use in America's juvenile justice system *only* when and if a great deal more high-quality research on intervention practices has been conducted and much more unequivocally has shown such habilitative interventions to be ineffective. Our course now should be, as the 1979 Panel on the Rehabilitation of Criminal Offenders enjoined, evaluation research designed and carried out with vigor, rigor, imagination, systematization, and, especially, we would add, full reflection of what we believe will prove to be the main avenue of success in the search for effective delinquency interventions, that is, prescriptive programming.

Prescriptive Programming

Our central belief and operating assumption with regard to all habilitative interventions for juvenile delinquents, including the particular intervention that forms most of the substance of this book, is that effective intervention is differential intervention. Simple to define in general terms, but quite difficult to implement effectively, prescriptive programming recognizes that different juveniles will be responsive to different change methods. The central question in prescriptive programming with juvenile delinquents is *Which types of youth, meeting with which types of change agents, for which types of interventions will yield optimal outcomes?* This is a view that runs counter to the prevailing "one-true-light" assumption underlying most intervention efforts directed toward juvenile offenders. The one-true-light assumption, the antithesis of a prescriptive viewpoint, holds that specific treatments are sufficiently powerful to override substantial individual differences and aid heterogeneous groups of patients.

Research in all fields of psychotherapy has shown the one-true-light assumption to be erroneous (Goldstein, 1978; Goldstein & Stein, 1976). Palmer (1975) has shown it to be especially in error with regard to aggressive and delinquent adolescents. Palmer reviewed a study by Martinson (1974) that examined a large number of diverse intervention efforts designed to alter the deviant behavior of juvenile offenders. Martinson concluded in his review that "with few and isolated exceptions, the rehabilitative efforts that have been reported so far have had no appreciable effect on recidivism" (p. 25), but Palmer pointed out that this conclusion was based on the one-true-light assumption. In each of the dozens of studies reviewed by Martinson, there were homogeneous subsamples of adolescents for whom the given treatments under study had worked. Martinson had been unresponsive to the fact that when homogeneous subsamples are combined to form a heterogeneous full sample, the various positive, negative, and no-change treatment outcome effects of the subsamples cancel each other out. Thus the full sample appears no different than an untreated group. But when smaller, more homogeneous subsamples are examined separately, many treatments do work. The task then is not to continue the futile pursuit of the one treatment that works for all, but instead to discern which treatments administered by which treatment providers work for whom and for whom they do not.

Both the spirit and substance of the "many-true-lights" prescriptive programming viewpoint have their roots in analogous thinking and programming in change endeavors with populations other than juvenile delinquents. In work with emotionally disturbed adults and children, for example, there is Kiesler's (1969) grid model matching treaters, treatments, and clients; Magaro's (1969) individualization of psychotherapy offered and psychotherapist offering it as a function of patient social class and premorbid personality; and our own factorial, tridifferential research schema for enhancing the development of prescriptive matches (Goldstein, 1978; Goldstein & Stein, 1976). In elementary and secondary education contexts, examples of prescriptive programming include Keller's (1966) personalized instruction; Cronbach and Snow's (1977) aptitude-treatment interactions; Hunt's (1972) matching of student conceptual level and teacher instructional style; and Klausmeier, Rossmiller, and Sailey's (1977) individually guided education model.

These ample precedents, however, are not the only beginnings of concern with prescriptive programs in juvenile corrections. In addition to these precedents, early research specifically with juvenile delinquents also points to the value of prescriptive programming. Several of the early findings of successful outcomes for specific interventions with subgroups of juvenile delinquents appear to be almost serendipitous side results of studies searching for overriding, one-true-light effects, a circumstance slightly diminishing their generalizability. Nonetheless, it is worth noting the differential effectiveness of each of the two most widely used interventions with juvenile delinquents—individual and group psychotherapy.

Individual psychotherapy has been shown to be effective with highly anxious delinquent adolescents (Adams, 1962), the socially withdrawn (Stein & Bogin, 1978), those displaying at most a moderate level of psychopathic behavior (Carney, 1966; Craft, Stephenson, & Granger, 1964), and those who display a set of characteristics summarized by Adams (1961) as "amenable." Adolescents who are more blatantly psychopathic, who manifest a low level of anxiety, or those who are "nonamenable" in Adams's terms are appropriately viewed as poor candidates for individual psychotherapy interventions.

Many group approaches have been developed in attempts to aid delinquent adolescents. Some of the more popular have been Activity Group Therapy (Slavson, 1964), Guided Group Interaction (McCorkle, Elias, & Bixby, 1958), and Positive Peer Culture (Vorrath & Brendtro, 1974). Research demonstrates that such approaches are indeed useful for older, more sociable and person-oriented adolescents (Knight, 1969), for those who tend to be confrontation-accepting (Warren, 1974), for the more neurotic-conflicted (Harrison & Mueller, 1964), and for the acting-out neurotic (California Department of the Youth Authority, 1967). Juveniles who are younger, less sociable, or more delinquent (Knight, 1969) or who are confrontation-avoiding (Warren, 1974) or psychopathic (Craft et al., 1964) are less likely to benefit from group intervention. Other investigations also report differentially positive results for such subsamples of delinquents receiving individual or group psychotherapy as "immature-neurotic" (Jesness, 1965), short-term rather than long-term incarceration (Bernstein & Christiansen, 1965), "conflicted" (Glaser, 1973), and those "reacting to an adolescent growth crisis" (Warren, 1974).

Other investigators, studying these and other interventions, continue to succumb to their own one-true-light beliefs and suggest or imply that their nondifferentially applied approach is an appropriate blanket prescription, useful with all delinquent subtypes. Keith (1984) writes in this manner as he reviews the past and current use of psychoanalytically oriented psychotherapy with juvenile delinquents. Others assume an analogously broad, nonprescriptive stance toward group psychotherapy (Lavin, Trabka, & Kahn, 1984), family therapy (Curry, Wiencrot, & Koehler, 1984), and behavior modification—although in this last instance there in fact exists very substantial evidence that the sets of interventions comprising behavior modification do have very broad effectiveness, at least for the acquisition of new behaviors (Davidson & Seidman, 1974; Mayer, Gensheimer, Davidson, & Gottschalk, 1986). Yet even here, and perhaps especially here, there is a great deal of prescriptive research to be done. The good results of behavior modification used as a blanket prescription offer the promise of even better outcomes if behavior modification is employed in the form of differential prescriptions. As Redner, Snellman, and Davidson (1983) observe:

> Yes, behavioral interventions with delinquent populations seem successful, particularly with program related and prosocial behaviors. However, one can neither specify optimal conditions for the behavioral treatment of delinquents nor claim that behavioral interventions are extremely successful in reducing recidivism for any length of time. This area of research has consistently omitted the experimental manipulation of such potentially important variables as the role of the change agent, *participant characteristics*, and setting characteristics, which would allow one to make suggestions for optimal intervention conditions. (p. 218, italics added)

The utility of the differential intervention perspective with juvenile delinquents apparently also extends appropriately to interventions that are less directly psychotherapeutic and more singularly correctional/administrative in nature. There is evidence that probation, for example, may yield better outcomes for adolescent offenders who are neurotic (Empey, 1969), who display a reasonable level of prosocial behavior (Garrity, 1956) or social maturity (Sealy & Banks, 1971), or who are, in the terminology of the Interpersonal Maturity System, "Cultural Conformists" (California Department of the Youth Authority, 1967). Probation appears to be a substantially less useful prescriptive intervention when the youth is nonneurotic (Empey, 1969), manipulative (Garrity, 1956), or low in social maturity (Sealy & Banks, 1971).

Diversion from the juvenile justice system is a more recent correctional/administrative intervention than probation, so less opportunity has existed for its differential utilization and examination. Yet even here, as Gensheimer, Mayer, Gottschalk, and Davidson (1986) demonstrate in their meta-analysis of existing studies of the efficacy of diversion, while *overall* results do not support its value on efficacy criteria of recidivism; self-reported delinquency; program, academic, social, or vocational behaviors; school or work attendance; self-esteem levels; or global ratings of adjustment, there may well be prescriptive exceptions to these negative combined results, just as these exceptions exist for subpopulations of delinquents receiving psychotherapy. Younger delinquents appear to profit more from diversion than older adolescents. Those delinquents in diversion programs for lengthy periods change more than those involved for shorter periods. The prescriptive programming strategy, if more fully applied here, would perhaps more discerningly identify other types of youth and additional diversion program characteristics that yield higher levels of outcome efficacy. Such a result is obscured, as we noted earlier, when adolescents of all types or programs of all types are aggregated into large samples for overall analyses of effects.

In our exploration of prescriptive programming to this point we have focused on two of the three classes of variables that combine to yield optimal prescriptions—the interventions and types of youth to whom the interventions are directed. But optimal prescriptions should be tridifferential, specifying type of intervention by type of client by type of change agent. It is this last class of variable we now wish to briefly address. Interventions, *as received by the youths to whom they are directed,* are never identical to the procedures as specified in a textbook or treatment manual. The intervention received is as specified in a manual—as interpreted and implemented by the change agent—as perceived and experienced by the youth. The change agent looms large in this sequence and, just as we have all along dismissed the idea that all delinquents are equivalent, so too must we get beyond practices that treat all change agents as the same. Who administers the intervention does make a difference, an assertion for which there already exists supporting, if preliminary, evidence in the context of administering interventions to juvenile delinquents. Grant and Grant (1959) report finding internally oriented change agents to be highly effective with high-maturity offenders, but detrimental to low-maturity offenders. Palmer (1973) found "relationship/self-expression" change agents achieved their best results with "communicative-alert, impulsive-anxious, or verbally hostile-defensive" youths, and did least well with "dependent-anxious" ones. Change agents characterized as "surveillance/self-control" did poorly with "verbally hostile-defensive" or "defiant-indifferent" delinquents, but quite well with the "dependent-anxious." Agee (1979) reported similar optimal pairings. In her work, delinquents and the change agents responsible for them were each divided into expressive and instrumental subtypes.

The expressive group contained adolescents who were overtly vulnerable, hurting, and dependent. The instrumental group contained youths who were defended against their emotions, independent, and nontrusting.

Expressive staff members were defined as open with expressing their feelings and working with the feelings of others. They typically value therapy and personal growth and see this as an ongoing process personally and for the youths they treat. Unlike the expressive delinquent youngsters though, they have resolved past problems and are good role models because of their ability to establish warm, rewarding interpersonal relationships.

Instrumental staff members were defined as not being as comfortable with feelings as the expressive staff members were. They are more likely to be invested in getting the job done than processing feelings and are more alert to behavioral issues. They appear self-confident, cool, and somewhat distant, which impresses the instrumental delinquent.

Agee (1979) indeed reports evidence suggesting the outcome superiority of (1) expressive-expressive and (2) instrumental-instrumental youth-change agent pairings, a finding in substantial part confirmed in our own examination of optimal change agent empathy levels when working with delinquent youth (Edelman & Goldstein, 1984).

This book describes the first several stages of a longer, ongoing prescriptive programming effort, and hence we have devoted a great deal of this initial chapter to the prescriptive programming strategy and its evidential support to date. In this chapter's final section we wish to begin introducing the reader to the intervention that has been the target of our development and evaluation and describe how these efforts reflect the initial stages of this prescriptive programming perspective.

AN INTRODUCTION TO AGGRESSION REPLACEMENT TRAINING

Any and every act of juvenile delinquency has multiple causes, both within and external to the youth himself. With regard to internal causes, as we will elaborate in considerable detail in the chapters that follow, there is ample evidence to support the belief that delinquents frequently possess a series of interlocking and often reciprocally compounding deficiencies. They rather characteristically are weak or lacking in much of the broad array of personal, interpersonal, and social-cognitive *skills* that collectively constitute effective prosocial behavior. Their not infrequent impulsiveness and overreliance on aggressive means for goal attainment frequently reflects deficiency in *anger control*. In the cognitive realm, chronically delinquent adolescents have been shown to characteristically reason at the more egocentric, concrete, and, in a sense, more primitive levels of *moral reasoning*. Our overriding belief in selecting the individual interventions that as a group constitute Aggression Replacement Training (ART) was that it was these three core deficiencies to which we optimally should respond. While there are many other internal and external antecedents of delinquent behavior than those we addressed in ART, we predicted that much of the outcome variance associated with efforts to change such behavior would occur in the domains of enhanced prosocial skill proficiency, heightened anger control, and advancing levels of moral reasoning.

ART, therefore, consists of three coordinated interventions. *Structured Learning* is a set of procedures designed to enhance prosocial skill levels (Goldstein, 1973, 1981). It grows directly from the social learning, behavior-deficit model advanced by Bandura (1969, 1973) and consists of a series of social learning instructional procedures. Concretely, in Structured Learning, small groups of delinquent adolescents are (1) shown several examples of expert use of the behaviors that constitute the skills in which they are deficient (i.e., *modeling*); (2) given several guided opportunities to practice and rehearse these competent behaviors (i.e., *role playing*); (3) provided with praise, reinstruction, and related feedback on how well their role-playing skill enactments matched the expert model's portrayals (i.e., *performance feedback*); and (4) encouraged to engage in a series of activities designed to increase the chances that skills learned in the training setting will endure and be available for use when needed in school, home, community, institution, or other real-world settings (i.e., *transfer training*). By these means—modeling, role playing, performance feedback, and transfer training—instruction is offered in a curriculum of 10 prosocial skills. The historical development of Structured Learning, its current status, and its research foundation are described in detail in Chapter 2. A complete presentation of its constituent procedures and skills curriculum comprises Chapter 3.

Anger Control Training, the second component of ART, was developed by Feindler and her research group (Feindler, Marriott, & Iwata, 1984) at Adelphi University, based in substantial part on the earlier anger control and stress inoculation research, respectively, of Novaco (1975) and Meichenbaum (1977). Anger Control Training, in complement to Structured Learning's goal of prosocial behavior facilitation, teaches antisocial behavior inhibition, that is, the reduction, management, or control of anger and aggression. It does so by training youths to respond to provocations ("hassles") which heretofore had elicited anger with, instead, a chain of responses consisting of (1) triggers—identifying internal (self-statement) and external events that function as one's anger stimuli; (2) cues—kinesthetic or other physiological sensations or experiences signifying anger arousal; (3) reminders—the first of several anger-reducing techniques taught (in this instance, how to generate arousal-reducing self-statements); (4) reducers—techniques such as backward counting, deep breathing, peaceful imagery, and reflection on long-term consequences; (5) utilization of the appropriate Structured Learning skill alternative to anger or aggression; (6) self-evaluation—of the utilization and results of Steps 1 through 5 in the anger control sequence. The background, development, and evidential basis for Anger Control Training is the focus of Chapter 4; its procedures and curriculum constitute Chapter 5.

Moral Education is the third intervention comprising ART. Armed with both the enhanced ability to respond to the real world prosocially and the skills necessary to stifle or at least diminish impulsive anger and aggression, will the chronically acting-out youth in fact choose to use these skills? To enhance the likelihood of this choice, one must enter, we believe, into the realm of moral values. In a long and pioneering series of investigations, Kohlberg (1969, 1973) has demonstrated that exposing youths to a series of moral dilemmas in a discussion-group context that includes youths reasoning at differing levels of moral thinking arouses an experience of cognitive conflict whose resolution will frequently advance a youth's moral reasoning to that of the higher level peers in the group. While such moral reasoning stage advancement is a reliable finding, as with other single interventions, efforts to utilize it by itself as a means of enhancing actual overt moral behavior have yielded only mixed success at best (Arbuthnot & Gordon, 1983; Zimmerman, 1983); perhaps, we would speculate, because such youths did not have in their behavioral repertoires either the actual skill behaviors for acting prosocially or for successfully inhibiting the antisocial behaviors. We thus reasoned that Kohlbergian Moral Education has marked potential for enhancing prosocialness and reducing antisocialness in youths who have successfully undergone both Structured Learning and Anger Control Training. Chapter 6 examines theory and research bearing upon Moral Education in considerable detail, and Chapter 7 provides a complete presentation of its procedures, curriculum, and materials.

As research reviewed in the following chapters will make clear, each of the three intervention sequences that constitutes ART results in substantial change in those to whom it is directed. But in each instance there are limitations on the change obtained. Both Structured Learning and Anger Control Training yield reliable and considerable immediate and short-term alteration in their respective target behaviors, but neither has shown equally reliable longer term effects yet. Moral Education, as noted above, seems to impinge with consistency upon values, but much less frequently can changes in moral behavior be shown. Therefore, we reasoned that the combination of these three interventions, in fact, *this* combination in particular, might yield more reliable and longer term positive outcomes than each can or has done individually. In asserting this hypothesis, we rely on three different if overlapping rationales—the generally superior potency of multimodal interventions, the utility of construction treatment strategies, and the likely fruitfulness of incremental prescription building. With regard to the first of these rationales, multimodal intervention packages, we have commented elsewhere that

> behavior change in our view may result from interventions which are explicitly targeted on overt behavior, or which seek to diminish emotional responses which inhibit use of behaviors already in the person's behavioral repertoire, or which provide information about the consequences of alternative behaviors. Behavioral, affective, and cognitive interventions each in these differing ways possess potential for altering overt behaviors. Which, and how many of these alternative intervention routes will correspond to any given youngster's channels of accessibility will obviously vary from youngster to youngster. We believe, however, that it generally will prove efficacious to take more than one route simultaneously. The source and maintainers of aggression are diverse and multi-channeled. So too must its remediation be. Structured Learning is our *behavioral* intervention; Anger Control Training is *affective* in its substance; Moral Education is *cognitive* in nature. Guided by our multimodal philosophy, it is our hypothesis that these interventions will yield outcomes superior to those resulting from single-channel interventions. (Goldstein, Glick, Reiner, Zimmerman, Coultry, & Gold, in press)

In our development, implementation, and evaluation of ART, we have also sought to execute a constructive treatment strategy, an approach to intervention research and development described well by Kazdin (1980):

> The constructive treatment strategy refers to developing a treatment package by adding components to enhance therapy.... With the constructive approach the investigator usually begins with a basic treatment component that is relatively narrow or circumscribed in focus. Research is conducted that adds various ingredients to the basic treatment to determine what enhances treatment effects. As research continues, effective components are retained and a large treatment package is constructed. (p. 87)

Finally, ART, consistent with one of this chapter's major themes, is in its development and investigation an ongoing example of incremental prescription building. Describing this treatment-enhancement strategy elsewhere, we observed:

Bergin and Strupp (1972) have urged an incremental prescriptive strategy, one in which partial or tentative prescriptions are replicated, combined, and empirically examined in such a manner that one can ascertain whether the percent of outcome variance accounted for is, as predicted, progressively increasing. Klett and Moseley (1963) champion a similar incremental strategy. They propose a prescription-building process in which (a) active treatment ingredients are identified, (b) their weighting vis-à-vis outcome variance is determined, (c) ingredients are combined into new sets and combinations, and (d) the new prescriptive combinations are offered, evaluated, reweighted and so forth. (Goldstein & Stein, 1976, p. 19)

Central to the notions of multimodal intervention, constructive treatment strategy, and incremental prescription building is the belief that the development of effective habilitative interventions for juvenile delinquency is a process optimally without end, an ongoing search for ever more effective solutions. It is a process exemplified by this book, for ART is much more than a beginning and much less than an end in this search. Where our effort now lies, what we have accomplished thus far, and where we hope our future explorations will take us is what this book is all about.

FORMAT OF THIS BOOK

This book presents the ART program as it was used in our research with juvenile delinquents. We worked with small groups (6-12) of boys and used a 10-week training format, involving weekly classes for each component of ART. The following chapters present all of the procedures and materials needed to implement the program in schools and in delinquency facilities.

We present background research on Structured Learning, Anger Control Training, and Moral Education, and a training manual for each with guidelines for the trainer in Chapters 2 through 7. Chapter 8 describes in detail how we implemented and evaluated the program in two treatment facilities and our results. Chapter 9 presents future directions for both the use and evaluation of ART and the expansion of such training to the community. Chapter 10 will be of special interest to administrators of youth facilities. It presents details of how the Annsville Youth Center in New York implemented the program. Annsville's statement of program description and philosophy is also included. Appendix A presents instruments that can be used for assessment and research. The "transfer coach" in Appendix B presents methods for aiding the transfer of skills learned in ART to the real world.

Chapter 2

The Behavioral Component of ART: Structured Learning

Until the early 1970s, there were primarily three major clusters of psychotherapies designed to alter the behavior of aggressive, unhappy, ineffective, or disturbed individuals: psychodynamic/psychoanalytic, humanistic/client-centered, and behavior modification. Each of these diverse orientations found concrete expression in individual and group interventions targeted to aggressive adolescents: the psychodynamic in psychoanalytically oriented individual psychotherapy (Guttman, 1970), activity group therapy (Slavson, 1964), and the varied array of treatment procedures developed by Redl and Wineman (1957); the humanistic/client-centered in the applications to juvenile delinquents (e.g., Truax, Wargo, & Silber, 1966) of the client-centered psychotherapy of Carl Rogers (1957), the therapeutic community applications of Jones (1953), Guided Group Interaction (McCorkle et al., 1958), Positive Peer Culture (Vorrath & Brendtro, 1974), and the school discipline approach of Dreikurs, Grunwald, and Pepper (1971); and behavior modification in a wide variety of interventions reflecting the systematic use of contingency management, contracting, and the training of teachers and parents as behavior change managers (O'Leary, O'Leary, & Becker, 1967; Patterson, Cobb, & Ray, 1973; Walker, 1979). Though each of these intervention philosophies differs from the others in several major respects, one of their significant commonalities is the shared assumption that the client had somewhere within himself, as yet unexpressed, the effective, satisfying, nonaggressive, or prosocial behaviors whose expression was among the goals of the intervention. Such latent potentials would be realized by the client in all three approaches if the change agent were sufficiently skilled in reducing or removing obstacles to such realization. The psychodynamic therapist sought to do so by calling forth and interpreting unconscious material blocking progress-relevant awareness. The client-centered change agent, who, in particular, believed that the potential for change resides within the client, sought to free this potential by providing a warm, empathic, maximally accepting helping environment. And the behavior modifier, by means of one or more contingency management procedures, attempted to assure that when the latent desirable behaviors or approximations thereof did occur, the client would receive appropriate contingent reinforcement, thus increasing the probability that these behaviors would recur. Therefore, whether sought by means of interpretation, therapeutic climate, or contingent reward, all three approaches assumed that somewhere within the individual's repertoire resided the desired, effective, sought-after goal behaviors.

PSYCHOLOGICAL SKILLS TRAINING

In the early 1970s, an important new intervention approach began to emerge, psychological skills training, an approach resting upon rather different assumptions. Viewing the "helpee" more in educational, pedagogic terms than as a client in need of counseling or psychotherapy, the psychological skills trainer assumed he was dealing with an individual lacking, deficient, or at best weak in the skills necessary for effective and satisfying personal and interpersonal functioning. The task of the skills trainer became, therefore, not interpretation, reflection, or reinforcement but the active and deliberate teaching of desirable behaviors. Rather than an intervention called psychotherapy, between a patient and psychotherapist, or counseling, between a client and a counselor, what emerged was an intervention called training, between a trainee and a psychological skills trainer.

The roots of the psychological skills training movement lie in both education and psychology. The notion of literally seeking to teach desirable behaviors has often, if sporadically, been a significant goal of the American educational establishment. The Character Education Movement of the 1920s and more contemporary Moral Education and Values Clarification programs are but a few of several possible examples. Add to this institutionalized educational interest in skills training the hundreds of interpersonal and planning skills courses taught in the more than 2,000 community colleges across the United States and the hundreds of self-help books oriented toward similar skill-enhancement goals that are available to the public, and it becomes clear that the formal and informal educational establishment provided fertile soil and explicit stimulation within which the psychological skills training movement could grow.

Much the same can be said for American psychology, as its prevailing philosophy and concrete interests also laid the groundwork for the development of this new movement. The learning process has above all else been the central theoretical and investigative concern of American psychology since the late 19th century. This focal interest also assumed major therapeutic form in the 1950s, as psychotherapy practitioners and researchers alike came to view psychotherapeutic treatment more and more in learning terms. The very healthy and still expanding field of behavior modification grew from this joint learning-clinical focus and may be appropriately viewed as the immediately preceding context from which psychological skills training emerged. Concurrent with the growth of behavior modification, psychological thinking increasingly shifted from a strict emphasis on remediation to one equally concerned with prevention, and the bases for this shift included movement away from a medical model concept toward what may most aptly be called a psychoeducational theoretical stance. Both of these thrusts—heightened concern with prevention and a psychoeducational perspective—gave strong added impetus to the viability of the psychological skills training movement.

Perhaps psychology's most direct contribution to psychological skills training came from social learning theory and, in particular, from the work conducted or inspired by Albert Bandura. Regarding the same broad array of modeling, behavioral rehearsal, and social reinforcement investigations that helped stimulate and direct the development of our own approach to skills training, Bandura (1973) comments:

> The method that has yielded the most impressive results with diverse problems contains three major components. First, alternative modes of response are repeatedly modeled, preferably by several people who demonstrate how the new style of behavior can be used in dealing with a variety of . . . situations. Second, learners are provided with necessary guidance and ample opportunities to practice the modeled behavior under favorable conditions until they perform it skillfully and spontaneously. The latter procedures are ideally suited for developing new social skills, but they are unlikely to be adopted unless they produce rewarding consequences. Arrangement of success experiences particularly for initial efforts at behaving differently, constitute the third component in this powerful composite method. . . . Given adequate demonstration, guided practice, and success experiences, this method is almost certain to produce favorable results. (p. 253)

Other events of the 1970s provided still further stimulation for the growth of the skills training movement. The inadequacy of prompting, shaping, and related operant procedures for adding *new* behaviors to individuals' behavioral repertoires was increasingly apparent. The widespread reliance upon deinstitutionalization that lay at the heart of the community mental health movement resulted in the discharge from public mental hospitals of approximately 400,000 persons, the majority of whom were substantially deficient in important daily functioning skills. In addition, it had become clear, especially to us, that what the American mental health movement had available to offer clients from lower socioeconomic levels was grossly inadequate in meeting their psychotherapeutic needs. These factors—relevant supportive research, the incompleteness of operant approaches, large populations of grossly skill-deficient individuals, and the paucity of useful interventions for large segments of American society—along with historically supportive roots in both education and psychology, suggested to several researchers and practitioners the need for a new intervention, something prescriptively responsive to the several deficiencies of existing interventions. Psychological skills training was the answer, and a movement was launched.

Our involvement in this movement, a psychological skills training approach we have termed Structured Learning, began in the early 1970s. At that time, and for several years thereafter, our studies were conducted in public mental hospitals with long-term, highly skill-deficient, chronic patients, especially those preparing for deinstitutionalization into the community. As our research program progressed and demonstrated with regularity successful skill-enhancement effects (Goldstein, 1981), we shifted our focus from teaching a broad array of interpersonal and daily living skills to adult psychiatric inpatients to a more explicit concern with skill training for aggressive individuals. Our trainee groups included spouses engaged in family disputes violent enough to warrant police intervention (Goldstein, Monti, Sardino, & Green, 1977; Goldstein & Rosenbaum, 1982), child-abusing parents (Goldstein, Keller, & Erné, 1985; Solomon, 1977; Sturm, 1980), and, most especially, overtly aggressive adolescents (Goldstein, Sherman, Gershaw, Sprafkin, & Glick, 1978; Goldstein, Sprafkin, Gershaw, & Klein, 1980).

SKILL DEFICIENCY AND JUVENILE DELINQUENCY

A substantial body of literature has in fact directly demonstrated that delinquent and other aggressive children and teenagers display widespread interpersonal, planning, aggression management, and other psychological skill deficiencies. Freedman, Rosenthal, Donahoe, Schlundt, and McFall (1978) examined the comparative skill competence levels of a group of juvenile delinquents and a matched group (age, IQ, socioeconomic background) of nonoffenders in response to a series of standardized role-play situations. The offender sample responded in a consistently less skillful manner. Spence (1981) constituted comparable offender and nonoffender samples and videotaped interviews of each adolescent with a previously unknown adult. The offender group evidenced significantly less eye contact, appropriate head movement, and speech, as well as significantly more fiddling and gross body movement. Conger, Miller, and Walsmith (1965) add further to this picture of skill deficiency. They conclude from their evidence that juvenile delinquents, as compared to nondelinquent cohorts

> had more difficulty in getting along with peers, both in individual one-to-one contacts and in group situations, and were less willing or able to treat others courteously and tactfully, and less able to be fair in dealing with them. In return, they were less well liked and accepted by their peers. (p. 442)

Not only are delinquents discriminable from their nondelinquent peers on a continuum of skill competence, but much the same is true for youngsters who are "merely" chronically aggressive. Patterson, Reid, Jones, and Conger (1975) observe:

> The socialization process appears to be severely impeded for many aggressive youngsters. Their behavioral adjustments are often immature and they do not seem to have learned the key social skills necessary for initiating and maintaining positive social relationships with others. Peer groups often reject, avoid, and/or punish aggressive children, thereby excluding them from positive learning experiences with others. (p. 4)

Mussen, Conger, Kagan, and Gerwitz (1979) confirm this observation. Boys who became delinquent in the Mussen et al. longitudinal study were appraised by their teachers as less well-adjusted socially than their classmates as early as third grade. They appeared less friendly, responsible, or fair in dealing with others, and more impulsive and antagonistic to authority. Poor peer relations—showing less friendliness toward classmates, being less well-liked by peers—was a further developmental predictor of later delinquency. Thus, it may be safely concluded that psychological skill deficiencies of diverse—especially interpersonal—types markedly characterize both predelinquent and delinquent youths, to a degree that significantly differentiates them from their nondelinquent or nonaggressive peers. Furthermore, as Spence (1981) notes, the relationship between delinquent behavior and psychological skill deficits is a complex one:

> On the one hand it seems likely that adolescents who are delinquent in social skills may well resort to offending as a means of

achieving the peer status and respect they would be unable to obtain by more socially acceptable means. Similarly, it seems probable that children who experience difficulty in interactions with teachers and/or peers at school are more likely to truant, and thereby become more likely to commit offenses. To complicate matters further, evidence also suggests that when apprehended by the police, adolescents who are deficient in social skills will be more likely to be prosecuted or convicted for the offense than their socially skilled peers. (p. 108)

It is clear that the juvenile offender characteristically displays substantial deficits in a broad array of prosocial psychological skills. The remediation of such deficits looms as an especially valuable goal. As noted earlier, our attempts to do so during the past decade have utilized a skills training intervention we have termed Structured Learning.

RESEARCH EVALUATION

Since 1970, our research group has conducted a systematic research program oriented toward evaluating and improving the effectiveness of Structured Learning. Approximately 60 investigations have been conducted involving a wide variety of trainee populations and trainers. These include chronic adult schizophrenics (Goldstein, 1973; Goldstein, Sprafkin, & Gershaw, 1976; Liberman, 1970; Orenstein, 1973; Sutton-Simon, 1973), geriatric patients (Lopez, 1977; Lopez, Hoyer, Goldstein, Gershaw, & Sprafkin, 1982), child-abusing parents (Fischman, 1984, 1985; Goldstein, Keller, & Erné, 1985; Solomon, 1977; Sturm, 1980), young children (Hummel, 1980; Spatz-Norton, 1985; Swanstrom, 1974), such change-agent trainees as mental hospital staff (Berlin, 1976; Goldstein & Goedhart, 1973; Lack, 1975; Robinson, 1973; Schneiman, 1972), police (Goldstein, et al., 1977), persons employed in industrial contexts (Goldstein & Sorcher, 1973a, 1973b), and, in recent years, aggressive and other behaviorally disordered adolescents.

With regard to adolescent trainees, Structured Learning has been successful in enhancing such prosocial Structured Learning skills as empathy, negotiation, assertiveness, following instructions, self-control, conflict resolution, and perspective taking. Beyond these demonstrations that Structured Learning enhances prosocial skill competencies, our adolescent studies have also highlighted other aspects of the teaching of prosocial behaviors. Fleming (1976), in an effort to capitalize upon adolescent responsiveness to peer influence, demonstrated that gains in negotiating skill are as great when the Structured Learning group leader is a respected peer as when the leader is an adult. Litwack (1976), more concerned with the skill-enhancing effects of an adolescent's anticipating that he will later serve as a peer leader, showed that such helper role expectation increases the degree of skill acquired. Apparently, when the adolescent expects to teach others a skill, his own level of skill acquisition benefits, a finding clearly relevant to Riessman's (1965) helper therapy principle. Trief (1976) demonstrated that successful use of Structured Learning to increase the perspective-taking skill (i.e., seeing matters from other people's viewpoints) also leads to consequent increases in cooperative behavior. The significant transfer effects both in this study and in the Golden (1975), Litwack (1976), and Raleigh (1977) investigations have been important signposts in planning further research on transfer enhancement in Structured Learning.

As in earlier efforts with adult trainees, the value of teaching certain skill combinations has begun to be examined. Aggression-prone adolescents often get into difficulty when they respond with overt aggression to authority figures with whom they disagree. Golden (1975), responding to this type of event, successfully used Structured Learning to teach such adolescents resistance-reducing behavior, defined as a combination of reflection of feeling (the authority figure's) and assertiveness (forthright but nonaggressive statement of one's own position). Jennings (1975) was able to use Structured Learning successfully to train adolescents in several of the verbal skills necessary for satisfactory participation in more traditional, insight-oriented psychotherapy. Guzzetta (1974) was successful in providing means to help close the gap between adolescents and their parents by using Structured Learning to teach empathic skills to parents. But the major findings of our adolescent studies for our present purposes pertain to skill-enhancement effectiveness. The overall conclusions that may justifiably be drawn from these several empirical evaluations (conclusions identical to those one may draw for adult Structured Learning studies) are twofold.

Skill Acquisition

Across diverse trainee populations (clearly including aggressive adolescents in urban secondary schools and juvenile detention centers) and target skills, skill acquisition is a reliable training outcome, occurring in well over 90 percent of Structured Learning trainees. While pleased with this outcome, we are acutely aware of the manner in which therapeutic gains demonstrable in the training context are rather easily accomplished—given the potency, support, encouragement, and low threat value of trainers—but that the more consequential outcome question by far pertains to trainee skill performance in real-world contexts (i.e., skill transfer).

Skill Transfer

Across diverse trainee populations, target skills, and applied (real-world) settings, skill transfer occurs with approximately 45 to 50 percent of Structured Learning trainees. Goldstein and Kanfer (1979) as well as Karoly and Steffen (1980) have indicated that across several dozen types of psychotherapy involving many different types of psychopathology the average transfer rate on follow-up is between 15 percent and 20 percent of patients seen. The near 50 percent rate consequent to Structured Learning is a significant improvement upon this collective base rate, although it must immediately be underscored that this cumulative average transfer finding also means that the gains shown by half of our trainees were limited to in-session acquisition. Of special consequence, however, is the consistently clear manner in which skill transfer in our studies was a function of the explicit implementation of laboratory derived transfer-enhancing techniques, such as those described in the next chapter.

Concurrent with or following our development of the Structured Learning approach to psychological skills training, a number of similar programmatic attempts to enhance social competency emerged. Those that focused at least in large part on aggressive youngsters and their prosocial training include Life Skills Education (Adkins, 1970, 1974), Social Skills Training (Argyle, Trower, & Bryant, 1974), AWARE: Activities for Social Development (Elardo & Cooper, 1977), Relationships Enhancement (Guerney, 1977), Teaching Conflict Resolution (Hare, 1976), Developing Human Potential (Hawley & Hawley, 1975), ASSET (Hazel, Schumaker, Sherman, & Sheldon-Wildgen, 1981), Interpersonal Communication (Heiman, 1973), and Directive Teaching (Stephens, 1976). The instructional techniques that constitute each of these skills training efforts derive from social learning theory and typically consist of instructions, modeling, role playing, and performance feedback—with ancillary use in some instances of contingent reinforcement, prompting, shaping, or related behavioral techniques. Developing in part out of the empirical tradition of behavior modification, psychological skills training efforts, not surprisingly, came under early and continuing research scrutiny. Table 2 summarizes research by other investigators examining psychological skills training involving aggressive adolescent and preadolescent subjects.

Results

The 30 investigations that constitute Table 2 and our own research program, summarized earlier, comprise essentially all of the psychological skills training studies conducted to date with aggressive youngsters. Two-thirds of the studies are of multiple-group design; the remainder are single-subject studies. As noted earlier, psychological skills training is operationally defined in almost an identical manner across all of these investigations: usually a combination of modeling, role playing, and performance feedback, and in addition, in some instances, one or more transfer-enhancement procedures. Study subjects are either adjudicated juvenile delinquents, status offenders, or chronically aggressive youngsters studied in secondary school settings. While target skills have varied across investigations, for the most part they have concerned interpersonal behaviors, prosocial alternatives to aggression, and aggression-management or aggression-inhibition behaviors. As Spence (1981) notes, the single-case studies have tended toward microskill training targets (eye contact, head nods, and the like), and the multiple-group studies have sought to teach more macroskill competencies (e.g., coping with criticism, negotiation, problem solving). Results of the studies have been quite consistently positive for skill acquisition. Aggressive adolescents are able to learn a broad array of previously unavailable interpersonal, aggression-management, affect-relevant, and related psychological competencies via the training methods examined here. Evaluation for maintenance and transfer of acquired skills yields a rather different outcome. Many studies test for neither. Those that do evaluate long-term acquisition and generalization provide an inconsistent picture. As noted earlier, our own investigative efforts in this regard (Goldstein, 1981) point to the not surprising conclusion that generalization of skill competency across settings (transfer) and time (maintenance) is very much a direct function of the degree to which the investigator/trainer implemented as a part of the training effort procedures explicitly designed to enhance transfer and/or maintenance.

To summarize our view of empirical efforts to date: Psychological skills training with aggressive adolescents rests on a firm investigative foundation. A variety of investigators, designs, subjects, settings, and target skills is providing a healthy examination of the effectiveness of such training. Skill acquisition is a reliable outcome, but the social validity of this consistent result is tempered substantially by the frequent failure—or at least, indeterminacy—of transfer and maintenance.

Table 2. Psychological Skills Training Research with Adolescent and Preadolescent Trainees

Investigator	Design	Treatment	Trainees	N	Setting	Target Skill	Outcome
Bornstein, Bellack, & Hersen (1980)	Single case: Multiple baseline	Instructions Modeling Role play Feedback	Aggressive adolescent inpatients	4	Psychiatric hospital	Assertiveness	Increase in skill performance contingent on training, and decrease in aggression; maintained at 6 months
Braukmann, Fixsen, Phillips, Wolf, & Maloney (1974)	Single case: Multiple baseline	Instructions Modeling Role play Feedback	Juvenile delinquents	6	Family group home	Interview skills (posture, eye contact, etc.)	Increase in skill performance contingent on training
Braukmann, Maloney, Phillips, & Wolf (1973)	Single case: Multiple baseline	Instructions Modeling Role play Feedback	Juvenile delinquents	2	Family group home	Heterosexual interaction skills (head nods, attending, etc.)	Increase in skill performance contingent on training, and increase in female contact at parties
De Lange, Lanham, & Barton (1981)	Multiple group: Training, no training	Modeling Role play Feedback	Juvenile delinquents	50	Residential institution	Assertiveness	No significant between-condition differences
Elder, Edelstein, & Narick (1979)	Single group: Multiple baseline	Instructions Modeling Role play Feedback	Aggressive adolescent	4	Psychiatric hospital	Assertiveness, anger control	Increase in skill performance contingent on training, and decrease in aggression; maintained at 6 months

Study	Design	Procedures	Population	N	Setting	Target skills	Results
Greenleaf (1977)	Multiple group: Training (present vs. absent), transfer programming (present vs. absent), attention control, brief instructions control	Modeling Role play Feedback	Aggressive adolescents	43	Secondary school	Helping others	Both training conditions superior to controls on study skill acquisition and maintenance
Gross, Brigham, Hopper, & Bologna (1980)	Single group: Multiple baseline	Instructions Modeling Role play Shaping	Juvenile delinquents	10	Group home	Prosocial responsiveness (responding to criticism, responding to teasing)	Increase in skill performance contingent on training, reduced truancy at post-training, 2 months, and 1 year
Hazel, Schumaker, Sherman, & Sheldon-Wildgen (1981)	Multiple group: Training, no training	Instructions Discussion Modeling Role play Feedback	Juvenile delinquents	24	Probation office	Giving feedback, negotiation, resisting peer pressure, etc.	Training superior to controls on study skills; maintained at 2 months
Hollin & Courtney (1983)	Multiple group: Training—8 weeks, training—4 days, no-training control, non-referred control	Instructions Modeling Role play Feedback	Juvenile delinquents	15	Residential institution	Conversation skills (eye contact, listening, initiating), conflict avoidance skills	No significant between-condition differences

Table 2. (cont.)

Investigator	Design	Treatment	Trainees	N	Setting	Target Skill	Outcome
Hollin & Henderson (1981)	Multiple group: Training, no training	Instructions Modeling Role play Feedback	Juvenile delinquents	14	Residential institution	Conversation skills, non-verbal communication skills	No significant between-condition differences
Hummel (1980)	Multiple group: Training (single or combined skills), varied or constant stimulus conditions	Modeling Role play Feedback	Aggressive adolescents	47	Secondary school	Negotiation, self-control	All training under varied stimulus conditions superior to all training under constant stimulus conditions
Kifer, Lewis, Green, & Phillips (1974)	Single case: Multiple baseline	Instructions Role play Feedback	Juvenile delinquents and their parents	3	Family group home	Negotiation skills (expressing opinion, reaching agreement)	Increase in skill performance contingent on training
Lee, Hallberg, & Hassard (1979)	Multiple group: Training, attention control, no-training control	Instructions Modeling Role play Feedback	Aggressive adolescents	30	Secondary school	Aggression-control skills, assertiveness	Training superior to controls on assertiveness, no significant between-condition differences on aggression-control skills

Study	Design	Techniques	Population	N	Setting	Target skills	Results
Litwack (1976)	Multiple group: Training and anticipation of serving as a trainer, training, brief instructions control	Modeling Role play Feedback	Aggressive adolescents	40	Secondary school	Following instructions, expressing a compliment	Both training conditions superior to controls on both study skills training and helper-role structuring
Maloney et al. (1976)	Single case: Multiple baseline	Role play Contingent reinforcement	Juvenile delinquents	4	Family group home	Conversation skills, (posture, volunteering answers)	Increase in skill performance contingent on training—by peers or by teaching parents
Matson et al. (1980)	Single group: Multiple baseline	Instructions Modeling Role play Feedback Contingent reinforcement	Aggressive adolescent inpatients	4	Residential institution	Conversation skills (e.g., eye contact, choosing content)	Increase in skill performance contingent on training, maintained at 3 months
Minkin et al. (1976)	Single case: Multiple baseline	Instructions Modeling Role play Feedback	Juvenile delinquents	4	Family group home	Conversation skills (asking questions, giving feedback)	Increase in skill performance contingent on training
Ollendick & Hersen (1979)	Multiple group: Training, discussion control, no-training control	Instructions Modeling Role play Feedback	Juvenile delinquents	27	Residential institution	Interpersonal accomodation skills, verbal and nonverbal	Training superior to controls on study skills, reduction in state anxiety, and increase in internal locus of control

Table 2. *(cont.)*

Investigator	Design	Treatment	Trainees	N	Setting	Target Skill	Outcome
Pentz (1980)	Multiple group: Training by teacher, parent or peer: aggressive versus passive trainees, brief instruction control, no-training control	Modeling Role play Feedback	Aggressive and unasser- tive adoles- cents	90	Secondary school	Assertiveness	All training conditions supe- rior to controls on study skill acquisition and transfer, and teacher trainers superior to parent or peer trainers on skill acquisition
Robin (1981)	Multiple group: Training, family therapy, wait-list control	Instructions Modeling Role play Feedback	Adolescents from con- flicted fami- lies	33	Clinic	Problem-solving commu- nication skills	Training superior to controls on all study skills, training therapy on behavioral skills; maintained at 10 weeks
Robin, Kent, O'Leary, Foster, & Prinz (1977)	Multiple group: Training, wait-list control	Instructions Discussion Modeling Role play	Adolescents from con- flicted fami- lies and their parents	24	Clinic	Problem-solving commu- nication skills	Training superior to controls on study skills, no transfer to home
Sarason & Ganzer (1973)	Multiple group: Training, discus- sion control, no- training control	Modeling Role play Feedback	Juvenile delinquents	192	Residential institution	Prosocial problem solving	Training superior to controls on study skills

Study	Design	Procedures	Population	N	Setting	Target skills	Results
Sarason & Sarason (1981)	Multiple group: Training—live modeling, training—video modeling, no-training control	Instructions Modeling Role play Feedback	Adolescents in school with high dropout and delinquency levels	127	Secondary school	Job interview, resisting peer pressure, asking for help, dealing with frustration	Training—live modeling superior to controls on job interview skills, and training (both types) superior to controls on problem-solving skills; no significant between-condition differences on other study skills
Shoemaker (1979)	Multiple group: Training, discussion control, no-training control	Instructions Discussion Role play Feedback Contingency reinforcement	Juvenile delinquents	30	Residential institution	Assertiveness	Training superior to controls on study skill, no generalization to interview situation
A.J. Spence & S.H. Spence (1980)	Multiple group: Training, attention control, no-training control	Modeling Role play Feedback	Juvenile delinquents	44	Residential institution	Nonverbal skills (e.g., eye contact). Interaction skills (e.g., dealing with teasing)	Training superior to controls on study skills; no maintenance at 6 months
S.H. Spence & J.S. Marzillier (1979)	Single case: Multiple baseline	Instructions Modeling Role play Feedback	Juvenile delinquents	5	Residential institution	Conversation skills (eye contact, head movement, listening)	Increase in nonverbal skills performance contingent on training; maintained at 2 weeks

Table 2. (cont.)

Investigator	Design	Treatment	Trainees	N	Setting	Target Skill	Outcome
S.H. Spence & J.S. Marzillier (1981)	Multiple group: Training, attention placebo control, no-training control	Instructions Modeling Role play Feedback	Juvenile delinquents	76	Residential institution	Coping with criticism and teasing, inviting friendships	Training superior to controls on study skills
Thelen, Fry, Dollinger, & Paul (1976)	Multiple group: Training, didactic control, baseline control	Modeling Role play Feedback	Juvenile delinquents	6	Group home	Conflict resolution skills (coping with accusations, expressing positive feelings)	Increase in skill performance contingent on training; not maintained at 2 weeks
Trief (1976)	Multiple group: (cognitive, affective, or combined aspects of skill), attention control, brief instructions control	Modeling Role play Feedback	Juvenile delinquents	58	Residential institution	perspective taking	All training conditions superior to controls on study skill acquisition and transfer
Werner et al. (1975)	Multiple group: Training, no-training control	Instructions Modeling Role play Feedback	Juvenile delinquents	6	Family group home	Prosocial communication with police officers (eye contact, cooperation, expression of reform)	Pre-post training increase on study skills for training and control groups

34

Chapter 3

Trainer's Manual for Structured Learning

The purpose of this manual is to provide the information needed to prepare and conduct effective Structured Learning groups.* The selection, preparation, and instruction of adolescent trainees will be our major focus. We will also attend to such organizational decisions as the optimal number, length, timing, spacing, and location of the Structured Learning sessions themselves, as well as such instructional matters as implementing the Structured Learning procedures (modeling, role playing, performance feedback, transfer training) in opening and later sessions. Finally, group management problems and their resolution will be discussed.

PREPARING FOR STRUCTURED LEARNING

Selecting Trainers

A wide variety of individuals have served successfully as Structured Learning trainers. Their educational backgrounds have been especially varied, ranging from high school degree only through various graduate degrees. While formal training in a helping profession is both useful and relevant to becoming a competent Structured Learning trainer, we have found characteristics such as sensitivity, flexibility, and instructional talent to be considerably more important than formal education. We have made frequent and successful use of trainers best described as paraprofessionals, particularly with trainees from lower socioeconomic levels. In general, we select trainers based upon the nature and demands of the Structured Learning group. Two types of trainer skills appear crucial for successfully conducting a Structured Learning group. The first might be described as general trainer skills, that is, those skills requisite for success in almost any training or teaching effort. These include:

---

*This chapter follows, in general outline, Goldstein, A. P., Sprafkin, R. P., Gershaw, N. J., & Klein, P. (1980). *Skillstreaming the adolescent: A structured learning approach to teaching prosocial skills.* Champaign, IL: Research Press.

35

1. Oral communication and teaching ability
2. Flexibility and resourcefulness
3. Enthusiasm
4. Ability to work under pressure
5. Interpersonal sensitivity
6. Listening skills
7. Knowledge of their subject (adolescent development, aggression management, peer pressures on adolescents, etc.)

The second type of skills necessary is specific trainer skills, that is, those skills relevant to Structured Learning in particular. These include:

1. Knowledge of Structured Learning—its background, procedures, and goals
2. Ability to orient both trainees and supporting staff to Structured Learning
3. Ability to plan and present live modeling displays
4. Ability to initiate and sustain role playing
5. Ability to present material in concrete, behavioral form
6. Ability to deal with group management problems effectively
7. Accuracy and sensitivity in providing corrective feedback

How can we tell if potential trainers are skilled enough to become effective group leaders? We use behavioral observation, actually seeing how competently potential trainers lead mock and then actual Structured Learning groups during our trainer preparation phase.

Preparing Trainers

We strongly believe in learning by doing. Our chief means of preparing trainers for Structured Learning group leadership is, first, to have them participate in an intensive, 2-day workshop designed to provide the knowledge and experience needed for a beginning competence at being a trainer. In the workshop, we use Structured Learning to teach Structured Learning. First, we assign relevant reading materials for background information. Next, trainees observe skilled and experienced Structured Learning group leaders model the central modeling display presentation, role playing, performance feedback, and transfer training procedures that constitute the core elements of the Structured Learning session. Then, workshop participants role play in pairs these group leadership behaviors and receive detailed feedback from the workshop leaders and others in the training group regarding the degree to which their group leadership behaviors matched or departed from those modeled by the workshop leaders. To assist workshop learning to transfer smoothly and fully to agency functioning, regular and continuing supervisory sessions are held after the workshop with the newly created Structured Learning group leaders. These booster/monitoring/supervision meetings, when added to the several opportunities available for trainer performance evaluation during the workshop itself, provide a large sample of behaviors upon which to base a fair and appropriate trainer selection decison.

Selecting Trainees

Who belongs in the Structured Learning group? We have long held that no therapy or training approach is optimal for all clients and that our effectiveness as helpers or trainers will grow to the degree that we become prescriptive in our helping efforts (Goldstein, 1978; Goldstein & Stein, 1976). As noted earlier, Structured Learning grew originally from a behavior-deficit view of the asocial and antisocial behavior comprising juvenile delinquency. If such behavior is due in substantial part to a lack of ability in a variety of alternative, prosocial skills of an interpersonal, personal, aggression-management, or related nature, our selection goal is defined for us. The Structured Learning group should consist of youngsters weak or deficient in one or more clusters of skills that constitute the ART Structured Learning skill curriculum. This selection process optimally will involve the use of interview, direct observation, and behavioral testing procedures and appropriate skill checklists (Goldstein et al., 1980). Since the ultimate goal of ART is change in overt behavior, the removal of skill deficits, and the learning of prosocial alternatives, the selection of trainees for Structured Learning is equivalent to their selection for ART. No further selection procedures are necessary.

Largely or entirely irrelevant to the selection decision are most of the usual bases for treatment or training selection decisions. If the clients are skill deficient and possess a few very basic group participation skills, we are largely unconcerned with their age, sex, race, social class, or, within very broad limits, even their mental health. At times we have had to exclude persons who were severely emotionally disturbed, too hyperactive for a 30-minute session, or so developmentally disabled that they lacked the rudimentary memory and imagery abilities necessary for adequate group participation. But such persons have been relatively few and quite far between. Thus, while Structured Learning is not a prescription designed for all juvenile delinquents or aggressive adolescents, its range of appropriate use is nevertheless quite broad.

ART Structured Learning Skills

The 10 Structured Learning skills used in ART were modified from *Skillstreaming the Adolescent* (Goldstein et al., 1980). These skills, listed below, were selected on two bases. First, in our collective experience with delinquent youth, these are skills typically quite weak or lacking. Second, the use of these skills as training curricula in many Structured Learning groups reveals this set of skills to be motivating and participation-enhancing for the large majority of trainees. The necessary steps that constitute each skill are presented at the end of this chapter.

1. Expressing a Complaint
2. Responding to the Feelings of Others (Empathy)
3. Preparing for a Stressful Conversation
4. Responding to Anger
5. Keeping out of Fights
6. Helping Others
7. Dealing with an Accusation
8. Dealing with Group Pressure
9. Expressing Affection
10. Responding to Failure

The ART programs described in this book were set at 10 weeks for evaluation purposes. In other applied settings, we and others are conducting ART programs that are open-ended in length, some running a full year. Thus, trainers will often wish to teach additional or alternate skills. Additional skills can be chosen—by the trainers, or in collaboration with the trainees—from the 50 skills for adolescents found in *Skillstreaming the Adolescent*, which are shown in the following list. Further directions and worksheets for selecting appropriate skills can be found in that book.

Group I. Beginning Social Skills
1. Listening
2. Starting a Conversation
3. Having a Conversation
4. Asking a Question
5. Saying Thank You
6. Introducing Yourself
7. Introducing Other People
8. Giving a Compliment

Group II. Advanced Social Skills
9. Asking for Help
10. Joining In

11. Giving Instructions
12. Following Instructions
13. Apologizing
14. Convincing Others

Group III. Skills for Dealing with Feelings
15. Knowing Your Feelings
16. Expressing Your Feelings
17. Understanding the Feelings of Others
18. Dealing with Someone Else's Anger
19. Expressing Affection
20. Dealing with Fear
21. Rewarding Yourself

Group IV. Skill Alternatives to Aggression
22. Asking Permission
23. Sharing Something
24. Helping Others
25. Negotiating
26. Using Self-control
27. Standing Up for Your Rights
28. Responding to Teasing
29. Avoiding Trouble with Others
30. Keeping Out of Fights

Group V. Skills for Dealing with Stress
31. Making a Complaint
32. Answering a Complaint
33. Sportsmanship After the Game
34. Dealing with Embarrassment
35. Dealing with Being Left Out
36. Standing Up for a Friend
37. Responding to Persuasion
38. Responding to Failure
39. Dealing with Contradictory Messages
40. Dealing with an Accusation
41. Getting Ready for a Difficult Conversation
42. Dealing with Group Pressure

Group VI. Planning Skills
43. Deciding on Something to Do
44. Deciding What Caused a Problem
45. Setting a Goal
46. Deciding on Your Abilities
47. Gathering Information

48. Arranging Problems by Importance
49. Making a Decision
50. Concentrating on a Task

Group Organization

The preparation phase of the Structured Learning group is completed by attention to those organizational details necessary for a smoothly initiated, appropriately paced, and highly instructional group to begin. Factors to be considered in organizing the group are number of trainees, number of trainers, number of sessions, and spacing of sessions.

Number of Trainees

Since trainee behavior in a Structured Learning group may vary greatly from person to person and group to group, it is not appropriate that we recommend a single, specific number of trainees as optimal. Ideally, the number of trainees will permit all to role play, will lead to optimal levels of group interaction, and will provide a diverse source of performance feedback opportunities. In our experience with delinquent adolescents, these goals have usually been met when the group's size was five to seven trainees.

Number of Trainers

The role playing and feedback that make up most of each Structured Learning session are a series of "action-reaction" sequences in which effective skill behaviors are first rehearsed (role played) and then critiqued (feedback). Thus, the trainer must both lead and observe. We have found that one trainer is hard pressed to do both of these tasks well at the same time, and we strongly recommend that each session be led by a team of two trainers. One trainer can usually pay special attention to the main actor, helping the actor "set the stage" and enact the skill's behavioral steps. While this is occurring, the other trainer can attend to the remainder of the group and help them as they observe and evaluate the unfolding role play. The two trainers can then exchange these responsibilities on the next role play.

Number of Sessions

Structured Learning groups typically seek to cover one skill in one or two sessions. The central task is to make certain that every trainee in the group role plays the given skill correctly at least once, preferably more than once. Most Structured Learning groups have met this curric-

ulum requirement by holding sessions once or twice per week. Groups
have varied greatly in the total number of meetings they have held. At
least 10 meetings of the Structured Learning group are necessary for the
ART program.

Spacing of Sessions

The goal of Structured Learning is not merely skill learning or acquisition; much more important is skill transfer. Performance of the skill in
the training setting is desired, but performance of it in the facility or
community is crucial. Several aspects of Structured Learning, discussed
later in this manual, are designed to enhance the likelihood of such skill
transfer. Session spacing is one such factor. As will be described later,
after the trainee role plays successfully in the group and receives thorough performance feedback, he is assigned homework, that is, the task
of carrying out in the real world the skill he just performed correctly in
the group. In order to ensure ample time and opportunity to carry out
this very important task, Structured Learning sessions must be scheduled at least a few days apart.

Length and Location of Sessions

One-hour sessions are the typical Structured Learning format, though
both somewhat briefer and somewhat longer sessions have been successful. In general, the session goal that must be met is successful role
playing and clarifying feedback for all participants, be it in 45 minutes,
1 hour, or 1 1/2 hours.

In most agencies, a reasonably quiet and reasonably comfortable
office, classroom, or similar setting can be found or created for the use
of Structured Learning groups. We suggest no special requirements for
the meeting place beyond those that make sense for any kind of group
instruction—that it be free of distraction and at least minimally
equipped with chairs, chalkboard, and adequate lighting. How shall the
room be arranged? Again, no single, fixed pattern is required, but one
functional and comfortable layout is the horseshoe or U-shaped arrangement, which we have often employed—sometimes with and sometimes
without tables. Figure 1 depicts this room arrangement. Note how in this
group arrangement all observing trainees and the main actor can watch
the trainer point to the given skill's behavioral steps written on the
chalkboard while the role play is taking place. In this manner, any necessary prompting is provided immediately and at the same time that the
role play is serving as an additional modeling display for observing
trainees.

Figure 1. A Functional Room Arrangement for Structured Learning

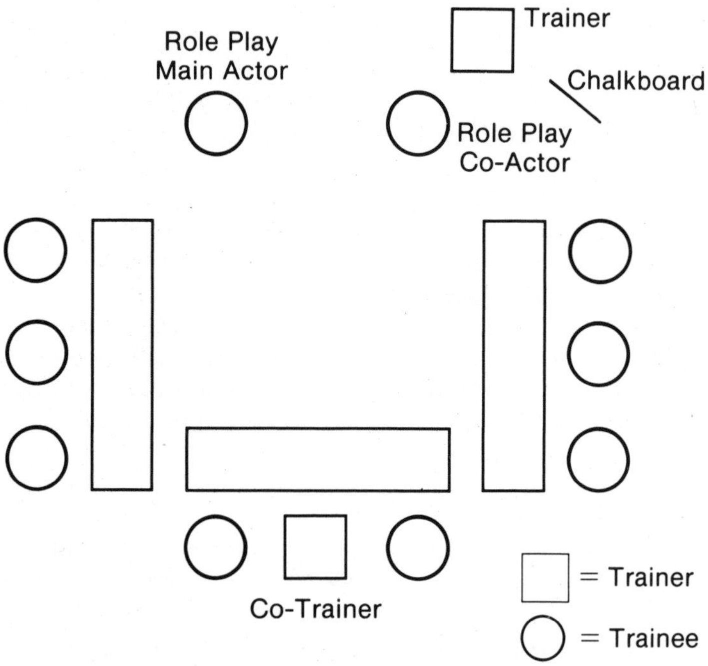

Meeting with the Trainees
Before the First Session

A final step that must be taken before holding the first session of a new Structured Learning group is preparing the trainees who have been selected for what they ought to expect and what will be expected of them. What this premeeting might include follows.

1. *Describing what the purposes of the group will be as they relate to the trainee's specific skill deficits.* For example, the trainer might say, "Remember when you lost privileges because you thought Henry had insulted you and you got in a shoving match with him? Well, in Structured Learning, you'll be able to learn what to do in a situation like that so you can handle it without fighting and still settle calmly whatever is going on."

2. *Describing briefly the procedure that will be used.* While we believe that trainees typically will not have a full understanding of what

Structured Learning is and what it can accomplish until after the group has begun and they have experienced it, verbal, pregroup structuring of procedures is a useful beginning. It conveys at least a part of the information necessary to help trainees know what to expect. The trainer might say, "In order to learn to handle these problem situations better, we're going to see and hear some examples of how different people handle them well. Then you will actually take turns trying some of these ways right here. We'll let you know how you did, and you'll have a chance to practice on your own."

3. *Describing some of the hoped-for benefits of active trainee participation in the group.* If the trainer has relevant information from a trainee, the possible benefits described might appropriately be improved proficiency in the particular Structured Learning skills in which the trainee rates herself as especially deficient.

4. *Describing group rules.* These rules include whatever the trainer believes the group members must adhere to in order to function smoothly and effectively with regard to attendance, punctuality, confidentiality, completion of homework assignments, and so forth. At this premeeting stage, rule structuring should be brief and tentative. Reserve a fuller discussion of this matter for the group's first session, in which all members can be encouraged to participate and in which rule changes can be made by consensus.

CONDUCTING THE STRUCTURED LEARNING GROUP

We now wish to turn to a detailed, step-by-step description of the procedures that constitute the Structured Learning session. The opening session will be considered first. The elements of this session that get the Structured Learning group off to a good start will be emphasized. The section then will describe the procedures that constitute the bulk of most Structured Learning sessions—modeling, role playing, performance feedback, and transfer training. Then an outline that can be followed for sessions after the first will be presented.

The Opening Session

The opening session is designed to create a safe, nurturing, nonthreatening environment for trainees, stimulate their interest in the group, and give more detailed information to them than was provided in their individual orientations. The trainers open the session with a brief familiarization period of warmup, to help participants become comfortable when interacting with the group leaders and with one another. Content for this initial phase should be interesting and nonthreatening to the trainees. Next, trainers introduce the Structured Learning program by providing trainees with a brief description of what skill training is about. Typically, this introduction covers such topics as the importance of interpersonal skills for effective and satisfying living, examples of skills that will be taught, and how these skills can be useful to trainees in their everyday lives. It is often helpful to expand this discussion of everyday skill use to emphasize the importance of the undertaking and the personal relevance of learning the skill to the participants. The specific training procedures (modeling, role playing, performance feedback, and transfer training) are then described at a level that the group can easily understand. We recommend that trainers describe procedures briefly, with the expectation that trainees will understand them more fully once they have actually participated in their use. A detailed outline of the procedures that ideally make up this opening session follows.

Outline of Opening Session Procedures

A. Introductions
   1. Trainers introduce themselves.
   2. Trainers invite trainees to introduce themselves. As a way of relaxing trainees and beginning to familiarize them with one another, the trainer can elicit from each trainee some nonprivate information such as neighborhood of residence, school background, special interests or hobbies, and so forth.
B. Overview of Structured Learning
   Although some or all of this material may have been discussed in earlier individual meetings with trainees, a portion of the opening session should be devoted to a presentation and group discussion of the purposes, procedures, and potential benefits of Structured Learning. The discussion of the group's purposes should stress the probable remediation of those skill deficits that trainees in the group are aware of, concerned about, and eager to change. The procedures that make up the typical Structured Learning session should be explained again and discussed with give and take from the group. The language used to explain the procedures should be geared to the trainees' level of understanding, that is, "show," "try," "discuss," and "practice," respectively, for the words "modeling," "role playing," "performance feedback," and "transfer training." Perhaps heaviest stress at this point should be placed on presenting and examining the potential benefits to trainees of their participation in Structured Learning. Concrete examples of the diverse ways that skill proficiencies could, and probably will, have a positive effect on the lives of trainees should be the focus of this effort.

C. Group Rules

The rules that will govern participation in the Structured Learning group should be presented by the trainers during the opening session. If appropriate, this presentation should permit and encourage group discussion designed to give members a sense of participation in the group's decision making. That is, members should be encouraged to accept and live by those rules they agree with and seek to alter those they wish to change. Group rules may be necessary and appropriate concerning attendance, lateness, size of the group, and time and place of the meetings. This is also a good time to provide reassurance to group members about concerns they may have, such as confidentiality, embarrassment, and fear of performing.

Following introductions, the overview of Structured Learning, and the presentation of group rules, the trainers should proceed to introducing and modeling the group's first skill, conducting role plays on that skill, giving performance feedback, and encouraging transfer training. These activities make up all subsequent Structured Learning sessions.

Modeling

The modeling display presented to trainees should depict the behavioral steps that constitute the skill being taught in a clear and unambiguous manner. All of the steps making up the skill should be modeled, in the correct sequence. Generally, the modeling will consist of live vignettes enacted by the two trainers, although trainees may be involved in the modeling display in some instances. (If available, an audio or audiovisual modeling display, instead of live modeling, may be presented.) When two trainers are not available, a reasonably skillful trainee may serve as a model along with the trainer. In all instances, it is especially important to rehearse the vignettes carefully prior to the group meeting, making sure that all of the skill's steps are enacted correctly and in the proper sequence.

Trainers should plan their modeling display carefully. Content should be selected that is relevant to the immediate life situations of the trainees in the group. At least two examples should be modeled for each skill so that trainees are exposed to skill use in different situations. Thus, two or more different content areas are depicted. We have found that trainers usually do not have to write out scripts for the modeling display but can instead plan their roles and likely responses in outline form and rehearse them in their preclass preparations. These modeling display outlines should incorporate the guidelines that follow:

1. Use at least two examples of different situations for each demonstration of a skill. If a given skill is taught in more than one group meeting, develop two more new modeling displays.
2. Select situations that are relevant to the trainees' real-life circumstances.
3. The main actor, that is, the person enacting the behavioral steps of the skill, should be portrayed as a person reasonably similar in age, socioeconomic background, verbal ability, and other salient characteristics to the people in the Structured Learning group.
4. Modeling displays should depict only one skill at a time. All extraneous content should be eliminated.
5. All modeling displays should depict all the behavioral steps of the skill being modeled in the correct sequence.
6. All displays should depict positive outcomes. Displays should always end with reinforcement to the model.

In order to help trainees attend to the skill enactments, Skill Cards containing the name of the skill being taught and its behavioral steps (the cards must be made by the trainers) are distributed prior to the modeling display. Trainees are told to watch and listen closely as the models portray the skill. Particular care should be given to helping trainees identify the behavioral steps as they are presented in the context of the modeling vignettes. Trainers should also remind the trainees that in order to depict some of the behavioral steps in certain skills, the actors will occasionally be "thinking out loud" statements that would ordinarily be thought silently, and that this process is done to facilitate learning.

Role Playing

Following the modeling display, discussion should focus on relating the modeled skill to the lives of trainees. Trainers should invite comments on the behavioral steps and how these steps might be useful in real-life situations that trainees encounter. It is most helpful to focus on current and future skill use rather than only on past events or general issues involving the skill. Role playing in Structured Learning is intended to serve as behavioral rehearsal or practice for future use of the skill. Role playing of past events that have little relevance for future situations is of limited value to trainees. However, discussion of past events involving skill use can be relevant in stimulating trainees to think of times when a similar situation might occur in the future. The hypothetical future situation rather than a reenactment of the past event would be selected for role playing.

Once a trainee has described a situation in her own life in which the skill might be helpful, that trainee is designated the main actor. She chooses a second trainee (the co-actor) to play the role of the other person (mother, peer, staff member, etc.) in her life who is relevant to the situation. The trainee should be urged to pick as a co-actor someone who resembles the real-life person in as many ways as possible—physically, expressively, etc. The trainers then elicit from the main actor any additional information needed to set the stage for role playing. To make role playing as realistic as possible, the trainers should obtain a description of the physical setting, a description of the events immediately preceding the role play, a description of the manner the co-actor should display, and any other information that would increase realism.

It is crucial that the main actor use the behavioral steps that have been modeled. This is the main purpose of the role playing. Before beginning the actual role playing, the trainer should go over each step as it applies to the particular role-play situation, thus preparing the main actor to make a successful effort. The main actor is told to refer to the Skill Card on which the behavioral steps are printed. As noted previously, the behavioral steps are written on a chalkboard visible to the main actor as well as the rest of the group during the role playing. Before the role playing begins, trainers should remind all of the participants of their roles and responsibilities: The main actor is told to follow the behavioral steps; the co-actor, to stay in the role of the other person; and the observers, to watch carefully for the enactment of the behavioral steps. At times, feedback from other trainees is facilitated by assigning each one a single behavioral step to focus upon and provide feedback on after the role play. For the first several role plays, the observers also can be coached on kinds of cues (posture, tone of voice, content of speech, etc.) to observe.

During the role play, it is the responsibility of one of the trainers to provide the main actor with whatever help, coaching, and encouragement she needs to keep the role playing going according to the behavioral steps. Trainees who "break role" and begin to explain their behavior or make observer-like comments should be urged to get back into the role and explain later. If the role play is clearly going astray from the behavioral steps, the scene can be stopped, needed instruction can be provided, and then the role play can be restarted. One trainer should be positioned near the chalkboard in order to point to each of the behavioral steps in turn as the role play unfolds, thus helping the main actor (as well as the other trainees) to follow each of the steps in order. The second trainer should sit with the observing trainees to be available as needed to keep them on task.

The role playing should be continued until all trainees have had an opportunity to participate in the role of main actor. Sometimes this will require two or three sessions for a given skill. As we suggested before, each session should begin with two new modeling vignettes for the chosen skill, even if the skill is not new to the group. It is important to note once again that while the framework (behavioral steps) of each role play in the series remains the same, the actual content can and should change from role play to role play. It is the problem as it actually occurs, or could occur, in each trainee's real-life environment that should be the content of the given role play.

There are a few more ways to increase the effectiveness of role playing. Role reversal is often a useful role-play procedure. A trainee role playing a skill may on occasion have a difficult time perceiving her co-actor's viewpoint and vice versa. Having them exchange roles and resume the role play can be most helpful in this regard. At times, the trainer can also assume the co-actor role in an effort to give the trainee the opportunity to handle types of reactions not otherwise role played during the session. For example, it may be crucial to have a difficult co-actor realistically portrayed. The trainer as co-actor may also be particularly helpful when dealing with less verbal or more hesitant trainees.

Performance Feedback

A brief feedback period follows each role play. This helps the main actor find out how well he followed or departed from the behavioral steps. It also examines the psychological impact of the enactment on the co-actor and provides the main actor with encouragement to try out the role-played behaviors in real life. The trainer should ask the main actor to wait until he has heard everyone's comments before responding to any of them.

The co-actor is asked about his reactions first. Next the observers comment on how well the behavioral steps were followed and other relevant aspects of the role play. Then the trainers comment in particular on how well the behavioral steps were followed and provide social reinforcement (praise, approval, encouragement) for close following. To be most effective in their use of reinforcement, trainers should follow these guidelines:

1. Provide reinforcement only after role plays that follow the behavioral steps.
2. Provide reinforcement at the earliest appropriate opportunity after role plays that follow the behavioral steps.
3. Vary the specific content of the reinforcements offered, for

example, praise particular aspects of the performance, such as tone of voice, posture, phrasing, etc.

4. Provide enough role-playing activity for each group member to have sufficient opportunity to be reinforced.
5. Provide reinforcement in an amount consistent with the quality of the given role play.
6. Provide no reinforcement when the role play departs significantly from the behavioral steps (except for "trying" in the first session or two).
7. Provide reinforcement for an individual trainee's improvement over previous performances.
8. Always provide reinforcement to the co-actor for being helpful, cooperative, etc.

In all aspects of feedback, it is crucial that the trainer maintain the behavioral focus of Structured Learning. Both trainer and trainee comments should point to the presence or absence of specific, concrete behaviors and not take the form of general evaluations or broad generalities. Feedback, of course, may be positive or negative in content. Negative comments should always be followed by a constructive comment as to how a particular fault might be improved. At minimum, a "poor" performance can be praised as "a good try" at the same time that it is being criticized for its real faults. If at all possible, trainees failing to follow the relevant behavioral steps in their role play should be given the opportunity to role play these same behavioral steps again after receiving corrective feedback. At times, as a further feedback procedure, we have audio- or videotaped entire role plays. Giving trainees post-role-play opportunities to observe themselves on tape can be an effective aid, enabling them to reflect on their own verbal and nonverbal behavior and its impact upon others.

Since a primary goal of Structured Learning is skill flexibility, role play enactments that depart somewhat from the behavioral steps may not be "wrong." That is, a different approach to the skill may in fact work in some situations. Trainers should stress that they are trying to teach effective alternatives and that the trainees would do well to have the behavioral steps being taught, or as collaboratively modified, in their repertoire of skill behaviors, available to use when appropriate.

Transfer Training

Several aspects of the training sessions already described have been designed primarily to make it likely that learning in the training setting will transfer to the trainees' actual real-life environments. Techniques for enhancing transfer training as they are used in the sessions follow.

Provision of General Principles

It has been demonstrated that transfer of training is facilitated by providing trainees with general mediating principles governing successful or competent performance in both the training and applied real-world settings. This has been operationalized in laboratory contexts by providing subjects with the organizing concepts, principles, strategies, or rationales that explain the stimulus-response relationships operating in both the training and application settings. General principles of skill selection and utilization are provided to Structured Learning trainees verbally, visually, and in written form.

Overlearning

Overlearning involves training in a skill beyond what is necessary to produce initial changes in behavior. The overlearning, or repetition of successful skill enactment, in the typical Structured Learning session is quite substantial. Each skill taught and its behavioral steps are:

1. Modeled several times
2. Role played one or more times by the trainee
3. Observed live by the trainee as every other group member role plays
4. Read by the trainee from a chalkboard and a Skill Card
5. Practiced in real-life settings one or more times by the trainee as part of his formal homework assignment

Identical Elements

In perhaps the earliest research on transfer enhancement, Thorndike and Woodworth (1901) concluded that when one habit encouraged another, it was to the extent that they shared identical elements. More recently, Ellis (1965) and Osgood (1953) have emphasized the importance for transfer of similarity between stimulus aspects of the training and application tasks. The greater the similarity of physical and interpersonal stimuli in the Structured Learning setting and the homework and community or other setting in which the skill is to be applied, the greater the likelihood of transfer. Structured Learning is made similar to real life in several ways. These include:

1. Designing the live modeling displays to be highly similar to what trainees face in their daily lives through the representative, relevant, and realistic portrayal of the models, protagonists, and situations

2. Designing the role plays to be similar to real-life situations through the use of props, the physical arrangement of the setting, and the choice of realistic co-actors
3. Conducting the role plays to be as responsive as possible to the real-life interpersonal stimuli to which the trainees must actually respond later with the given skill
4. Rehearsing of each skill in role plays as the trainees actually plan to use it
5. Assigning of homework

Stimulus Variability

Positive transfer is greater when a variety of relevant training stimuli are employed (Callantine & Warren, 1955; Duncan, 1958; Shore & Sechrest, 1961). Stimulus variability may be implemented in Structured Learning sessions by use of:

1. Rotation of group leaders across groups
2. Rotation of trainees across groups
3. Role playing of a given skill by trainees with several different co-actors
4. Role playing of a given skill by trainees across several relevant settings
5. Completion of multiple homework assignments for each given skill

Real-life Reinforcement

Given successful implementation of both appropriate Structured Learning procedures and the transfer enhancement procedures, positive transfer may still fail to occur. As Agras (1967), Gruber (1971), Patterson and Anderson (1964), Tharp and Wetzel (1969), and dozens of other investigators have shown, stable and enduring performance in application settings of newly learned skills is very much at the mercy of real-life reinforcement contingencies. We have found it useful to implement several supplemental programs outside of the Structured Learning setting that can help to provide the rewards trainees need to maintain new behaviors. These programs include provision for both external social rewards (provided by people in the trainee's real-life environments) and self-rewards (provided by the trainees themselves). A particularly useful tool for transfer enhancement, a tool combining the possibilities of identical elements, stimulus variability, and real-life reinforcement, is the skill homework assignment.

When possible, we urge use of a homework technique we have found to be successful with most groups. In this procedure, trainees are instructed to try in their own real-life settings the behaviors they have practiced during the session. The name of the person(s) with whom they will try the skill, the day, the place, etc. are all discussed. The trainee is urged to take notes on his attempt to use the skill on the Homework Report form (Figure 2). This form requests detailed information about what happened when the trainee attempted the homework assignment, how well he followed the relevant behavioral steps, the trainee's evaluation of his performance, and thoughts about what the next assignment might appropriately be.

It has often proven useful to start with relatively simple homework behaviors and, as mastery is achieved, work up to more complex and demanding assignments. This provides both the trainer and the people who are the targets of the homework with an opportunity to reinforce each approximation of the more complex target behavior. Successful experiences at beginning homework attempts are crucial in encouraging the trainee to make further attempts at real-life use of the skill.

The first part of each Structured Learning session is devoted to presenting and discussing these homework reports. When trainees have made an effort to complete their homework assignments, trainers should provide social reinforcement, while failure to do homework should be met with some chagrin and expressed disappointment, followed by support and encouragement to complete the assignment. It cannot be stressed too strongly that without these or similar attempts to maximize transfer, the value of the entire training effort is in severe jeopardy.

Later Sessions

Much of the foregoing procedural material may be conveniently summarized for purposes of review by the following outline.

Outline of Later Session Procedures

A. Homework review.
B. Trainer presents overview of the skill.
    1. Introduces skill briefly prior to showing modeling display.
    2. Asks questions that will help trainees define the skill in their own language.
       Examples:—"Who knows what _____ is?"
              —"What does _____ mean to you?"
              —"Who can define _____ ?"
    3. Postpones lengthier discussion until after trainees view the modeling display. If trainees want to engage in further discussion,

Figure 2. Homework Report

Name _____ Date _____

Group Leaders _____

Fill in During This Class

1. Homework assignment:

    a. Skill:

    b. Use with whom:

    c. Use when:

    d. Use where:

2. Steps to be followed:

Fill in Before Next Class

3. Describe what happened when you did the homework assignment:

4. Steps you actually followed:

5. Rate yourself on how well you used the skill (check one):

    Excellent ____   Good ____   Fair ____   Poor ____

6. Describe what you feel should be your *next* homework assignment:

the trainer might say, "Let's wait until after we've seen some examples of people using the skill before we talk about it in more detail."

    4. Makes a statement about what will follow the modeling display.
Example:—"After we see the examples, we will talk about times when you've had to use _____ and times when you may have to use that skill in the future."

    5. Distributes Skill Cards, asking a trainee to read the behavioral steps aloud.

    6. Asks trainees to follow each step in the modeling display as the step is depicted.

C. Trainer presents modeling display.

    1. Provides two relevant examples of the skill in use, following its behavioral steps.

D. Trainer invites discussion of skill that has been modeled.

    1. Invites comments on how the situation modeled may remind trainees of situations involving skill usage in their own lives.
Example:—"Did any of the situations you just saw remind you of times when you have had to _____ ?"

    2. Asks questions that encourage trainees to talk about skill usage and problems involving skill usage.
Examples:—"What do you do in situations where you have to _____ ?"
      —"Have you ever had to _____ ?"
      —"Have you ever had difficulty _____ ?"

E. Trainer organizes role play.

    1. Asks a trainee who has volunteered a situation to elaborate on his remarks, obtaining details on where, when, and with whom the skill might be useful in the future.

    2. Designates this trainee as a main actor, and asks the trainee to choose a co-actor (someone who reminds the main actor of the person with whom the skill will be used in the real-life situation).
Examples:—"What does _____ look like?"
      —"Who in the group reminds you of _____ in some way?"

    3. Gets additional information from the main actor, if necessary, and sets the stage for the role playing (including props, furniture arrangement, etc.).
Examples:—"Where might you be talking to _____ ?"
      —"How is the room furnished?"
      —"Would you be standing or sitting?"
      —"What time of day will it be?"

4. Rehearses with the main actor what he will say and do during the role play.

    Examples:—"What will you say for step one of the skill?"

        —"What will you do if the co-actor does ____ ____ ?"

5. Gives each group member some final instructions as to his part just prior to role playing.

    Examples:—To the main actor: "Try to follow all of the steps as best you can."

        —To the co-actor: "Try to play the part of _____ as best you can. Say and do what you think _____ would do when _____ follows the skill's steps."

        —To the other trainees in the group: "Watch how well _____ follows the steps so that we can talk about it after the role play."

F. Trainer instructs the role players to begin.

  1. One trainer stands at the chalkboard and points to each step as it is enacted and provides whatever coaching or prompting is needed by the main actor or co-actor.

  2. The other trainer sits with the observing trainees to help keep them attending to the unfolding role play.

  3. In the event that the role play strays markedly from the behavioral steps, the trainers stop the scene, provide needed instruction, and begin again.

G. Trainer invites feedback following role play.

  1. Asks the main actor to wait until he has heard everyone's comments before talking.

  2. Asks the co-actor, "In the role of _____ , how did _____ make you feel? What were your reactions to him?"

  3. Asks observing trainees: "How well were the behavioral steps followed?" "What specific things did you like or dislike?" "In what ways did the co-actor do a good job?"

  4. Comments on the following of the behavioral steps, provides social reward, points out what was done well, and comments on what else might be done to make the enactment even better.

  5. Asks main actor: "Now that you have heard everyone's comments, how do you feel about the job you did?" "How do you think that following the steps worked out?"

H. Trainer helps role player to plan homework.

  1. Asks the main actor how, when, and with whom he might attempt the behavioral steps prior to the next class meeting.

2. As appropriate, the Homework Report may be used to get a written commitment from the main actor to try out his new skill and report back to the group at the next meeting.

3. Trainees who have not had a chance to role play during a particular class may also be assigned homework in the form of looking for situations relevant to the skill that they might role play during the next class meeting.

MANAGING PROBLEM BEHAVIORS IN THE STRUCTURED LEARNING GROUP

As is true for any type of treatment, training, or teaching group, management problems sometimes occur during Structured Learning. Group management problems, at a general level, are any behaviors shown by one or more group members that interfere with, inhibit, deflect, or slow down the skills training procedures or goals that are the basic purposes of Structured Learning. In the present section we will describe problems as they may occur in the Structured Learning group. Some occur very rarely, others with somewhat greater frequency. All of the problems that we are presently aware of are included in our presentation to most fully prepare trainers for behaviors they may have to deal with in the actual groups. Our coverage should be considered comprehensive, but not exhaustive, since every time we have concluded that "we've seen everything" in the Structured Learning group, something new and challenging comes along. Our proposals for dealing with group management problems will usually suffice, but skilled trainers will be called upon from time to time to deal creatively and imaginatively with new challenges as they arise in even the most productive Structured Learning groups. Most methods for reducing group management problems will only need to be employed as a temporary bridge between initial trainee resistance or reluctance and that point in the process at which the trainee feels Structured Learning participation to be useful, valuable, and personally relevant. These techniques, derived from research on skills training group management as well as from our own experiences and those of others with such groups, should help trainers to deal with almost any difficulties that may arise in the Structured Learning group.

Types of Group Management Problems

Described next is the full range of group management problems that in reported experience have occurred in Structured Learning groups whose members are delinquent or chronically aggressive adolescents.

Inactivity

Minimal participation. Minimal participation involves trainees who seldom volunteer, provide only brief answers, and in general give the trainers a feeling that they are "pulling teeth" to keep the group at its various skills training tasks.

Apathy. A more extreme form of minimal participation is apathy, in which almost whatever the trainers do to direct, enliven, or activate the group is met with disinterest, lack of spontaneity, and little if any progress toward group goals.

Falling asleep. While it is quite rare, trainees do fall asleep from time to time. The sleepers need to be awakened and the trainers might wisely inquire into the cause of the tiredness, since boredom in the group, lack of sleep, and physical illness are all possible reasons, each one requiring a different trainer response.

Active Resistance

Participation, but not as instructed. Trainees displaying this type of group management problem are "off target." They may be trying to role play, serve as co-actor, give accurate feedback, or engage in other tasks required in Structured Learning, but their own personal agendas or misperceptions interfere, and they wander off course to irrelevant or semirelevant topics.

Passive-aggressive isolation. Passive-aggressive isolation is not merely apathy, in which the trainees are simply disinterested in participating. Nor is it participation but not as instructed, in which trainees actively go off task and raise personal agendas. Passive-aggressive isolation is the purposeful, intentional withholding of appropriate participation, an active shutting down of involvement. It can be thought of as a largely nonverbal crossing of one's arms in order to display deliberate nonparticipation.

Negativism. When displaying negativism, trainees signal more overtly, by word and deed, the wish to avoid participation in the Structured Learning group. They may openly refuse to role play, provide feedback, or complete homework assignments. Or, they may not come to sessions, come late to sessions, or walk out in the middle of a session.

Disruptiveness. Disruptiveness encompasses active resistance behaviors more extreme than negativism, such as openly and perhaps energetically ridiculing the trainers, other trainees, or aspects of the

Structured Learning process. Or, disruptiveness may be shown by gestures, movements, noises, or other distracting nonverbal behaviors characteristically symbolizing overt criticism and hostility.

Hyperactivity

Digression. Digression is related to "participation, but not as instructed," but in our experience is a more repetitive, more determined, and more strongly motivated moving away from the purposes and procedures of Structured Learning. Here, the trainees are feeling strongly some emotion, such as anger or anxiety or despair, and are determined to express it. Or the skill portrayed by the trainers or other trainees may set off associations with important recent experiences, which the trainees feel the need to present and discuss. Digression is also often characterized by "jumping out of role" in the role play. Rather than merely wandering off track, in digression the trainees *drive* the train off its intended course.

Monopolizing. Monopolizing involves subtle and not so subtle efforts by trainees to get more than a fair share of time during a Structured Learning session. Long monologues, requests by the trainees to unnecessarily role play again, elaborate feedback, and attention-seeking efforts to "remain on stage" are examples of such monopolizing behavior.

Interruption. Similar to monopolizing, but more intrusive and insistent, interruption is literally breaking into the ongoing flow of a modeling display, role play, or feedback period with comments, questions, suggestions, observations, or other statements. Interruptions may be overly assertive or angry on the one hand or take a more pseudobenevolent guise of being offered by a "trainer's helper." In either event, such interruptions more often than not retard the group's progress toward its goals.

Excessive restlessness. This is a more extreme, more physical form, of hyperactivity. The trainees may fidget while sitting, rock their chairs, get up and pace, smoke a great deal, drink soft drink after soft drink, or display other nonverbal, verbal, gestural, or postural signs of restlessness. Such behavior will typically be accompanied by digression, monopolizing, or interrupting behavior.

Cognitive Inadequacies and Emotional Disturbance

Inability to pay attention. Closely related at times to excessive restlessness, the inability to pay attention is often an apparent result of internal or external distractions, daydreaming, or other pressing agendas that command the trainees' attention. Inability to pay attention except for brief time spans may also be due to one or more forms of cognitive impairment.

Inability to understand. Cognitive deficits due to developmental disability, intellectual inadequacy, impoverishment of experience, disease processes, or other sources may result in aspects of the Structured Learning process not being understood, or being misunderstood, by the trainees. Failure to understand can, of course, also result from errors in the clarity and complexity of statements presented by the trainers.

Inability to remember. Material presented in the Structured Learning group may be both attended to and understood by the trainees, but not remembered. This may result not only in problems of skill transfer, but also in group management problems when what is forgotten includes rules and procedures for trainee participation, homework assignments, and so forth.

Bizarre behavior. This type of group management problem is not common, but when instances of it do occur it can be especially disruptive to group functioning. It may not only pull other trainees off task, but it may also frighten them or make them highly anxious. The range of bizarre behaviors possible is quite broad, and includes talking to oneself or inanimate objects, offering incoherent statements to the group, becoming angry for no apparent reason, hearing and responding to imaginary voices, and exhibiting peculiar mannerisms.

Reducing Group Management Problems

Most Structured Learning sessions proceed rather smoothly, but the competent trainer is a prepared trainer. Preparation includes both knowing what problems might occur, as well as corrective steps to take when they do occur. The remainder of this section will be devoted to examining an array of methods for reducing group management problems.

Simplification Methods

Reward minimal trainee accomplishment. Problematic trainee behavior can sometimes be altered by a process similar to what has been called "shaping." For example, rather than responding positively to trainees only when they enact a complete and accurate role play, reward in the form of praise and approval may be offered for lesser but still successful accomplishments. Perhaps only one or two behavioral steps were role played correctly. Or, in the extreme example of rewarding minimal trainee accomplishment, praise may be offered for "trying" after a totally unsuccessful role play or even for merely paying attention to someone else's role play.

Shorten the role play. A more direct means for simplifying the trainees' task is to ask less of them. One way of doing so is to shorten the role play, usually by asking trainees to role play only some (or one) of the behavioral steps that constitute the skill being taught.

Have trainer "feed" sentences to the trainee. With trainees having a particularly difficult time participating appropriately in the Structured Learning group, especially for reasons of cognitive inadequacy, the trainer may elect to take on the role of coach or prompter. There are a variety of ways this may be accomplished, perhaps the most direct of which involves a trainer standing immediately behind the trainee and whispering the particular statements that constitute proper enactment of each behavioral step for the trainee to then say out loud.

Have trainee read a prepared script. We personally have never used this approach to group management problems, but others report some success with it. In essence, it removes the burden of figuring out what to say completely from the trainees and makes easier the task of getting up in front of the group and acting out the skill's behavioral steps. Clearly, as with all simplification methods, using a prepared script should be seen as a temporary device, used to move trainees in the direction of role playing with no such special assistance from the trainers.

Have trainee play co-actor role first. An additional means of easing trainees into the responsibility of being the main actor in a role play is to have them play the role of the co-actor at first. This accustoms them more gradually to getting up before the group and speaking, because the "spotlight" is mostly on someone else. As with the use of a prepared script, this method should be used temporarily only. Before moving on to the next skill, *all* trainees must always take on the role of the main actor with the particular skill.

Elicitation of Response Methods

Call for volunteers. Particularly in the early stages of the life of a Structured Learning group, trainee participation may have to be actively elicited by the group's trainers. As trainees actually experience the group's procedures, find them personally relevant and valuable, and find support and acceptance from the trainers and from other group members, the need for such elicitation typically diminishes. The least directive form of such trainer activity is the straightforward calling for volunteers.

Introduce topics for discussion. Calling for volunteers, essentially an invitation to the group as a whole, may yield no response in the highly apathetic group. Under this circumstance, introducing topics for the group to discuss that appear relevant to the needs, concerns, aspirations, and particular skill deficiencies of the participating members will often be an effective course of action to pursue.

Call on a specific trainee. The largely nondirective elicitation methods already presented may be followed by a more active and directive trainer intervention if unsuccessful, that is, calling upon a particular trainee and requesting that trainee's participation. In doing so, it is often useful to select for such purposes a trainee who by means of attentiveness, facial expression, eye contact, or other nonverbal signaling communicates potential involvement and interest.

Reinstruct trainees by means of prompting and coaching. The trainer may have to become still more active and directive than mentioned already and, in a manner similar to our earlier discussion of feeding role play lines to a trainee, prompt and coach the trainee to adequate participation. Such assistance may involve any aspect of the Structured Learning process—attending to the modeling display, following a skill's behavioral steps during the role playing, providing useful performance feedback after someone else's role play, completing the homework assignments in the proper manner, and so forth.

Threat Reduction Methods

Employ additional live modeling by the trainers. When the Structured Learning trainers engage in live modeling of the session's skill, they are doing more than just the main task of skill enactment. Such trainer behavior also makes it easier for trainees to similarly get up and risk less-than-perfect performances in an effort to learn the skill. For trainees who are particularly anxious, inhibited, or reluctant to role play, an additional portrayal or two of the same skill by the trainers may put them at ease. Such additional live modeling will also prove useful to those trainees having difficulty role playing because of cognitive inadequacies.

Postpone trainee's role playing until last. This recommendation is a straightforward extension of the one just presented. The threat of role playing may be reduced for a trainee if he is not required to role play until both the trainers' live modeling and role playing by all other trainees are completed. It is crucial, though, that no trainee deficient in the session's skill be excused completely from role playing that skill. To do so would run counter to the central, skill-training purpose of Structured Learning.

Provide reassurance to the trainee. This method of dealing with group management problems involves the trainers' providing one or more trainees with brief, straightforward, simple, but very often highly effective, messages of encouragement and reassurance. "You can do it," "We'll help you as you go along," "Take it a step at a time" are but a few examples of such frequently valuable reassurance.

Provide empathic encouragement to the trainee. This is a method we have used often, with good results. In the case of trainee reluctance to role play, for example, the trainer may provide empathic encouragement by proceeding through the following steps:

Step 1. Offer the resistant trainee the opportunity to explain in greater detail her reluctance to role play and listen nondefensively.

Step 2. Clearly express your understanding of the resistant trainee's feelings.

Step 3. If appropriate, respond that the trainee's view is a viable alternative.

Step 4. Present your own view in greater detail, with both supporting reasons and probable outcomes.

Step 5. Express the appropriateness of delaying a resolution of the trainer-trainee difference.

Step 6. Urge the trainee to tentatively try to role play the given behavioral steps.

The identical procedure may be used effectively with a wide range of other trainee resistances.

Clarify threatening aspects of the trainee's task. Clarifying threatening aspects of tasks requires deeper explanations, repetition of earlier clarifications, and provision of further illustrations. In all instances, the task involved remains unchanged, but what is required of trainees to complete the task is further presented and made clear.

Restructure threatening aspects of the trainee's task. Unlike the method just discussed, in which the task remains unchanged and the trainers seek to clarify the trainee's understanding of it, in the present method the trainers may alter the trainee's task if it is seen as threatening. Behavioral steps may be altered, simplified, moved around, deleted, or added. Role plays may be shortened, lengthened, changed in content, merged with other skills, or otherwise changed. Aspects of performance feedback may be changed, too—the sequence of who delivers it, its generality versus specificity, its timing, its length, its focus. *No* aspect of Structured Learning as presented in this manual should be considered unchangeable. *All* treatment, training, and teaching methods should perpetually be open to revision as needed in the judgment of their skilled and sensitive users. Most certainly, this also includes Structured Learning.

Termination of Response Methods

Urge trainee to remain on task. Gently, but firmly, trainees who wander off the group's task may at times be brought back on track. The trainers can do this by reminders, cajoling, admonishing, or simply clearly pointing out to trainees what they are doing incorrectly and what they ought to be doing instead.

Ignore trainee behavior. Certain inappropriate trainee behaviors can be terminated most effectively by simply ignoring them. This withdrawal of reinforcement, or extinction process, is best applied to those problem behaviors that the group can tolerate while still remaining on task as the extinction process is taking place. Behaviors such as pacing, whispering to oneself, and occasional interruptions are examples of behaviors perhaps best terminated by simply ignoring them. Behaviors that are more disruptive to the group's functioning, or even dangerous, will have to be dealt with more frontally.

Interrupt ongoing trainee behavior. This problem management method requires directive and assertive trainer behavior. We recommend interrupting ongoing trainee behavior primarily when other methods fail. Interrupting trainees' inappropriate, erroneous, or disruptive behavior should be carried out firmly, unequivocally, and with the clear message that the group has its tasks and they must be gotten on with. In its extreme form, interrupting trainee behavior may even require removing trainees from groups for a brief or for an extended period of time.

This consideration of problem behaviors and their reduction completes our presentation of the procedures that constitute Structured Learning. We close this chapter with the skill steps employed in our 10-session ART program.

ART Structured Learning Skills

Skill 1. Expressing a Complaint

1. Define what the problem is and who is responsible for it.
2. Decide how the problem might be solved.
3. Tell that person what the problem is and how it might be solved.
4. Ask for a response.
5. Show that you understand his/her feelings.
6. Come to agreement on the steps to be taken by each of you.

Skill 2. Responding to the Feelings of Others (Empathy)

1. Observe the other person's words and actions.
2. Decide what the other person might be feeling and how strong the feelings are.
3. Decide whether it would be helpful to let the other person know you understand his/her feelings.
4. Tell the other person, in a warm and sincere manner, how you think he/she is feeling.

Skill 3. Preparing for a Stressful Conversation

1. Imagine yourself in the stressful situation.
2. Think about how you will feel and why you will feel that way.
3. Imagine the other person in the stressful situation. Think about how that person will feel and why.
4. Imagine yourself telling the other person what you want to say.
5. Imagine what he/she will say.
6. Repeat the above steps using as many approaches as you can think of.
7. Choose the best approach.

Skill 4. Responding to Anger

1. Listen openly to what the other person has to say.
2. Show that you understand what the other person is feeling.
3. Ask the other person to explain anything you don't understand.
4. Show that you understand *why* the other person feels angry.
5. If it is appropriate, express your thoughts and feelings about the situation.

Skill 5. Keeping Out of Fights

1. Stop and think about why you want to fight.
2. Decide what you want to happen in the long run.
3. Think about other ways to handle the situation besides fighting.
4. Decide on the best way to handle the situation and do it.

Skill 6. Helping Others

1. Decide if the other person might need and want your help.
2. Think of the ways you could be helpful.
3. Ask the other person if he/she needs and wants your help.
4. Help the other person.

Skill 7. Dealing with an Accusation

1. Think about what the other person has accused you of.
2. Think about why the person might have accused you.
3. Think about ways to answer the person's accusations.
4. Choose the best way and do it.

Skill 8. Dealing with Group Pressure

1. Think about what the other people want you to do and why.
2. Decide what you want to do.
3. Decide how to tell the other people what you want to do.
4. Tell the group what you have decided.

Skill 9. Expressing Affection

1. Decide if you have good feelings about the other person.
2. Decide whether the other person would like to know about your feelings.
3. Decide how you might best express your feelings.
4. Choose the right time and place to express your feelings.
5. Express affection in a warm and caring manner.

Skill 10. Responding to Failure

1. Decide if you have failed.
2. Think about both the personal reasons and the circumstances that have caused you to fail.
3. Decide how you might do things differently if you tried again.
4. Decide if you want to try again.
5. If it is appropriate, try again, using your revised approach.

Chapter 4

The Affective Component of ART: Anger Control Training

Although not all acts of aggression are preceded by anger by the per-petrator nor are all instances of anger necessarily followed by overt aggression, it is nonetheless true that very frequently anger leads to and is the sufficient antecedent of overt aggressive behavior. As we noted earlier, ART is multimodal in its intended thrust. Thus its behavior replacement goal is sought not only by the explicit teaching via Struc-tured Learning of prosocial alternative behaviors, but, as this chapter will describe, also by a parallel affect-oriented effort to eliminate or reduce the antecedent anger arousal.

ORIGINS OF ANGER CONTROL TRAINING

To best understand this component of ART, labeled Anger Control Train-ing, we begin this chapter in what at first may seem to be a setting quite distant from the study of anger and its management—the experimental psychology laboratory of the Russian psychologist Luria. In an extended series of investigations, Luria (1961) explored the manner in which in the course of normal development the child comes to regulate much of his external behavior by means of internal speech. Little and Kendall (1979) succinctly describe this unfolding pattern:

> The process of development of verbal control of behavior thus seems to follow a standard developmental sequence. First, the initiation of motor behavior comes under control of adult verbal cues, and then the inhibition of responses is controlled by the speech of adults. Self-control emerges as the child learns to respond to his own verbal cues, first to initiate responses and then to inhibit them.
>
> The 3- or 4-year-old child normally can follow rather com-plicated instructions given by an adult, and it is at this age that the child is said to begin to regulate his own behavior on the basis of verbal self-instructions.... Between the ages of $4\frac{1}{2}$ and $5\frac{1}{2}$, the child's self-verbalizations shift from overt to covert (primarily internal) speech. (p. 101)

In addition to Luria's seminal research, a number of other investigators have examined and confirmed this verbal mediation process (Allport, 1924; Bem, 1967; Kohlberg, Yaeger, & Hjertholm, 1968; Mussen, 1963; Vygotsky, 1962; Waring, 1927). But as with all normative developmental processes, there are children in whom the expected sequence fails to occur, occurs only in part, or occurs in distorted or incomplete form. If the studies cited lead to the conclusion that "there is considerable evidence to support the belief that self-control develops largely as a function of a child's development of [internal] language mechanisms" (Little & Kendall, 1979, p. 104), what of the youngsters in whom this sequence fails to fully or correctly unfold? As we shall see, it is precisely such youngsters who—deficient in the ability to regulate overt behavior by internal speech—display the arrays of behavior associated with such terms as hyperactivity, impulsivity, poor self-control, acting-out, and the like. However, as we shall also see, such impulsive behavior in these very same, poorly self-controlled youngsters may be reduced by externally imposed interventions that very closely replicate the normal developmental sequence described by Luria.

Donald Meichenbaum and his research group have been especially active in research in this area. Their initial investigations sought to establish further the relationship between impulsivity and poor verbal control of overt behavior. Meichenbaum and Goodman (1969), using what has become a standard measure for determining impulsivity/reflectivity, that is Kagan's (1966) Matching Familiar Figures Test, found that those youngsters who respond on the Kagan test quickly and make many errors (the impulsive youngsters) indeed exercise diminished verbal control over their overt behavior as compared to youngsters who take their time and make fewer errors (the reflective youngsters). But just what do reflective and impulsive youngsters say to themselves, and how does their self-directed speech differ? To answer such questions, Meichenbaum and Goodman (1971) observed and recorded the play behavior and private speech of sixteen 4-year-olds, who were matched for age, intelligence, and socioeconomic status. Half of the children were reflective and half of the children were impulsive on the Kagan measure. Their results indicated that the private speech of the cognitively impulsive preschoolers was largely comprised of the most immature, self-stimulatory content. Reflective preschoolers, in comparison, manifested significantly more outer-directed and self-regulatory speech and significantly more inaudible mutterings. The investigators thus concluded from their observational studies that cognitively reflective preschoolers use their private speech in a more mature, more instrumental, and more self-guiding fashion than impulsive preschoolers do.

Other investigators concerned with self-directed speech in impulsive children reported concurring results (Dickie, 1973; Kleiman, 1974), and Camp (1977) extended the finding to a different category of youngsters often deficient in the developmental sequence described by Luria. Camp found that "aggressive boys fail to employ verbal mediational activity in many situations where it would be appropriate, and when it does occur, covert mediational activity may fail to achieve functional control over behavior" (p. 151).

The nature of the normative developmental sequence described by Luria and found wanting in impulsive youngsters by Meichenbaum and others led Meichenbaum (1977) to seek to duplicate the sequence as a remedial intervention for youngsters deficient in such self-regulatory skills. He comments:

> Could we systematically train hyperactive, impulsive youngsters to alter their problem-solving styles, to think before they act, in short, to talk to themselves differently? Could we, in light of the specific mediational deficits observed, teach the children how to (a) comprehend the task, (b) spontaneously produce mediators and strategies, and (c) use such mediators to guide, monitor, and control their performances? This was the challenge that sparked the development of self-instructional training. (p. 31)

SELF-INSTRUCTIONAL TRAINING FOR THE IMPULSIVE YOUNGSTER

In research on self-instructional training, the typical sequence of instructional procedures is:

1. The therapist models task performance and self-instructs out loud while the child observes.
2. The child performs the task, instructing himself out loud as he does so.
3. The therapist models task performance and whispers self-instructions while the child observes.
4. The child performs the task, instructing himself in a whisper as he does so.
5. The therapist performs the task using covert self-instructions, with pauses and behavioral signs of thinking such as raising her eyes toward the ceiling or stroking her chin.
6. The child performs the task using covert self-instructions.

Meichenbaum and Goodman's (1971) initial use of these procedures yielded decreased impulsivity and enhanced reflectiveness (i.e., increased response time and decreased error rate) in samples of hyperactive youngsters in comparison to appropriate control conditions. They indeed could learn, as the investigators put it, "to stop, look, and listen." This early research also showed that observing a model utilize covert self-instructions was not sufficient to obtain the desired outcome; the youngster had to covertly self-instruct also.

Other investigators reported essentially confirming results vis à vis impulsiveness and hyperactivity (Bornstein & Quevillon, 1976; Camp, Blom, Hebert, & VanDoorninck, 1977; Douglas, Parry, Marton, & Garson, 1976; Palkes, Stewart, & Kahana, 1968) and began extending the apparent utility of self-instructional training to other, often related, types of problem behaviors. These include problematic classroom behaviors (Monahan & O'Leary, 1971; Robin, Armel, & O'Leary, 1975), tolerance for resisting temptation (Hartig & Kanfer, 1973), pain (Turk, 1976), anxiety (Meichenbaum, Gilmore, & Fedoravicius, 1971), and, as we shall examine in detail shortly, anger and aggression.

Beyond confirmation of effectiveness, a number of these studies provide valuable information regarding conditions under which self-instructional training effects may be maximized. Bender (1976), for example, showed enhanced reduction in impulsivity when the child's covert self-instructions included explicit strategies rather than just general instructions. Kendall (1977), proceeding further in this direction toward concrete instructions, recommended that the content of self-instructions used by impulsive youngsters optimally should consist of the following:

1. Problem definition, for example, "Let's see, what am I supposed to do?"
2. Problem approach, for example, "Well, I should look this over and try to figure out how to get to the center of the maze."
3. Focusing of attention, for example, "I better look ahead so I don't get trapped."
4. Coping statements, for example, "Oh, that path isn't right. If I go that way I'll get stuck. I'll just go back here and try another way."
5. Self-reinforcement, for example, "Hey, not bad. I really did a good job."

As is true for all psychological and educational interventions, not all tests of the efficacy of self-instructional training have yielded results confirming its value. Nonconfirming investigations include those of Heath (1978), Higa (1973), Weinreich (1975), and Williams and Akamatsu (1978). As our first chapter made clear, and as these several nonconfirming studies concretely highlight, all interventions—including self-instructional training—are optimally offered *prescriptively*. Self-instructional training appears to yield its hoped-for effects with some youngsters but not with others, and under some conditions but not under others. In a seminal discussion of this perspective titled "Outcome Inconsistency and Moderator Variables," Kendall and Braswell (1985) marshaled evidence from a large number of investigations to indicate that the effectiveness of self-instructional training was influenced by the youngster's age, sex, socioeconomic status, cognitive level, attributional style, and apparent motivation. The importance of these and other prescriptive moderator variables upon performance in the context of self-instructional training has also been emphasized by Copeland (1981, 1982); Pressley (1979); Braswell, Kendall, and Urbain (1982); and Kopel and Arkowitz (1975).

SELF-INSTRUCTIONAL TRAINING FOR
THE AGGRESSIVE YOUNGSTER

In 1975, Novaco sought to apply the self-instructional training approach to the management of anger. By way of definition, he comments:

> The arousal of anger is here viewed as an affective stress reaction. That is, anger arousal is a response to perceived environmental demands—most commonly, aversive psychosocial events.... Anger is thought to consist of a combination of physiological arousal and cognitive labeling of that arousal as anger.... Anger arousal results from particular appraisals of aversive events. External circumstances provoke anger only as mediated by their meaning to the individual. (Novaco, 1979, pp. 252-253)

It is important to note in this definition the central role of affective arousal in forming the definition of anger. Novaco's attempt to apply self-instructional training to the management of anger was based not only upon the general success of such training in altering self-regulatory processes, but also upon a separate series of studies consistently showing the marked influence (increases and decreases) of covert self-verbalization upon a variety of arousal states. Rimm and Litvak (1969), for example, found that affectively loaded implicit self-statements increased both respiration rate and depth. Schwartz (1971), using similar procedures, found increased heart rate to result, and May and Johnson (1973) reported similar findings, plus an effect of inner speech on skin conductance. Russell and Brandsma (1974) also found such skin conductance changes.

These findings, viewed in the context of the work of Luria, Meichenbaum, and others, led Novaco (1975) to conclude that "a basic premise is that anger is fomented, maintained, and influenced by the self-statements that are made in provocation situations" (p. 17). The intervention he constructed and examined for its anger control value consisted of three stages. In the first, *cognitive preparation*, the trainee is taught about the cognitive, physiological, and behavioral aspects of anger, its positive and negative functions, and especially its antecedents. During the second stage, *skill acquisition*, trainees learn alternative coping skills to utilize in response to provocations. It is here that special emphasis is placed upon self-instruction. The third phase, *application training*, makes use of imaginal and role-play inductions of anger and homework assignments to facilitate practice of the coping skills acquired—particularly skill in self-instruction. To operationalize this three-stage intervention, Novaco (1975) construed the process of self-instructing to control anger as necessarily responsive to all phases of the provocation sequence: (1) preparation for provocation, (2) impact and confrontation, (3) coping with arousal, and (4) reflecting on the provocation. Table 3 provides examples of the self-statements relevant to each phase which were rehearsed by Novaco's subjects in his evaluation of self-instruction for anger management.

Novaco's (1975) initial research subjects were 34 persons who were both self-identified and externally assessed as having serious anger-control problems. Four treatment conditions were established: self-instructional training plus relaxation training, each of these two conditions separately, and an attention-control condition. The effect of these interventions was measured by self-report and physiological indices, subject response to role-played provocations, and by anger diary ratings. Results indicated that across these outcome criteria the combined treatment, and to a lesser extent the self-instructional treatment alone, led to significant decreases in anger and significantly improved anger management. Novaco was able to later replicate this success both in a clinical case study (Novaco, 1977) and in a group comparison study involving probation officers (Novaco, 1978). Atrops (1978), Crain (1977), and Schrader, Long, Panzer, Gillet, and Kornbath (1977) have each reported successful use of Novaco's self-instructional training with chronically angry adolescent or adult offenders. This result is buttressed substantially by numerous other investigations demonstrating a decrease in anger or aggression as a result of self-statements whose contents were a more benign, cognitive reinterpretation of the provoking experiences (Green & Murray, 1973; Kaufmann & Feshbach, 1963; Mallick & McCandless, 1966; McCullough, Huntsinger, & Nay,

Table 3. Examples of Self-Statements Rehearsed in Self-Instructional Training for Anger Management

Preparing for provocation

This is going to upset me, but I know how to deal with it.

What is it that I have to do?

I can work out a plan to handle this.

I can manage the situation. I know how to regulate my anger.

If I find myself getting upset, I'll know what to do.

There won't be any need for an argument.

Try not to take this too seriously.

This could be a testy situation, but I believe in myself.

Time for a few deep breaths of relaxation. Feel comfortable, relaxed, and at ease.

Easy does it. Remember to keep your sense of humor.

Impact and Confrontation

Stay calm. Just continue to relax.

As long as I keep my cool, I'm in control.

Just roll with the punches; don't get bent out of shape.

Think of what you want to get out of this.

You don't need to prove yourself.

There is no point in getting mad.

Don't make more out of this than you have to.

I'm not going to let him get to me.

Look for the positives. Don't assume the worst or jump to conclusions.

It's really a shame she has to act like this.

For someone to be that irritable, he must be awfully unhappy.

If I start to get mad, I'll just be banging my head against the wall. So I might as well just relax.

There is no need to doubt myself. What he says doesn't matter.

I'm on top of this situation and it's under control.

Coping with arousal

My muscles are starting to feel tight. Time to relax and slow things down.

Getting upset won't help.

It's just not worth it to get so angry.

I'll let him make a fool of himself.

I have a right to be annoyed, but let's keep the lid on.

Note. Adapted from Novaco, R.W. (1975). *Anger control: The development and evaluation of an experimental treatment* (pp. 95–96). Lexington, MA: D.C. Heath.

Table 3. *(cont.)*

Time to take a deep breath.

Let's take the issue point by point.

My anger is a signal of what I need to do. Time to instruct myself.

I'm not going to get pushed around, but I'm not going haywire either.

Try to reason it out. Treat each other with respect.

Let's try a cooperative approach. Maybe we are both right.

Negatives lead to more negatives. Work constructively.

He'd probably like me to get really angry. Well I'm going to disappoint him.

I can't expect people to act the way I want them to.

Take it easy, don't get pushy.

Reflecting on the provocation
  a. When conflict is unresolved

Forget about the aggravation. Thinking about it only makes you upset.

These are difficult situations, and they take time to straighten out.

Try to shake it off. Don't let it interfere with your job.

I'll get better at this as I get more practice.

Remember relaxation. It's a lot better than anger.

Can you laugh about it? It's probably not so serious.

Don't take it personally.

Take a deep breath.

  b. When conflict is resolved or coping is successful

I handled that one pretty well. It worked!

That wasn't as hard as I thought.

It could have been a lot worse.

I could have gotten more upset than it was worth.

I actually got through that without getting angry.

My pride can sure get me into trouble, but when I don't take things too seriously, I'm better off.

I guess I've been getting upset for too long when it wasn't even necessary.

I'm doing better at this all the time.

1977; Moon & Eisler, 1983; Schlichter & Horan, 1981; Snyder & White, 1979; Stein & Davis, 1982) although, as we noted with respect to the self- instructional training of impulsive youngsters, there are exceptions to its successful use with high-anger individuals (Coats, 1979; Urbain & Kendall, 1981).

Just as Meichenbaum needed to view the remediation of impulsivity in the light of Luria's insights about the normal development of self-regulation, and as Novaco needed Meichenbaum's impulsivity research results in order to extend self-instructional training to chronically angry individuals, the final psychologist in the lineage of Anger Control Training whose work we will summarize built upon the substantial foundation provided by Novaco. Eva Feindler and her research group have contributed greatly to the development of anger control training, both with important research findings and substantial refinements in technique (Feindler, 1979; Feindler & Fremouw, 1983; Feindler, Latini, Nape, Romano, & Doyle, 1980; Feindler, et al., 1984). This series of investigations provides consistent additional support for the anger-control potency of the cognitive preparation, skill acquisition, application training sequence examined earlier by Novaco, especially for the self-instructional components. In addition, these investigations provided refinement of the Novaco three-stage sequence into a chain in which clients learn (1) *triggers*—the external events and internal appraisals that serve as provocations to anger arousal; (2) *cues*—the physiological and kinesthetic sensations that signal to the individual her level of anger arousal; (3) *reminders*—the self-instructional statements that may function to reduce anger arousal, for example, the statements on Table 3; (4) *reducers*—techniques that in combination with reminders may reduce anger arousal, for example, deep breathing, backward counting, peaceful imagery, and consideration of long-term consequences; and (5) *self-evaluation*—the opportunity to self-reinforce and/or self-correct depending on how well or poorly Steps 1-4 were implemented. Finally, in addition to the empirical evidence provided and procedural refinements created and examined, Feindler sounds a welcome prescriptive note:

> Further delineation is needed on individual subject variables that may predict appropriateness for self-control treatment or account for differential responses to treatment. Variables such as age, length of residential treatment, nature of aggressive acts, attributional style, cognitive ability, level of social skills, family stability, and degree of peer involvement in antisocial acts may all help to predict adolescent responsiveness to treatment. (Feindler & Fremouw, 1983, p. 482)

In our own work on Anger Control Training and our use of it as one of three constituent procedures of ART, we thus stand on a series of broad and creative shoulders—Luria, Meichenbaum, Novaco, Feindler, and others. Our own relevant research findings (see Chapter 8) and our efforts to refine the technology of anger control still further (see Chapter 5) we hope will prove worthy additions to this ongoing research and development progression.

Chapter 5

Trainer's Manual for Anger Control Training

Anger and aggressive behavior are clearly major problems for many delinquent adolescents.* Not only do anger and aggression themselves cause difficulty for adolescents and those attempting to work with them, but the adolescents' frequent preference for using such behavior in conflict situations interferes with the use of whatever positive and constructive behavior they may possess or be taught. The goal of the Anger Control Training program described in this chapter is to teach adolescents (1) to understand what causes them to feel angry and act aggressively and (2) techniques they can use to reduce their anger and aggression. Many adolescents believe that in many situations they have no choice: The only way for them to respond is with aggression. Although they may perceive situations in this way, it is the goal of Anger Control Training to give them the skills necessary to make a choice. By learning what causes them to become angry and by learning how to use a series of anger reduction techniques, adolescents will become more able to stop their almost "automatic" aggressive responses long enough to consider constructive alternatives.

CONDUCTING THE ANGER CONTROL TRAINING GROUP

Anger Control Training is designed to be taught by one or two trainers with groups of 6 to 10 adolescents. Successful trainers of Anger Control Training groups ideally are very much the same types of individuals who succeed in running effective Structured Learning groups. They should possess, in general, the positive personal and good teacher qualities noted earlier as desirable for trainers of Structured Learning groups. In

---

*This chapter follows, in general outline, Feindler, E. L. (1981). *The art of self-control.* Unpublished manuscript, Adelphi University, Garden City, NY.

addition, they should be knowledgeable about and well practiced in Anger Control Training procedures and able to deal effectively with their own personal anger management.

The Anger Control Training program described in this chapter is comprised of 10 weekly sessions of 1 hour each. Anger Control Training requires active participation by trainees, both during the training sessions themselves and by completing assigned homework between sessions. Anger Control Training is an active process for the trainer as well. The trainer is required to model (demonstrate) the proper use of the anger reduction techniques that are the core of the program, guide (lead the role playing) trainees' practice of the program's anger reducers, and provide feedback about how successful this practice was in matching the trainer's modeling. The following guidelines are applicable to conducting this training sequence.

Modeling

All modeling begins with the trainer stating the particular anger control technique or chain of techniques that he will demonstrate and then describing a conflict situation in which the technique(s) may be used. If there are two trainers available, they should both do the modeling, with one trainer being the "main actor" who demonstrates the technique(s) and the other being the "co-actor" who represents the person who provokes the main actor. When two trainers are not available, a group member may serve as the co-actor. In such cases it is important to briefly rehearse with the co-actor in order to provide a realistic example of a provocation in a conflict situation.

Once the conflict situation has been briefly described, the two actors then act out the scene, with the main actor *carefully and clearly using the anger control technique(s)*. Following the completion of the scene, the trainer summarizes the technique(s) he used and briefly discusses them with the trainees. The following are some general guidelines for modeling:

1. Use at least two examples for each demonstration.
2. Try to select scenes that are relevant to trainees.
3. All scenes should result in positive outcomes, never in aggressive acts.
4. The main actor should be portrayed as a person reasonably similar in age, socioeconomic background, verbal ability, and other salient characteristics to the people in the Anger Control Training group.

Role Playing

Following each modeling presentation, trainees are asked to take part in role plays in which they practice the just-modeled anger control technique or chain of techniques in situations they have recently encountered or expect to encounter in the near future. The Hassle Log (a worksheet introduced later in the chapter) is an ideal source for such situations. Once a trainee describes the conflict situation from his Hassle Log, he becomes the main actor in the role play and chooses a second trainee (the co-actor) to play the part of the other person in the conflict. The trainer then asks for enough information (time, place, etc.) from the main actor to set the stage for the role play. The scene is then played out with the main actor applying the anger control technique(s) as accurately as possible.

In Anger Control Training trainees will learn a number of anger reduction techniques, some of which will be more useful than others for different trainees. One trainee may need only one technique to control his anger, while others may need two, three, or more techniques in combination. Since the role playing that runs throughout the program is aimed at giving the trainees practice at handling real-life conflict situations, the trainer is encouraged to help trainees try out in the role plays *all* of the different techniques so that each person can identify which are most useful to him. As the program progresses and the role plays call for anger reducers, the main actor should use any or all of the anger reduction techniques that he feels are helpful and/or necessary to achieve greater self-control and personal power.

Some general role playing guidelines for trainers follow:

1. Just before beginning, remind the trainees of their parts: The main actor must use the anger control technique(s) and the co-actor should try to stay in his described role in the scene.
2. Instruct the observing group members to pay attention to whether the anger control technique(s) are being used properly by the main actor.
3. As the role play unfolds, if either actor "breaks role," stop the scene and encourage him to get back into role.
4. If the role play is clearly departing from the anger control technique(s) to be practiced, stop the role play, give whatever instructions are needed, and then restart the role play.
5. The role playing should continue until *each* trainee has had the opportunity to be the main actor and practice using the technique(s) in a situation he has really encountered or is about to encounter.

Performance Feedback

After each role play there should be a brief feedback period that points out to the main actor how well he used the technique(s) being practiced. This also provides the main actor with a chance to see how the use of the anger control technique(s) affected the co-actor, and provides the encouragement to try the technique(s) outside of the training sessions. The feedback should be sequenced in the following manner: (1) The co-actor is asked about his reactions; (2) the observers are asked to comment on how well the technique was used; and (3) the trainers comment on how well the technique was used and provide reinforcement (praise, approval, encouragement). There are several guidelines for providing reinforcement effectively:

1. Provide reinforcement only after role plays in which the technique was used properly.
2. Provide reinforcement to the co-actor for his help and cooperation.
3. Provide a degree of reinforcement that matches the quality of the role play.
4. Provide no reinforcement when the role play departs significantly from using the specific technique.
5. Provide reinforcement for a trainee's improvement in the use of the techniques from the previous role plays.

After all of the feedback, give the main actor an opportunity to make comments on both the role play and the feedback he has just received.

Managing Problem Behaviors

Problem behaviors will sometimes interfere with management of the Anger Control Training group. Group management problems, such as inactivity, active resistance, hyperactivity, cognitive inadequacies, and emotional disturbance are discussed in the Structured Learning trainer's manual, Chapter 3. Problems that occur in the two groups are likely to be similar, and trainers can refer to Chapter 3 for methods of reducing group management problems.

PROGRAM SESSIONS

With this general background, we will look at the outline of each of the 10 sessions, presented in Table 4. Then we will review each session's structure in more detail.

Table 4. General Overview of Anger Control Training

Week 1: Introduction
1. Explain the goals of Anger Control Training and "sell it" to the youngsters.
2. Explain the rules for participating and the training procedures.
3. Give initial assessments of the A-B-Cs of aggressive behavior: (A) What led up to it? (B) What did you do? (C) What were the consequences?
4. Review goals, procedures, and A-B-Cs; give out binders.

Week 2: Cues and Anger Reducers 1, 2, and 3
1. Review first session.
2. Introduce the Hassle Log.
3. Discuss how to know when you are angry (cues).
4. Discuss what to do when you know you are angry.
   - Anger reducer 1: deep breathing
   - Anger reducer 2: backward counting
   - Anger reducer 3: pleasant imagery
5. Role play: cues + anger reducers.
6. Review Hassle Log, cues, and anger reducers 1, 2, and 3.

Week 3: Triggers
1. Review second session.
2. Discuss understanding what makes you angry (triggers).
   - External triggers
   - Internal triggers
3. Role play: triggers + cues + anger reducer(s).
4. Review triggers, cues, and anger reducers 1, 2, and 3.

Week 4: Reminders (Anger Reducer 4)
1. Review third session.
2. Introduce reminders.
3. Model using reminders.
4. Role play: triggers + cues + reminders + anger reducer(s).
5. Review reminders.

Week 5: Self-Evaluation
1. Review fourth session.
2. Introduce self-evaluation.
   - Self-rewarding
   - Self-coaching
3. Role play: triggers + cues + reminders + anger reducer(s) + self-evaluation.
4. Review self-evaluation.

Table 4. *(cont.)*

Week 6: Thinking Ahead (Anger Reducer 5)
1. Review fifth session.
2. Introduce thinking ahead.
   - Short- and long-term consequences
   - Most and least serious consequences
   - Internal, external, and social consequences
3. Role play: "if-then" thinking ahead.
4. Role play: triggers + cues + reminders + anger reducer(s) + self-evaluation.
5. Review thinking ahead.

Week 7: The Angry Behavior Cycle
1. Review sixth session.
2. Introduce the Angry Behavior Cycle.
   - Identifying your own anger-provoking behavior
   - Changing your own anger-provoking behavior
3. Role play: triggers + cues + reminders + anger reducer(s) + self-evaluation.
4. Review the Angry Behavior Cycle.

Week 8: Rehearsal of Full Sequence
1. Review seventh session.
2. Introduce using new behaviors (skills) in place of aggression.
3. Role play: triggers + cues + reminders + anger reducer(s) + SL skill + self-evaluation.

Week 9: Rehearsal of Full Sequence
1. Review Hassle Logs.
2. Role play: triggers + cues + reminders + anger reducer(s) + SL skill + self-evaluation.

Week 10: Overall Review
1. Review Hassle Logs.
2. Recap anger control techniques.
3. Role play: triggers + cues + reminders + anger reducer(s) + SL skill + self-evaluation.
4. Reinforce for participation and encourage to continue.

Week 1: Introduction

Explaining Program Goals

In the first session it is necessary to introduce the program, "sell it" to the trainees, and get their commitment to participate. The basic introduction involves talking with the trainees about how being angry and aggressive can at times lead to trouble for them with authorities (police, school), with peers, and even with regard to how they feel about themselves. The following strategies will help the trainer to "sell" to the trainees the idea that learning to achieve greater control of their anger is a worthwhile task.

The trainer can give examples of admired people who have excellent self-control, for example, Bruce Lee and Sugar Ray Leonard. These people would not/could not be successful by being out-of-control. These examples help make the point that having more self-control *does not* mean that the trainees will be pushed around or be "wimps."

After providing the examples, the trainer explains how greater self-control means greater personal power. Trainees are *more powerful* when they are in control of their reactions to others, despite the attempts of others to provoke them. By being aggressive, they allow others to control them.

Explaining Rules and Procedures

It is essential to present procedural matters at the outset of the program. The trainer begins by explaining that meetings will be held once a week for 10 weeks on (*day*) at (*time*) and will last 1 hour. At these meetings, each trainee is expected to participate actively, cooperatively, and with respect for the other trainees. Homework will be given and used as the material for the next session; therefore, completion of the homework is required for the success of the program. The homework will require each trainee to complete a "Hassle Log" each week. The Hassle Log is a worksheet trainees fill out about one or more conflict situations they are involved in (see Week 2).

Different techniques for anger reduction will be taught by (1) explanations and demonstrations by the trainer and (2) practice in the form of role playing by trainees. Trainees will get to role play the anger control techniques in the situations they bring to each session on their Hassle Logs, so that the next time that situation or a similar one occurs, they will have the choice to do something other than get angry.

Giving Initial Assessments of the A-B-Cs

The trainer should explain to the group how each conflict situation has three steps: (A) What triggered the problem? What led up to it?, (B) What did you do? (the actual response to "A"), and (C) What were the consequences to you and to the other person? Then the trainer gives examples of how he has handled some conflicts, being sure to point out the "A," "B," and "C" steps. Finally, trainees give examples, and the trainer helps them identify the "A," "B," and "C" steps operating in the situation.

Reviewing

A brief review of the reasons for developing greater self-control, the rules and procedures of the group, and the A-B-Cs ends the meeting. Finally, the trainer gives out binders that the trainees will use to hold all of the program materials and reminds them of their commitment to the program.

Week 2: Cues and Anger Reducers 1, 2, and 3

Reviewing the First Session

Trainees should be reminded that they increase their personal power by having control over their reactions to others. Again, providing examples of popular sports figures who demonstrate exceptional self-control that leads to their success is helpful. The trainer should review the rules and procedures, emphasizing that this program will involve learning anger control techniques by watching them being demonstrated and then practicing them. Then the trainer goes over the A-B-C model of conflicts, reminding the group of the three steps in each conflict. The trainer gives an example and asks a few trainees for examples that occurred in the past week.

Introducing the Hassle Log

The trainer shows the group an example of the Hassle Log (Figure 3) and asks someone different to read each item. Then he explains the importance of the log: (1) It provides an accurate picture of conflicts that occur during the week; (2) it helps trainees learn about what makes them angry and how they handle these situations (so that they can work to change those that they handle poorly, that cause them trouble, and that leave them feeling bad about themselves); and (3) it provides material for role playing in future sessions (using situations that really happen makes practicing the anger control techniques much more effective than using "made-up" situations). At this point, the trainer gives an example of a conflict and how to fill out the Hassle Log for it. The Hassle Log should be filled out for situations that trainees handle well in addition to those in which they become angry or aggressive. The trainer makes sure each trainee understands how to complete the Hassle Log by having each of them fill out a log in the session for a recent hassle. Then the trainer checks the logs and corrects any misunderstanding of the instructions. Trainees receive a stack of Hassle Logs to keep in their binders and are instructed to fill them out as soon as possible after an incident.

Figure 3. Hassle Log

Name _____ Date _____

Morning _____ Afternoon _____ Evening _____

Where were you?

Classroom	_____	Bathroom	_____	Off grounds	_____
Dorm	_____	Team office	_____	Halls	_____
Gym	_____	Dining room	_____	On a job	_____
Recreation room	_____	Outside/on grounds	_____	Other	_____

What happened?

Somebody teased me.   _____

Somebody took something of mine.   _____

Somebody told me to do something.   _____

Somebody was doing something I didn't like. _____

I did something wrong.   _____

Somebody started fighting with me.   _____

Other: _____

Who was that somebody:

Another resident _____   Aide _____   Teacher _____

Another adult _____   Counselor _____

What did you do?

Hit back	_____	Told peer	_____
Ran away	_____	Ignored it	_____
Yelled	_____	Used Anger Control	_____
Cried	_____	_____	
Broke something	_____	_____	
Was restrained	_____	Used Structured	
Told aide or counselor	_____	Learning skill	_____
Walked away calmly	_____	_____	
Talked it out	_____	_____	

How did you handle yourself?

1	2	3	4	5
Poorly	Not so well	Okay	Good	Great

How angry were you?

	Really	Moderately	Mildly angry but	Not angry
Burning _____	angry _____	angry _____	still okay _____	at all _____

Discussing Cues

Every person has physical signs that can let him know he is angry: for example, muscle tension, a knot in the stomach, clenched fists, grinding teeth, or a pounding heart. The trainer should give some examples of the signs that let him know when he is angry and explain that individuals must know they are angry before they can use self-control to reduce the anger. Next, the trainees try to identify their own and each other's warning signs by role playing short conflict situations. The trainer gives feedback on how well each trainee could identify the warning signs or cues.

Discussing Anger Reducers 1, 2, and 3

Now that the trainees have begun to be able to identify their anger warning signs (cues), they can start to make use of anger reduction techniques to increase their self-control and personal power when they notice themselves getting angry. Any or all of the three anger reducers can be a first step in a chain of new behaviors giving the trainees greater self-control and the time needed to decide how to respond most effectively. The key sequence here is that noticing the cues leads to use of an anger reducer. As the trainer presents each of the three anger reducers, he models its use, has the trainees role play the sequence "cues + anger reducer," and then gives feedback on the role plays.

Anger reducer 1: deep breathing. Taking a few slow, deep breaths can help in making a more controlled response in a pressure situation. Examples from sports of taking a few deep breaths (e.g., in basketball—before taking important foul shots, and in boxing) can be presented. Trainees are reminded about their signs of being angry and how deep breathing can reduce tension by relieving physical symptoms of tension. Then the trainer models, has trainees role play, and gives feedback on the sequence of "cues + deep breathing."

Anger reducer 2: backward counting. A second method of reducing tension and increasing personal power is to silently count backward (at an even pace) from 20 to 1 when faced with a pressure situation. Trainees should be instructed to turn away from the provoking person or situation, if appropriate, while counting. Counting backward is a way of gaining time to think about how to respond most effectively. The trainer models, helps trainees role play, and gives feedback on the sequence of "cues + backward counting."

Anger reducer 3: pleasant imagery. A third way of reducing tension in an anger-arousing situation is to imagine a peaceful scene that has a calming effect (e.g., You are lying on the beach. The sun is warm, and there is a slight breeze.). The trainees are encouraged to think of scenes *they* find relaxing. Then the trainer models, helps the trainees role play, and gives feedback on the sequence of "cues + pleasant imagery."

Reviewing

The trainer reviews the Hassle Log and reminds the group of the importance of completing it. Each member's warning signs of anger (cues) and the three anger reducers are reviewed. Homework is given in which the trainees will attempt to use each of the three anger reducers during one situation in the coming week in which they notice that they are getting angry. Trainees will note on their Hassle Logs for that situation which anger reducer they used.

Week 3: Triggers

Reviewing the Second Session

The trainer reviews the cues and anger reducers taught in Session 2 by going over the completed Hassle Logs for those situations in which trainees used one of the three anger reducers assigned in the homework from the last session. Reinforcement is provided for those trainees who successfully used the reducers following the identification of the warning signs (cues) of being angry. The trainer checks to be sure the Hassle Logs are filled out properly.

Discussing Triggers

The trainer reviews the idea that each conflict situation has an "A" (trigger), a "B" (behavior), and a "C" (consequence). In this session, the focus will be on the "A" step, or trigger. The goal is to help trainees identify things that trigger, or arouse, their anger. Both external and internal triggers will be described.

External triggers are things done by one person that make another person angry. External triggers may be something others say to a trainee (e.g., being told what to do or being called a name) or they may be non-verbal (e.g., being pushed or an obscene gesture). The trainer helps trainees identify one or more external triggers (verbal or nonverbal) that led to their becoming angry or aggressive during the last few weeks. Almost always, it takes more than just an external trigger to lead to anger arousal and aggressive behavior: What youngsters think or say to themselves (*internal triggers*) when faced with an external trigger is of crucial importance in whether or not they become angry. Youngsters will often say things to themselves such as "That s.o.b. is making fun of me,"

"He's making me look like a wimp," or "I'm going to tear that guy's head off." These self-statements are the internal triggers that often combine with external triggers to lead to aggressive behavior. Helping trainees identify their internal triggers sets the stage for the next session, in which they will learn how to replace internal triggers that make them angry with positive self-statements, or reminders, that reduce their anger in conflict situations.

Role Playing

The trainer models, helps the trainees role play, and gives feedback on the chain "triggers (external and internal) + cues + anger reducer(s) (any or all of 1, 2, and 3)." For these role plays and all others, *situations from the Hassle Logs are used.* In this session's role playing, the emphasis is on identifying the internal triggers. Some situations that may be useful for this role play include: (1) sports situations in which someone is deliberately tripped or fouled, (2) getting into trouble for something one didn't do, and (3) feeling lied to by a peer or adult.

Reviewing

The trainer reviews the chain of events taught so far, including the idea of internal and external triggers, the cues for recognizing anger, and the use of anger reducers 1, 2, and 3.

Week 4: Reminders (Anger Reducer 4)

Reviewing the Third Session

The trainer briefly reviews the definitions of internal and external triggers by going through the completed Hassle Logs with the group and having them identify the internal and external triggers for one hassle for each of the trainees.

Introducing Reminders

Reminders are statements that can be used to help increase success in pressure situations of all types. Some examples of reminders that can be used during pressure situations in sports are: (1) "Bend your knees and follow through" when making a foul shot in a basketball game and (2) "Watch out for his left" or "Jab and then hook" when boxing. Trainees should suggest several reminders of this type that they do use or could use. The trainer describes and gives several examples of how reminders can also be very helpful in pressure situations in which trainees must try very hard to keep calm (e.g., confrontations with police, court appearances). Finally, trainees generate a list of reminders they have used or could use in recent pressure or conflict situations involving anger (drawn from the Hassle Logs). These reminders can be written on the board. Some possible reminders include:

- Take it easy.
- Cool it.
- Slow down.
- Chill out.
- Ignore it.
- Take a deep breath.

Modeling Using Reminders

The trainer should model the use of appropriate reminders to increase self-control and personal power in conflict situations, as opposed to using internal triggers (e.g., "Cool it" versus "I'll kill him"). At first, it is useful for trainees to say the reminders out loud, but over time and practice, the goal is to be able to "say" them silently—that is, to think them. This goal can be accomplished by gradually decreasing the frequency of saying a reminder out loud and increasing the frequency of saying a reminder silently. The trainer explains that a reminder should be used at the right time (not too early and not too late) and emphasizes that trainees must *make a choice* to use a reminder in a conflict situation.

Role Playing

The trainer models the chain "triggers + cues + reminders + anger reducer(s)." Then trainees role play conflict situations from their Hassle Logs in which the main actor (1) identifies the external and internal triggers, (2) identifies the cues of anger, and (3) uses reminders and anger reducers 1, 2, and 3 (any or all). If the main actor is having trouble using the reminders, it may be helpful for the trainer to quietly say examples of them to him at the proper time. Focus in the role play should be on going from "out loud" reminders to silent ones. The trainer gives feedback on the role plays, particularly on the use of the reminders and anger reducers.

Reviewing

The trainer summarizes the use of reminders, their timing, and the rationale for their use. Then trainees are given index cards and asked to select and write down three reminders that they feel they might use in the coming week. As homework, trainees are instructed to use each of these reminders during hassles that arise during the week and to note in the Hassle Log for that situation the reminder they used.

Week 5: Self-Evaluation

Reviewing the Fourth Session

The trainer reviews reminders by having each trainee relate a hassle from the past week in which she used a reminder from the ones written down in the last session and assigned as homework. The group is reminded about the A-B-C model and each trainee is asked about the consequences to herself and to others of having used the reminder. Again out loud and silent reminders are distinguished. The outcome of using the reminder is evaluated: Did the reminder work? If not, what went wrong?

Introducing Self-Evaluation

Self-evaluation is a way for trainees to (1) judge for themselves how well they have handled a conflict, (2) reward themselves for handling it well (self-rewarding), or (3) help themselves find out how they could have handled it better (self-coaching). Basically, self-evaluation uses a set of reminders that can be used *after* a conflict situation. The trainer should present some statements that trainees can use to reward themselves (e.g., "I really kept cool" or "I was really in control") and to coach themselves when they have failed to remain in control in a conflict situation (e.g., "I need to pay more attention to my cues"). Then each trainee should generate a list of self-rewarding and self-coaching statements to use in the situations from the Hassle Logs. These statements are gone over individually and as a group.

Role Playing

The trainer models the chain "triggers + cues + reminders + anger reducer(s) + self-evaluation." The reminders technique (anger reducer 4) is so important that it should always be included in the role playing chain, in addition to choosing any or all of the other anger reducers taught so far. In this modeling, both self-rewarding and self-coaching self-evaluation statements are emphasized. Next, the trainer conducts role plays from Hassle Log situations in which the main actor carries out all of the following steps: (1) identifies external and internal triggers, (2) identifies cues of anger, (3) uses reminders plus anger reducer(s) 1, 2, and 3 (any or all), and (4) evaluates her performance, either rewarding or coaching herself. The trainer provides feedback on the role play with an emphasis on self-evaluation.

Reviewing

The two types of self-evaluation are reviewed. Then the trainer assigns homework requiring trainees to list on their Hassle Logs self-evaluation statements following conflicts (resolved or unresolved) that occur in the coming week.

Week 6: Thinking Ahead (Anger Reducer 5)

Reviewing the Fifth Session

The trainer reviews self-evaluation by going over the Hassle Logs for the self-rewarding and self-coaching statements written down as the homework assigned last session.

Introducing Thinking Ahead

Thinking ahead is another way of controlling anger in a conflict situation by judging the likely future consequences for current behavior. The trainer refers to the A-B-C model and explains that thinking ahead helps a trainee figure out what the "C" (consequence) will probably be before he decides what to do. The sentence, "If I do this now, then this will probably happen later" is a good way to estimate consequences.

The trainer should distinguish between short- and long-term consequences, encouraging trainees to consider the long-term results over the short-term ones (e.g., short term: "If I slug him now, he'll shut up" versus long term: "If I slug him now, my probation will probably get extended 3 months"). Trainees are asked to list short- and long-term consequences of specific aggressive acts they have engaged in during the last 2 months.

Next, trainees talk about the most and least serious consequences of being aggressive. Trainees are encouraged to list a series of consequences that might follow from an aggressive act they have engaged in within the last 2 months.

Finally, the trainer explains the difference between the internal and external consequences of being aggressive (e.g., external: going back to court, having to spend another 3 months in a facility; internal: feeling terrible about yourself, losing self-respect). The trainer also talks about social consequences, such as losing friends or being excluded from a group. Group members each list negative external, internal, and social consequences of being aggressive and enumerate the positive consequences of using self-control.

Role Playing: "If-Then" Thinking Ahead

The trainer models, helps trainees role play, and gives feedback on using the "if (I act aggressively), then (this will probably be the consequence)" thinking ahead procedure using situations from the Hassle Logs. Negative consequences are emphasized as additional reminders not to act aggressively.

Role Playing Anger Control Chain

The trainer models the chain presented so far "triggers + cues + reminders + anger reducer(s) + self-evaluation." Then he conducts role plays from the Hassle Log situations in which the main actor follows all of the above steps and uses any or all of anger reducers 1, 2, 3, and now 5 (thinking ahead). The trainer gives feedback on the role plays.

Reviewing

The reasons to use thinking ahead, the different types of consequences to aggression, and the "if-then" statements are reviewed. Then the trainer assigns as homework to use thinking ahead in two conflict situations in the coming week and to write the "if-then" statement on the Hassle Log for that situation.

Week 7: The Angry Behavior Cycle

Reviewing the Sixth Session

The trainer reviews thinking ahead by going over with the group the completed Hassle Logs in which the trainees wrote down the "if-then" statements used in conflict situations in the past week as part of their homework.

Introducing the Angry Behavior Cycle

Until this point in the program, the focus has been on what to do when someone else makes one angry. Naturally, there are things that *everyone* does that can make other people angry and lead to conflicts. Today's session will focus on what the trainees themselves do to make other people angry with them.

The trainer should give some examples of things that he does that are very likely to make others angry (e.g., calling someone a name, making fun of a person's appearance). Trainees then think about and list three things they do that make other people angry at them. (Each trainee should identify *at least* three things that he does that make others angry.) If the trainer feels the group can handle some confrontation, trainees can respectfully tell another group member what he does to make them angry.

The trainer gets an agreement from each trainee to try to change these problematic behaviors in the coming week, perhaps by using the thinking ahead procedure ("If I do this, then this person may get angry and the situation may get out of hand"). Changing even one behavior may prevent some conflicts and lead to trainees' being better liked or having more friends.

Role Playing

This role play is again designed to allow practice of all the anger control techniques taught so far. The trainer models the chain of "triggers + cues + reminders + anger reducer(s) + self-evaluation." Then the trainer conducts role plays of this chain from trainees' Hassle Logs with the main actor using any or all of anger reducers 1, 2, 3, and 5 in addition to all the other steps. He then gives feedback on the role plays.

Reviewing

The trainer reviews the behaviors that each trainee has identified as often making other people angry. Trainees are reminded of their agreement to try in the coming week to change at least one of the three behaviors they identified as being part of their Angry Behavior Cycle.

Week 8: Rehearsal of Full Sequence

Reviewing the Seventh Session

The trainer reviews the Angry Behavior Cycle—the idea that in addition to getting angry at what other people do, we do things that make other people angry. She goes over with the trainees their attempts at changing their own anger-provoking behavior, the procedures they agreed to try in the last session.

Introducing Using New Behaviors

So far, Anger Control Training has worked to teach the trainees what *not* to do (be aggressive) and how not to do it (the anger control techniques). While this is an important accomplishment, trainees also need to learn what *to do* in place of being aggressive. In other words, they need to know how to meet the demands of life situations effectively and in a satisfying manner without needing to resort to aggression. In the 7 weeks that have passed since the beginning of this program, trainees have also been in another weekly class, Structured Learning (SL), in which they have learned a series of new skills to use in getting along better with others and in handling life situations in an effective way. The last 3 weeks of Anger Control Training is the time to help the trainees practice putting together the anger control techniques and the new skills learned in the Structured Learning class. In this way, trainees will have considerable practice in knowing what not to do in conflict situations and in being able to behave in a constructive, satisfying, and non-aggressive way instead. The trainer explains to the group that this week and the next 2 weeks will be spent doing role plays that use all the anger control techniques and add some of the skills they have learned in the Structured Learning class.

Role Playing

The trainer conducts role plays from situations in trainees' Hassle Logs that follow the entire sequence: "triggers + cues + reminders + anger reducer(s) + SL skill + self-evaluation." Then she gives feedback on the role plays, focusing on how well all the steps were put together.

Week 9: Rehearsal of Full Sequence

Reviewing the Hassle Logs

The trainer goes over the completed Hassle Logs to reinforce how well the trainees are using all of the anger control techniques and beginning to add the use of the SL skills.

Role Playing

Role playing and feedback are continued using the entire series of steps: "triggers + cues + reminders + anger reducer(s) + SL skill + self-evaluation."

Week 10: Overall Review

Reviewing the Hassle Logs

The trainer goes over the completed Hassle Logs to continue reinforcing trainees' new ways of handling conflict situations. It may be helpful to bring to this session some Hassle Logs for each trainee from very early in the program to compare against those filled out for this last week.

Recapping Anger Control Techniques

All of the anger control techniques taught in the program should be briefly recapped: (1) increasing personal power through self-control; (2) the A-B-C model; (3) cues of being angry; (4) anger reducers 1, 2, and 3; (5) internal and external triggers; (6) using reminders; (7) self-evaluation; (8) thinking ahead; (9) the Angry Behavior Cycle; and (10) using the Structured Learning skill.

Role Playing

The trainer conducts role plays and gives feedback using the full chain: "triggers + cues + reminders + anger reducer(s) + SL skill + self-evaluation."

Reinforcing and Encouraging Continuation

If appropriate, the trainer lets the group know that they have learned how to control their anger, increase their personal power, be better liked and respected, and stay out of future trouble caused by aggression. Each of them now has a choice to make: to use or not to use what he has learned. There may, of course, be times in which they have no choice but to defend themselves with aggression. There are, however, many situations in which the trainees do have a choice; it's up to them to make it.

Chapter 6

The Cognitive Component of ART: Moral Education

Moral Education is the third component of Aggression Replacement Training, and in terms of its intended impact it is the cognitive component of the program. While its historical roots are diverse and include the thinking and investigative energy of numerous developmental, educational, social, and experimental psychologists, educators, and philosophers, its primary contemporary developer and proponent is Lawrence Kohlberg.

CRITICAL ASSUMPTIONS

Using primarily Piaget's cognitive developmental approach to moral development (Lickona, 1976; Piaget, 1932) along with moral philosophy as the foundation for his theory, Kohlberg postulated that investigations of moral reasoning should encompass those situations "in which conflicting interests and values lie, and [where] morality involves reasoning and problem solving abilities which can be used to resolve these conflicts" (cited in Edelman & Goldstein, 1981, p. 286). Specifying precisely what these reasoning and problem-solving abilities involve has been a major focus of Kohlberg's work for many years. From this research, Kohlberg (1971a) was able to delineate three criteria that could be used to determine if an act or decision involved a moral component: *prescriptivity*, meaning that the decision originates from an internal sense of duty; *universality*, meaning that the ethical demands of the decision can be recognized by everyone; and *primacy*, describing the notion that nonmoral considerations are evaluated after moral ones have been examined. While Kohlberg maintains that these criteria provide some insight into the meaning of morality, it is not until the concept of justice is incorporated that its essence unfolds.

In fact, Kohlberg argues that morality can be conceptualized primarily as the "principle of justice," which he describes as the basic understanding and acceptance of the value and equality of all human

97

beings and as a reciprocity in all human interactions (Edelman & Goldstein, 1981). Specifically, Kohlberg (1969) states that:

> Justice is not a rule or a set of rules; it is a moral principle. By a moral principle we mean a mode of choosing which is universal, a rule choosing which we want all people to adopt in all situations. . . . There are exceptions to rules, then, but no exception to principles. . . . There is only one principled basis for resolving claims: justice or equality. . . . A moral principle is not only a rule of action but a reason for action. As a reason for action, justice is called respect for persons. (pp. 69-70)

The importance of "justice" in Kohlberg's theory is further reflected in his description of the structure of the six stages of moral reasoning (see Table 5) and their contents (see Table 6). It becomes apparent from these tables that a "sense of justice" becomes progressively more integrated and increasingly complex for individuals as stage level progresses.

It is important to note that Kohlberg does not believe that an individual reasons at only one stage in all situations. Rather, he sees people as reasoning primarily at one stage and secondarily at adjacent stages, either one stage below or above the predominant stage (Kohlberg, 1969). It is within this formulation that Kohlberg explains an individual's variability in responses to the Moral Judgment Interview (a method he developed to assess levels of moral development). This interview involves the presentation of a series of stories, all of which incorporate a moral dilemma that can be resolved by a number of alternative actions. Generally, the dilemma involves a conflict between behaving by conforming to authority figures or legal-social rules versus responding in accordance with the welfare or needs of others (Arbuthnot & Faust, 1981). The participant is asked to determine which action the character in the story should take and why. Through a series of probe questions, it is believed that the participant's decision-making processes concerning the resolution of these dilemmas as they relate to specific moral issues (e.g., value of human life, laws and rules, punishment and justice, truth and contract, property rights) can be ascertained. In addition, Kohlberg maintains that this technique can be used to investigate the major hypotheses underlying his theory. It is a theory that rests upon a cognitive-developmental framework concerned with thinking about rules, laws, and principles (Arbuthnot & Faust, 1981), one that clearly differentiates between the content and structure of moral reasoning, with the former reflecting "what" one is thinking (i.e., opinions, what one actually states in the reasoning process) and the latter referring to "how" one thinks (i.e., the thinking process that determines what one says) (Arbuthnot & Faust, 1981). This suggests that although the content of an individual's response to a moral dilemma may vary, the structure or reasoning process generally remains constant at a particular point in time. Furthermore, this idea implies that while similarities may exist in the content of the responses of, for example, Stage 1 and Stage 2 persons, the reasoning processes underlying the responses will be different.

Also basic to the cognitive-developmental approach is the notion of developmental stages. Kohlberg's hypothesis of distinct stages of moral development suggests that, over the life span, there are qualitatively different ways of thinking and reasoning about moral issues. These qualitative changes are believed to emerge from transformations in the child's thought structure (Arbuthnot & Faust, 1981) and can be observed in the reasoning process. Implicit is the belief that these stages form an invariant sequence, with later stages representing more complex and abstract ways of reasoning (Kohlberg, 1973).

Evolving from the invariant sequence notion is the idea of hierarchical integrations, which has been described as a process in which the structures of an earlier stage serve as the building blocks for the structures of the next stage (Arbuthnot & Faust, 1981). While each successive stage represents a transformation of the preceding stage, the notion of hierarchical integrations entails that each successive stage is more differentiated (i.e., more complex and more specialized) and more integrated (i.e., structured parts are better organized) than the prior stage.

As with the concept of hierarchical integrations, each stage is also believed to represent a structured whole, meaning that every stage reflects an organized system of thought (Kohlberg, 1973). Kohlberg's theory also posits that the "highest stage" represents the theoretically "ideal" endpoint of development. Finally, the theory postulates that progression to more advanced stages is induced by cognitive conflict (Kohlberg, 1969).

It is the latter assumption that is particularly relevant to any intervention designed to enhance an individual's level of moral reasoning. Kohlberg (1969), Turiel (1974), and Piaget (1932) maintain that through the child's interpersonal interactions with adults and peers he is increasingly exposed to situations of value conflict that ultimately lead to cognitive conflict. Resolution of this conflict requires that the child experiment with alternative ways of reasoning that are typically representative of the next higher stage of moral judgment. This result suggests that environmental stimulation may promote, within certain limits, the development of moral reasoning (Arbuthnot & Faust, 1981).

In addition, the literature suggests that critical periods exist in which the child must actively explore other means of dealing with his

Table 5. Kohlberg's Six Stages of Moral Reasoning

I. Preconventional Level

At this level, the child is responsive to cultural rules and labels of good and bad and right or wrong, but interprets these labels in terms of either the physical or the hedonistic consequences of action (punishment, reward, exchange of favors) or in terms of the physical power of those who enunciate the rules and labels. The level comprises the following two stages:

Stage 1: Punishment and Obedience Orientation
The physical consequences of an action determine its goodness or badness regardless of the human meaning or value of the consequences. Avoidance of punishment and unquestioning deference to power are valued in their own right, not in terms of respect for an underlying moral order supported by punishment and authority (the latter being Stage 4).

Stage 2: Instrumental Relativist Orientation
Right action consists of that which instrumentally satisfies one's own needs and, occasionally, the needs of others. Human relations are viewed in terms similar to those of the marketplace. Elements of fairness, or reciprocity, and equal sharing are present, but they are always interpreted in a physical, pragmatic way. Reciprocity is a matter of "you scratch my back and I'll scratch yours," not of loyalty, gratitude, or justice.

II. Conventional Level

At this level, maintaining the expectations of the individual's family, group, or nation is perceived as valuable in its own right, regardless of immediate and obvious consequences. The attitude is one not only of *conformity* to personal expectations and social order, but of loyalty to it, of actively *maintaining,* supporting, and justifying the order and of identifying with the persons or groups involved in it. This level comprises the following two stages:

Stage 3: Interpersonal Concordance, or "Good Boy-Nice Girl" Orientation
Good behavior is that which pleases or helps others and is approved by them. There is much conformity to stereotypical images of what is majority or "natural" behavior. Behavior is frequently judged by intention: "He means well" becomes important for the first time. One earns approval by being "nice."

Note. From Kohlberg, L. (1971). Stages of moral development as a basis for moral education. In C.M. Beck, B.S. Crittendon, & E.V. Sullivan (Eds.), *Moral education: Interdisciplinary approaches* (pp. 86–88). Toronto: University of Toronto Press.

Stage 4: "Law and Order" Orientation
There is orientation toward authority, fixed rules, and the maintenance of the social order. Right behavior consists of doing one's duty, showing respect for authority, and maintaining the given social order for its own sake.

III. Postconventional, Autonomous, or Principled Level
At this level, there is a clear effort to define moral values and principles that have validity and application apart from the authority of the groups or persons holding these principles and apart from the individual's own iden- tification with these groups. This level again has two stages:

Stage 5: Social-Contract Legalistic Orientation
Generally, this stage has utilitarian overtones. Right action tends to be defined in terms of general individual rights and in terms of standards that have been critically examined and agreed upon by the whole society. There is a clear awareness of the relativism of personal values and opin- ions and a corresponding emphasis on procedural rules for teaching con- sensus. Aside from what is constitutionally and democratically agreed upon, the right is a matter of personal "values" and "opinion." The result is an emphasis upon the "legal point of view," but with an emphasis upon the possibility of changing law in terms of rational considerations of social utility (rather than freezing it in terms of Stage 4 "law and order"). Outside the legal realm, free agreement and contract are the binding elements of obligation. This is the "official" morality of the United States government and Constitution.

Stage 6: Universal Ethical-Principle Orientation
Right is defined by the decision of conscience in accord with self-chosen *ethical principles* appealing to logical comprehensiveness, universality, and consistency. These principles are abstract and ethical; they are not concrete moral rules like the Ten Commandments. At heart, these are uni- versal principles of justice, the reciprocity and equality of human rights, and respect for the dignity of human beings as individual persons.

environment in order to prevent fixation at more developmentally immature levels (Kohlberg, 1969; Piaget, 1932; Turiel, 1974). For example, Kohlberg and Kramer's (1969) research indicates that, for Americans, one such critical or transitional period occurs between the ages of 10 and 13. It is during this period that a child typically moves from a preconventional to a conventional level of moral reasoning. Fur- thermore, they suggest that it is important for children to exhibit at least some conventional moral reasoning during this period in order to pre-

Table 6. The Content of the Moral Reasoning Stages

Stage	What Is Right	Reasons for Doing Right	Social Perspective
	Level I—Preconventional		
Stage 1—Heteronomous morality	Avoidance of breaking rules backed by punishment; obedience for its own sake; avoidance of physical damage to persons and property.	Avoidance of punishment and the superior power of authority.	*Egocentric point of view.* Doesn't consider the interests of others or recognize that they differ from one's own. Doesn't relate two points of view. Actions are considered physically rather than in terms of psychological interests of others. Confusion of authority's perspective with one's own.
Stage 2—Individualism, instrumental purpose, and exchange	Following rules only when it is to someone's immediate interest; acting to meet one's own interests and needs and letting others do the same. Right is also what is fair, an equal exchange, a deal, an agreement.	Serving one's own needs or interests in a world where one recognizes that other people have their interests, too.	*Concrete individualistic perspective.* Aware that everybody has his own interest to pursue and that these interests conflict, so that right is relative (in the concrete individualistic sense).

Note. From Kohlberg, L. (1976). Moral stages and moralization: The cognitive-developmental approach. In T. Lickona (Ed.), *Moral development and behavior: Theory, research, and social issues* (pp. 34–35). New York: Holt, Rinehart, & Winston.

Level II—Conventional

	What is right	Social Perspective
Stage 3—Mutual interpersonal expectations, relationships, and interpersonal conformity	Living up to what is expected by the people one is close to or what others generally expect of people in one's role as son, daughter, brother, sister, or friend, etc. "Being good" is important and means having good motives and showing concern about others. It also means keeping mutual relationships, such as trust, loyalty, respect, and gratitude.	The need to be a good person in one's own eyes and those of others. Caring for others. Belief in the Golden Rule. Desire to maintain rules and authority that support stereotypical good behavior.	*Perspective of the individual in relationships with other individuals.* Aware of shared feelings, agreements, and expectations that take primacy over individual interests. Relates points of view through the concrete Golden Rule, putting oneself in the other guy's shoes. Does not yet consider generalized system perspective.
Stage 4—Social system and conscience	Fulfilling the actual duties to which one has agreed. Laws are to be upheld except in extreme cases where they conflict with other fixed social duties. Right is also defined as contributing to society, the group, or institution.	Keeping the institution going as a whole; avoiding the breakdown in the system that would occur "if everyone did it"; or obeying the imperative of conscience to meet one's defined obligations. (Easily confused with Stage 3 belief in rules and authority.)	*Differentiates societal point of view from interpersonal agreement or motives.* Takes the point of view of the system that defines roles and rules. Considers individual relations in terms of place in the system.

103

Table 6. (cont.)

Stage	What Is Right	Reasons for Doing Right	Social Perspective
	Level III—Postconventional, or Principled		
Stage 5—Social contract or utility and individual rights	Being aware that people hold a variety of values and opinions and that most values and rules are relative to the group. These relative rules should usually be upheld, however, in the interest of impartiality and because they are the social contract. Some nonrelative values and rights like *life* and *liberty*, however, must be upheld in any society and regardless of majority opinion.	A sense of obligation to law because of one's social contract to make and abide by laws for the welfare of all and for the protection of all people's rights. A feeling of contractual commitment, freely entered upon, to family, friendship, trust, and work obligations. Concern that laws and duties be based on rational calculation of overall utility, "the greatest good for the greatest number."	*Prior-to-society perspective.* Perspective of a rational individual aware of values and rights prior to social attachments and contracts. Integrates perspectives by formal mechanisms of agreement, contract objective impartiality, and due process. Considers moral and legal points of view; recognizes that they sometimes conflict and finds it difficult to integrate them.

| Stage 6—Universal ethical principles | Following self-chosen ethical principles. Particular laws or social agreements are usually valid because they rest on such principles. When laws violate these principles, one acts in accordance with the principle. Principles are universal principles of justice: The equality of human rights and respect for the dignity of human beings as individual persons. | The belief as a rational person in the validity of universal moral principles and a sense of personal commitment to them. | *Perspective of a moral point of view* from which social arrangements derive. Perspective is that of any rational individual recognizing the nature of morality or the fact that persons are ends in themselves and must be treated as such. |

vent fixation at a preconventional level. These ideas—that environmental stimulation can enhance moral reasoning and that critical transitional periods exist in the developmental sequence—suggest that the success of an intervention designed to promote moral reasoning may lie, in part, on the "readiness" of the individual to progress to higher stages of moral judgment.

The core postulates comprising Kohlberg's theory have received extensive critical scrutiny. Much of this research has yielded supportive evidence. Over the course of a longitudinal investigation of American boys between the ages of 10 and 16 from low- and middle-income families, Kramer (1968) and Kohlberg and Kramer (1969) found that moral reasoning did progress sequentially through stages. The longitudinal data also reveal that although the time period between testing was 4 years, potentially allowing the participants to move through more than one stage during that interval, only 10 percent of the boys evidenced changes beyond one stage. The results also indicated that relatively few participants reached the highest stages of moral development and that the rate of development varied for different individuals. Similar results have also been found by Turiel (1966) in an investigation of individuals' reasoning at Kohlberg's Stages 2, 3, or 4, and by Lee (1971). Using 5- to 8-year-old children, Kuhn (1976) also found progression to the subsequent stage at a 1-year follow-up.

Kohlberg's (Kohlberg & Kramer, 1969; Kohlberg & Turiel, 1971; Turiel, Edwards, & Kohlberg, 1977) cross-cultural research, which included the countries of Mexico, Turkey, India, Taiwan, Israel, and Canada, provided support for the invariant sequence hypothesis. For instance, the results of studies involving 10-, 13-, and 16-year-old urban, middle-class boys of the United States, Mexico, and Taiwan and a comparable age group of boys in villages in Turkey and the Yucatan indicated that the predicted age-related changes occurred (when the changes occurred at all) regardless of country. Based on these studies, Kohlberg and his collaborators concluded that the invariant sequence hypothesis was culturally universal, even though rates of development and highest stage attained remained variable (lower for comparable groups in Turkey and the Yucatan). They also maintained that these results support the notion that all individuals reason about similar moral values (i.e., life, love, laws, contract, and punishment), regardless of culture or subculture. These conclusions have aroused extensive and diverse criticism in the literature. While these objections will be addressed in detail later, at this time it is important to note that some of the criticisms are based upon methodological flaws, particularly in the scoring techniques developed and utilized by the Kohlberg group in these studies. Since that time, scoring methods have been revised and used in at least one reported replication study (Nisan & Kohlberg, 1978). In this study, the predicted sequence was found both for longitudinal and for cross-sectional data.

Further support for the invariant sequence hypothesis is provided by studies that have suggested that moral judgment is significantly correlated with age (Grinder, 1964; Stuart, 1967; Whiteman & Kosier, 1964). Specifically, Colby, Kohlberg, and Gibbs (1979) found that while at age 10 approximately 63 percent of the child's statements reflect Stage 2 reasoning, by age 24 to 26 only 5 percent of the statements reflect this stage. The results also indicated that there is an increase in percentage of Stage 3 reasoning with age, and that Stage 4 reasoning emerges at approximately age 13 to 14 and also increases with age. Other researchers have found similar distributions of stage responses (Arbuthnot, 1973, 1975; Arbuthnot & Faust, 1981; Faust & Arbuthnot, 1978; Haan, Smith, & Block, 1968; Kohlberg & Kramer, 1969). In studying these percentages, it is important to recognize that individual differences exist, with some of this variation accounted for by such factors as socioeconomic status, intelligence, and education. Thus, the percentages presented are most appropriately viewed as rough estimations of the relationship between age and moral reasoning stage.

Related to the invariant sequence hypothesis is the question of the possibility of regression in moral stages. It has been suggested that further support for the invariant sequence hypothesis can be advanced if this regression is not noted. At this time, there is considerable debate among researchers on this question. A number of investigators have observed a regression in moral reasoning, particularly among college students (Haan, Smith, & Block, 1968; Holstein, 1976; Kohlberg & Kramer, 1969; Kramer, 1968; Turiel, 1974). In studying this phenomenon, Kohlberg and Kramer (1969) noted that it generally appears between late high school and the early years of college among middle-class students whose moral reasoning scores during high school were quite advanced in comparison to their age-related peers. Theoretically, Turiel (1974) and Kohlberg and Kramer (1969) argue that what appears to be a regression really reflects a transitional period during which the individual experiments with alternative ways of reasoning about moral issues and which ultimately leads to the enhancement of the moral structure. They maintain that the structure does not regress, even though the content of the individual's response may resemble that of a Stage 2 reasoner.

In support of this contention, Kohlberg and Kramer (1969) report that all of their participants who had evidenced stage regression had returned to, at least, a mixture of Stage 4 and Stage 5 reasoning, and in some cases reached dominant Stage 5 reasoning. These results, in conjunction with the Nisan and Kohlberg (1978) finding cited previously and those results indicating positive correlations between age and moral reasoning, suggest that the invariant sequence hypothesis is still tenable in spite of the observed regressions in college students. However, the results of studies in the area of stage regression strongly imply that individuals are capable of lower stage reasoning even after progressing to higher stages. It is important to note that this idea is clearly reflected in some of Kohlberg's other theoretical hypotheses and in the empirical investigations evolving from them. For example, while the structural whole hypothesis has been supported to some extent, most of the research evidence indicates that individuals reason at more than one stage at specific points in time (Arbuthnot & Faust, 1981; Kohlberg, 1973). In fact, the results suggest that generally 50 percent of the individual's reasoning reflects the dominant stage, with the remaining statements representing reasoning at adjacent stages (either a lower or higher stage).

Many studies have shown that individuals understand reasoning at or below their own stage, but not more than one stage above their own (Rest, 1979; Rest, Turiel, & Kohlberg, 1969; Turiel, 1966). Rest (1979), for instance, asked adolescents to rewrite a number of moral statements in their own words and then to rank order them in terms of preference. The results indicated that participants correctly rewrote statements up to and representative of their own stage of reasoning, but not beyond that stage. However, although they were capable of comprehending reasoning below their own stage, participants typically gave these responses low preference ratings and preferred statements that reflected reasoning one stage higher than their present reasoning skills. Statements two stages beyond present reasoning ability were also given low preference scores. The fact that lower stage reasoning continues to be understood but not preferred has important implications for both the development of measures of moral reasoning, as well as interventions designed to advance moral reasoning levels.

A number of investigators have criticized Kohlberg's work on methodological, theoretical, and philosophical grounds. Most of these objections have evolved from the universally invariant sequence hypothesis, which Kohlberg claims has received support from both his 17-year longitudinal study and his cross-cultural work. Throughout these investigations, however, Kohlberg and his colleagues utilized the "aspect scoring system" for determining the participant's modal reasoning stage. Kurtines and Grief (1974) have criticized this scoring system on the basis of a lack of standardization of administration and scoring methods, which they claim has resulted in a lack of support for the validity and reliability of the Moral Judgment Interview. They also maintain that Kohlberg's failure to provide information concerning the interrater reliabilities emerging from his longitudinal research, his failure to specify the number of dilemmas used and the lack of a published scoring manual have made it difficult to investigate the theory for researchers outside of his immediate group.

As mentioned previously, when Kohlberg and other researchers found data dissonant to the invariant sequence hypothesis, they proceeded to modify the original scoring system. What emerged was a new scoring system called "issue scoring." Although the consistently high reliability coefficients reported imply that the Kohlberg issue scoring procedure has some utility for assessing moral reasoning, it has been suggested that other measures may be more appropriate to use in short-term intervention research. Some support for this contention has been provided by Carroll and Nelson (1979), Carroll and Rest (1981), Enright (1980), and Rest (1979), who have proposed or developed measures of moral reasoning designed to incorporate a number of intervention-related considerations. While it is not within the scope of this discussion to address these measures, the interested reader is referred to the aforementioned sources for a detailed discussion of their rationale and empirical bases. It is important, however, to reiterate that even though reliabilities are adequate for the revised scoring system, the fact remains that many of Kohlberg's theoretical conclusions were based upon studies utilizing the old scoring method. Thus, any interpretation based upon these studies must be advanced with caution; attention should be directed toward reanalyzing the original work using the new scoring procedure.

Thus far, our discussion has centered upon criticisms of Kohlberg's unstandardized administration protocol and scoring technique and the utility of his assessment procedure for research other than longitudinal developmental studies. Other criticisms have been voiced in the literature. In relation to Kohlberg's cross-cultural studies, for example, critics have commented on his failure to specify subject characteristics, sample sizes, or the methods used to establish the moral stages in different cultures (Kurtines & Grief, 1974); his failure to adequately sample diverse cultures to support his claim of universality (Fraenkel, 1976; Simpson, 1974); and his failure to determine if the values captured by the Moral Judgment Interview are deemed important within the particular culture investigated (this criticism is basic to the universal moral values assumption) (Simpson, 1974). He has been criticized for his failure to provide sufficient empirical evidence that a Stage 6 (postconventional reasoning level) even exists within the cultures studied (Simpson, 1974). Finally, not related solely to the cross-cultural research are philosophical objections to Kohlberg's description of the Stage 6 "ideal" moral individual (Peters, 1978; Simpson, 1974). Additional criticisms to Kohlberg's theory have emerged from the moral relativists (Raths, Harmin, & Simon, 1966), who maintain that moral principles are subjective, that values are not universal, and that Kohlberg's position of the "moral superiority" of the Stage 6 reasoner is an elitist point of view.

It is apparent that many of these criticisms call into question a number of Kohlberg's basic theoretical premises. Recently, supporters of the Kohlberg approach have made concerted efforts to respond to these criticisms. Concerning objections involving methodological and assessment issues, efforts have been made to more rigorously specify subject characteristics, sample sizes, and administration and scoring protocols, and, as previously mentioned, to develop new measures that tap broader aspects of moral reasoning. Specification of these procedures has enhanced opportunities for replication efforts.

The moderation of the criticisms concerning the existence of Stage 6 reasoning and of descriptions of the Stage 6 reasoner as the "ideal" moral individual cannot be so briefly summarized because, in contrast to the former objections, which represent methodological problems, the latter two involve theoretical considerations. In fact, attempts to resolve them have emerged primarily from philosophical sources. Edelman and Goldstein (1981) describe the Stage 6 individual as "someone who, in a totally rational and impartial way, considers and reasons through the conflicting interests and values of different individuals on the basis of an abstract respect for the universal equal rights of all people" (p. 308).

Thus, not only is there little empirical support for the existence of the Stage 6 individual (Edelman & Goldstein, 1981), but even if reasoning of this form does occur, it does not necessarily represent an "ideal" way to think. Although objections to Kohlberg's lack of consideration of "moral habits and moral feelings" have primarily revolved around the Stage 6 individual, it is a valid criticism for all six of the moral reasoning stages. Consequently, in line with Wilson's (1973) and Edelman and Goldstein's (1981) suggestion, an adequate definition of morality must incorporate its cognitive, affective, and behavioral components.

Wilson (1973), unlike Kohlberg, is one of the few investigators in the area of morality who has considered all three of these components. Briefly, he suggests that morality is comprised of the following aspects:

1. Concern and respect for other people as equals and consideration of the needs of others, as well as oneself. One attains these values by having the concept of a person which involves the recognition of the similarities and differences among human beings (cognitive component), claiming the concept as a moral principle by determining if the individual believes this is an important concept to use (cognitive component), by rule-supported feelings by determining if the person has any feelings of respect and consideration attached to human beings (affective component) and by helping others as a means of reflecting these feelings (behavioral component).
2. Awareness of feelings in oneself and others by determining if the individual has the concept of emotion (cognitive component) and the ability to identify and label emotions in oneself and others (affective and cognitive component).
3. Assessing the individual's knowledge of relevant hard facts (i.e., physical health, safety, laws) and the sources of these facts (Does the person have the knowledge to make moral decisions?).
4. Determination of the individual's ability to use the above components to make decisions in various moral situations (cognitive component).
5. Assessment of the person's ability to translate the moral decision into overt behavior (behavioral component). (pp. 41-64)

It is apparent that, while Wilson's definition encompasses the three major aspects of morality, its complexity and vagueness make it difficult to utilize in investigations of moral reasoning. To fill this gap, Edelman and Goldstein (1981) have offered another definition of morality, using Wilson's component analysis as its foundation:

Morality involves those skills, values and abilities that comprise (1) thinking or reasoning (problem solving, decision making) in a rational way, while (2) showing an awareness of, and consideration for the needs, interests and feelings of others as well as oneself, and (3) behaving constructively, i.e., in ways that benefit both self and others, in the problematic or conflictual social-interpersonal situations which one encounters in one's daily interactions with other people. Morality, then, involves cognitive (thinking), affective (feeling), and behavioral (doing) aspects which are necessarily interrelated. (p. 259)

It must also be noted that this definition does not in any way negate Kohlberg's conception of morality. Rather, this definition serves to include, yet transcend, Kohlberg's original ideas. In addition, it attempts to moderate those criticisms emerging from Kohlberg's belief in the "ideal" Stage 6 reasoning individual by incorporating the affective dimensions of morality.

INTERVENTION RESEARCH

Since the 1920s, researchers within the moral reasoning domain have extended their work into the intervention realm. This move was prompted by the belief that the traditional institutions—family, religion, and the schools—were no longer successful in preparing children for the moral conflicts they were confronted with (Arbuthnot & Faust, 1981; Edelman & Goldstein, 1981). Many researchers claim that these institutions promote rule-oriented reasoning (equating morality with conformity to conventions), rather than reasoning based on principles of justice (Arbuthnot & Faust, 1981; Edelman & Goldstein, 1981). Thus, when the rules of society change, the individual's rule-oriented reasoning no longer helps him to adequately resolve moral conflicts, and a "moral crisis" may ensue. A moral crisis is characterized by an increased frequency of antisocial behavior and value confusion and a discrepancy between one's behavior and verbalized values. It emerges not only from questioning what values are worthwhile, but also from questioning how to apply values in specific situations or when values conflict with each other (Arbuthnot & Faust, 1981; Edelman & Goldstein, 1981). Consequently, techniques were developed with the primary goal of enhancing moral reasoning and the secondary goal of reducing antisocial behavior. Most of the procedures were designed to be utilized within school settings. Historically, the more prominent programs have included Values Clarification (Kirschenbaum, 1975; Raths, Harmin, & Simon, 1966; Simon, Howe, & Kirschenbaum, 1972; Simon & Olds, 1976), certain applications of role playing (Arbuthnot, 1975; Matefy & Acksen, 1976; Tracy & Cross, 1973) and Moral Education (Blatt & Kohlberg, 1975; Grimes, 1974; Stanley, 1976; Sullivan, 1980). Our choice of Moral Education as the ART component intervention designed to enhance moral reasoning, rather than the alternatives listed, is securely based on quite substantial evidence that participation in Moral Education procedures can indeed effectively increase the participants' level of moral reasoning and, as we shall see, in a number of instances also cause changes in overt prosocial behaviors (Arbuthnot & Gordon, 1983; Blasi, 1980; Edelman

& Goldstein, 1981; Gibbs, Arnold, Ahlborn, & Cheesman, 1984; Zimmerman, 1983).

The practical application of Kohlberg's theory, presented in complete detail in Chapter 7, involves classroom discussions of moral dilemmas in which cognitively stimulating dilemmas are used to promote debate and discussions among students. Since classrooms are likely to be comprised of students reasoning at diverse stages, Kohlberg maintained that the moral discussions engaged in would induce cognitive conflict in an individual functioning at the lower stages and would provide role-taking opportunities which, over time, would result in a transition to the next higher stage of moral reasoning—at least for those students initially reasoning at the lower stages. While these teacher-led moral discussions are believed to prevent moral reasoning fixation in those students who lag behind their peers, supporters of Moral Education do not claim that it promotes the moral development of students who are progressing satisfactorily. Nevertheless, these higher stage reasoners are a crucial part of the Moral Education program, since during discussions they present statements that induce the cognitive conflict believed to be necessary for moral growth. While the presence of higher stage reasoners is an absolute necessity for the inducement of cognitive conflict, Edelman and Goldstein (1981) suggest that the potency of the cognitive conflict can be enhanced by considering such factors as the relevance the moral dilemma has for the individual, the extent to which the dilemma is presented in a context that promotes the mutual exchange of conflicting opinions, and the extent to which these opinions and underlying reasons reflect reasoning one stage higher than that of the lower reasoning individual.

Thus, it is apparent that Moral Education involves at least three conditions that are believed to enhance moral reasoning—role-taking opportunities through reciprocal social interaction, cognitive conflict regarding genuine moral dilemmas, and exposure to the next higher stage of reasoning (Edelman & Goldstein, 1981). These three basic principles, in conjunction with the notion that the teacher's role is that of promoting self-discovery of higher-stage reasoning, not moral indoctrination, form the basis for the specific procedures employed in Moral Education programs. After groups of from 8 to 15 individuals who reason at two or three consecutive moral reasoning stages are established, the teacher presents dilemmas that can induce cognitive conflict and that are relevant to the students. The trainer provides a rationale for Moral Education, describes what the group will be like, what her role is, and what the format will be for group participation (Arbuthnot & Faust,

1981). A four-step process ensues in which group members are asked to confront a moral dilemma, state a tentative position, examine the reasoning, and reflect on an individual position. Kohlberg and his collaborators maintain that these procedures, employed by a trainer who is able to establish a nonjudgmental climate, are the conditions necessary to promote moral development.

In fact, the research evidence suggests that moral dilemma discussion groups can successfully enhance moral reasoning stages. The results of a study involving 6th graders (11–12-year-olds) and 10th graders (15–16-year-olds) in which the experimenter led moral discussion groups (18 weekly 45-minute sessions) indicated that students in the experimental classrooms showed significantly more upward change in moral reasoning (one-third stage increase) as compared to various control group classrooms (Blatt & Kohlberg, 1975). In addition, participants in the experimental condition maintained the change at a 1-year follow-up. The changes observed were generally in the direction of the next higher stage, implying that true learning, rather than rote learning of phrases, had occurred. Similarly, the results of a study by Colby, Kohlberg, Fenton, Speicher-Dubin, and Lieberman (1977) indicated that students in a moral discussion group led by teachers in the context of a social studies class showed a significant upward change in moral reasoning as compared to students in control classrooms where no moral discussions were held. In addition, Colby et al. (1977) found that more change in moral reasoning occurred for students who were in the process of stage transition, who were in classrooms that consisted of students of diverse levels of moral reasoning, and who had teachers skilled in promoting reasoning at adjacent stages and who used a greater number of discussion periods. In a series of studies reported by Sullivan (1980), Moral Education programs were again found to enhance moral reasoning. The results of a study using elementary-school-age children indicated that while both the experimental group (twice weekly participation in a minicourse in ethics in which moral dilemma discussions were held for 1 academic year) and the control group (no participation in the ethics class) showed movement from primarily Stage 1 to Stage 3 reasoning on posttesting, only the experimental group evidenced some Stage 4 reasoning and had completely abandoned the use of Stage 1 reasoning. This developmental pattern was also evident at a 1-year follow-up (Sullivan, 1980).

In an earlier study using secondary-school-age children, Beck, Sullivan, and Taylor (1972) found that there were no differences between the experimental and control groups in moral reasoning on posttests. However, a 1-year follow-up indicated that students in the experimental group evidenced more postconventional reasoning than did those in the control group. The authors maintain that the 1-year interval between posttesting and follow-up provided opportunities for students to use their newly learned reasoning skills and thus to consolidate Stage 5 reasoning. In another study using high school students, results were less supportive (Sullivan & Beck, 1975). No differences in moral reasoning enhancement were found for the experimental and control groups. The discrepancy between the results of the last two studies can be found in an examination of the teaching methods employed. In the latter study, an ethics textbook, reflecting the interests of the teachers more than those of the students, was used, whereas in the former study a textbook was not employed. The authors argue that the use of a textbook created a more structured environment, which restricted the type of moral discussions that could evolve. These results suggest that the relevance of the moral dilemmas used has significant effects on the success of a Moral Education program.

Other studies using direct moral discussion of real-life situations have yielded positive results. Rundle (1977), using a 5th grade classroom in which moral issues were taught by the experimenter and a teacher (29 hours) within the context of classroom democracy, found that the experimental classroom (students discussed and modified classroom rules using democratic procedures) showed significantly more change (one-half stage) than students in either the classroom with no moral discussion or the one with moral discussion using hypothetical moral dilemmas. This again suggests that the efficacy of Moral Education programs is in part a function of the relevance of the dilemmas discussed. In addition, Rundle (1977) found that children in the experimental group performed significantly better on a cooperation task (brick-building) than those in the two control groups. It is important to recognize, however, that the group participating in moral discussion using hypothetical dilemmas was led by a teacher who had not received training in Moral Education procedures. Thus, the group differences may have resulted from differential levels of experience with Moral Education procedures rather than from exposure to real versus hypothetical dilemmas.

The work of Grimes (1974) indicated that moral discussion groups involving 5th and 6th grade children and their mothers can also lead to enhanced moral reasoning. Specifically, the results indicated that such group discussions between mothers (the experimenter had trained them in Moral Education prior to the initiation of the study) and their children led to more change (between one-third and one whole stage) than groups in which children, without their mothers, discussed hypothetical moral dilemmas (one-third stage increase) or groups which did not discuss moral dilemmas at all (no change). The authors maintain that the presence of the mother increased the frequency of moral dilemma discussions in the home. Stanley (1976) found similar results in a study involving parents and their adolescent children. Not only did the parent-adolescent group (10 weeks) show moral growth (one-third stage increase), but at a 1-year follow-up they had also continued to hold weekly family meetings involving family fairness discussions. In contrast, the parent-only group, as well as the control group, showed no significant pre-to-posttest gains.

More directly relevant to our decision to include Moral Education as one of the parts in the tripart intervention we call ART is the substantial evidence that it reliably increases moral reasoning level in juvenile delinquent populations (Arbuthnot & Gordon, 1983; Fleetwood & Parish, 1976; Gibbs, Arnold, Ahlborn, & Cheesman, 1984; Rosenkoetter, Landman, & Mazak, 1980). Although not all such Moral Education intervention attempts have yielded enhanced moral reasoning (Schmidlin, 1977; Wright & Dixon, 1977), given its overall intervention efficacy with delinquents and the moral reasoning deficiency typically displayed by juvenile delinquents when compared to nondelinquents (see next section), we nevertheless strongly concur with Arbuthnot and Gordon (1983) that the necessary technology is in place, and that "the task for the correctional education may be seen, then, not as one of conversion or rehabilitation, but one of development, or habilitation, of a moral reasoning framework which the offender, for whatever reason in his or her developmental history, has not yet acquired" (p. 133).

A number of conclusions can be drawn from the results of these studies employing Moral Education procedures: (1) moral dilemma discussion groups can lead to significantly more moral growth (one-third to one whole stage increase over one academic semester) than in various control groups; (2) this change occurs when a range of reasoning stages are represented in the classroom; (3) the teacher must help the student probe his reasoning in an environment that promotes openness and trust; (4) the moral discussion must create divided opinions and controversy among the students; (5) the most effective Moral Education interventions occur with discussion of real dilemmas in the context of a "real" group (e.g., the classroom, the family); and (6) delinquent individuals characteristically function at lower levels of moral reasoning than do nondelinquent cohorts, but can be trained to increase their levels of such reasoning ability as a result of participation in Moral Education.

What of the relationship between moral reasoning and overt behavior? Research concerned with this question has been considerable and of two types: seeking connections between level of moral reasoning and both antisocial and prosocial behaviors.

Moral Reasoning and Antisocial Behavior

While the study of moral behavior has primarily been undertaken in controlled laboratory settings and has usually involved the use of nondelinquent populations, there is research evidence to suggest that— with exceptions—a relationship exists between moral judgment and unsocialized behavior. These studies consistently yield positive correlations between aggressive behavior/delinquency and preconventional levels of moral reasoning. Specifically, Freudlich and Kohlberg (see Kohlberg, 1973) found that while 23 percent of working-class, nondelinquent adolescents reasoned at preconventional stages (usually characteristic of children under age 10), 83 percent of delinquent adolescents reasoned at Stages 1 or 2. Similar results were found by Fodor (1972) in an investigation using 14- to 17-year-old delinquent males (violations ranged from petty larceny to attempted homicide). Delinquents were found to score significantly lower on Kohlberg's Moral Judgment Interview as compared to nondelinquents. A study by Campagna and Harter (1975) also indicated that sociopathic males evidenced significantly more preconventional reasoning than a matched sample of nonsociopathic males. Hudgins and Prentice (1973) similarly found that 14- to 16-year-old nondelinquent males scored significantly higher (conventional level) on Kohlberg's moral dilemmas than a matched sample of delinquent males (preconventional level). Blasi (1980) has carefully examined the relevant research in this domain and concluded that in 10 of the 15 pertinent studies evidence indicates that delinquent individuals characteristically utilize developmentally lower levels of moral reasoning than do matched nondelinquents. Thus, while certainly not always the case, the thrust of relevant evidence indicates the two preconventional stages to be the typical level of moral reasoning among juvenile delinquents.

Moral Reasoning and Prosocial Behavior

In general, and again with not insignificant exceptions, the literature suggests that a positive relationship exists between stage level and such prosocial behaviors as honesty, as measured by cheating behavior (Harris, Mussen, & Rutherford, 1976; Kohlberg & Turiel, 1971; Krebs, 1967;

Schwartz, Feldman, Brown, & Heingartner, 1969); altruism, as reflected in helping people in distress, and generosity (McNamee, 1977; Ugurel-Semin, 1952); nonviolence, as measured by refusal to inflict pain on other people (Kohlberg & Turiel, 1971); and conformity behavior (Fodor, 1972; Saltzstein, Diamond, & Belenky, 1972).

There is considerable debate concerning the validity of using these behaviors to draw conclusions about the relationship between moral reasoning and "moral behavior." In studies of honesty, for example, the evidence suggests that more conventional than postconventional reasoners cheated on tasks when there were no explicit authoritative or group sanctions preventing it. Kohlberg and Turiel (1971) maintain that, because the postconventional reasoners define the situation as one which involves mutual trust and equality of opportunity, they are less likely to cheat. In contrast, the conventional reasoners maintained that there was no reason to resist cheating since the authority figure (i.e., experimenter) did not disapprove of this behavior. Thus, it seems that one of the consequences of a rule-oriented morality is that behavior is in part controlled by the prevailing rules of the situation (Arbuthnot & Faust, 1981).

Postconventional reasoners are believed to behave according to principles, not rules. Therefore, when conventional rules for behavior are no longer present in a situation, the conventional reasoner's behavior is more likely to break down as compared to those reasoning at the principled level. These ideas were partially confirmed in a study by Harris, Mussen, and Rutherford (1976) in which 5th grade boys were administered a resistance-to-temptation task based on the duplicating technique (participants are asked to score their own tests after they have been scored by the experimenter) used by Hartshorne and May (1928). The results indicated that honesty was positively, although not significantly, correlated with moral reasoning scores. In contrast, the Krebs (1967) study yielded significant positive correlations between moral reasoning and resistance to temptation as measured by a structured game in which it was easy to cheat. Although drawing conclusions from "box scores" of results across studies on any given topic is not without its own weaknesses, it is nevertheless useful to note that according to Blasi (1980), of the 17 studies seeking to identify a possible relationship between moral reasoning level and honesty, 7 support such an association, 7 do not, and 3 investigations report equivocal results.

McNamee (1977) conducted an experiment concerning altruism in which the participant could decide to help or not help a confederate drug user. Compliance with the experimenter's expectation was defined as the participant's willingness to help the confederate. The results indicated that while all participants reasoning at Stage 6 offered the confederate assistance, only 68 percent of Stage 5 reasoners, 38 percent of Stage 4 reasoners, and 28 percent of Stage 3 reasoners offered some kind of assistance (either a referral or personal assistance). These results indicate that behavioral choice differs for higher and lower stage reasoners. The results of a study by Ugurel-Semin (1952) provide further support for the relationship between moral reasoning and altruistic behavior. Specifically, the results indicated that for 4- to 16-year-old children in Istanbul, increases in moral judgment stage are associated with increasingly more mature justifications for their altruistic behavior. But as with the moral reasoning/honesty relationship, the connection between level of moral reasoning and altruistic behavior—all relevant evidence considered—is equivocal. Of 19 relevant studies, 11 confirm the relationship, 4 do not, and 4 are mixed in their findings (Blasi, 1980).

The results of a study by Kohlberg and Turiel (1971) on nonviolence again provide support for a positive relationship between moral reasoning and moral behavior. The investigators administered the Moral Judgment Interview to participants in Milgram's study of obedience to authority in which one participant is told by the researcher to administer increasingly painful shocks to another participant. While 75 percent of the Stage 6 reasoners refused to continue shocking the other participant, stating that the researcher did not have a right to inflict pain on another person, only 13 percent of the lower stage reasoners (including Stage 5) discontinued administering the shock. Although Stage 5 reasoners often felt uncomfortable with the experiment, they continued to shock because both they and the victim had made a commitment to the researcher to participate in the study. In contrast, the Stage 3 and Stage 4 participants continued shocking the victim because of the experimenter's definition of the situation. Thus, it is apparent that, even though similar decisions may be elicited by people reasoning at different stages, the reasoning process underlying these behavioral choices differs for individuals functioning at different levels of moral development. And, finally, in a study examining the relationship between moral reasoning and conformity behavior, Saltzstein, Diamond, and Belenky (1972) found that significantly more Stage 3 reasoners conformed to group opinion than those participants reasoning at Stage 4 or Stage 5. Yet again, as was the case for honesty and altruism, behaviors indicative of nonviolence and those reflective of resistance to conforming to group pressure are not consistent in the direction or the degree of their correlation with level of moral reasoning.

In summary, the results of the studies presented in this and the last section indicate that relationships may exist between moral reasoning stage and both antisocial and prosocial behavior, but that the magnitude and reliability of such relationships, however, appear to depend in part on the particular prosocial or antisocial behavior examined. As Blasi (1980) notes:

> The body of research reviewed here seems to offer considerable support for the hypothesis that moral reasoning and moral action are statistically related. This statement, however, should be qualified as soon as one looks at the findings in more detail. Empirical support, in fact, varies from area to area. It is strongest for the hypothesis that moral reasoning differs between delinquents and nondelinquents and that at higher stages of moral reasoning, there is greater resistance to the pressure of conforming one's judgment to others' views. The support is clear but less strong for the hypothesis that higher moral stage individuals tend to be more honest and more altruistic. Finally, there is little support for the expectation that individuals of the postconventional level resist more than others the social pressure to conform in their moral actions. (p. 37)

Discrepancies between Word and Deed in Real-Life Situations

The primary criticisms emerging from the use of such behaviors as cheating, altruism, and conformity to study the relationship between moral reasoning level and moral behavior have emerged within the Kohlberg group. Kohlberg (1969, 1973) and Turiel (1980) argue that these behaviors cannot always be viewed as representative of moral behavior because they do not take into consideration the individual's intentions and they do not reflect true moral dilemma situations. For example, Kohlberg (1969) argues that the invalidity of experiments utilizing honesty stems from the fact that they do not reflect true moral dilemmas. According to Kohlberg, a true moral dilemma involves a situation requiring the individual to choose between two courses of action in which "strong emotional reactions are activated." Kohlberg does not believe that cheating situations often evoke these emotions. Damon (1980) supports a similar view. He maintains that tests of cheating and lying, for instance, are trivial and do not capture an individual's true moral concerns.

Studies investigating the idea that people may reason and behave differently when confronted with a hypothetical versus a real-life moral dilemma have yielded inconsistent findings. In Blasi's (1980) review of evidence bearing upon this question, he found six studies that reported a significant positive relationship between moral reasoning and real-life behaviors, three investigations that yielded negative data, and three reporting mixed results. For example, in the McNamee (1977) study discussed earlier, no discrepancy was found between reasoning in concrete versus hypothetical moral conflicts. However, in a study by Gerson and Damon (1975) using 4- to 10-year-old children, there was considerable discrepancy between the stage of reasoning used in hypothetical versus concrete situations. The results indicated that lower levels of reasoning were employed in concrete situations of generosity (actual distribution of candy bars) as compared to hypothetical situations (hypothetical distribution of money). Similarly, Kohlberg, Kauffman, Scharf, and Hickey (1975) found that prisoners use lower stage reasoning when responding to concrete prison dilemmas as compared to standard hypothetical dilemmas.

The fact that individuals do not reason at only one stage makes these discrepant findings somewhat more interpretable. Nevertheless, these results also imply that extraneous variables may be operative in the reasoning process, having their effect on an individual's ultimate behavioral choice. This idea has received considerable support in the literature. For example, based upon a study that indicated that significantly more preconventional (70 percent) and conventional (55 percent) reasoners cheated than postconventional reasoners (15 percent), Kohlberg (1973) concluded that factors beyond moral judgment influence the translation of moral reasoning into moral action. This conclusion was based upon the fact that 15 percent of the principled reasoners still cheated, even though stage descriptions would suggest that they would not behave in this manner.

One factor believed to impact upon moral action is ego strength, defined as "attentional-will factors" (sense of will or purpose) (Grim, Kohlberg, & White, 1968). Kohlberg (1971b) suggests that ego strength may lead to impulse control and the ability to delay gratification. Specifically, Kohlberg (1971b) maintains that the mediational effects of ego strength factors may cause people "to differentially follow the moral judgments that they themselves make in the situation" (p. 381). Related to this factor is the question of the role of affect on moral behavior (Rothman, 1980). While little research has investigated the mediating role of affect, Ruma and Mosher (1967) found a positive relationship between the level of moral judgment of delinquents and the guilt they experienced about their behavior. Self-interest (Gerson & Damon, 1975) may be another variable accounting for a considerable percentage of the variance, in that it elicits different levels of personal investment in particular situations. The ability to role-take, perspective-take, or empathize may provide yet another link in the reasoning-behavior chain.

A host of situational factors has also been found to mediate moral behavior. These factors include the use of hypothetical versus concrete, real dilemmas (Gerson & Damon, 1975; Haan, 1975; Keasey, 1977; Straughan, 1975), demand characteristics of the situation or experiment (Adair & Schachter, 1972; Orne, 1962), and the parameters (type and variety) of the moral conflict within a particular situation (Damon, 1980). It has been suggested that situational factors are particularly potent in concrete situations of moral decision making since the individual often has considerable personal investment in the outcome of the dilemma (Rothman, 1980). Other factors proposed to account for the discrepancy between moral reasoning stage and moral behavior are age (increased consistency of moral behavior with increasing age) (Saltzstein, Diamond, & Belenky, 1972; Turiel & Rothman, 1972) and the confusion between moral behavior and socially conventional behavior (Turiel, 1980). Concerning the latter point, Turiel (1980) argues that a distinction must be made between moral issues, involving consideration of justice, and conventional concerns, involving issues related to the expectations of others in society (e.g., mode of dress, forms of address). He maintains that it is unreasonable to assume that one's conception of socially conventional issues should be related to one's conception of moral issues.

Thus, just as behavioral choices may vary for different individuals reasoning at the same stage, one person may behave differently across two situations even though her reasoning is the same. Nevertheless, although these factors are believed to influence the reasoning-behavior relationship, the degree of impact of each variable, alone or in combination, is as yet unknown. Furthermore, despite this impact, most researchers in the area of moral development continue to maintain that level of moral reasoning is the most influential factor and, in fact, the only distinctively moral factor impacting upon moral behavior (Kohlberg, 1973). Support for this contention awaits future research.

From this discussion, two conclusions can be drawn concerning the relationship between moral reasoning and moral behavior. First, it can be stated that advanced moral reasoning is a necessary but not sufficient condition for consistent moral behavior (Arbuthnot & Faust, 1981). In other words, while one can observe consistency between an individual's maturity of moral reasoning and maturity of behavior, one cannot always predict behavior from knowledge of the individual's reasoning stage in real-life situations. As Hoffman (1970) maintains, it seems reasonable to assume "that both specificity and generality can be found in moral behavior as in any other trait. Individuals do vary between their general predispositions toward honesty and dishonesty but their actual

behavior in moral conflict situations is not an all-or-none matter"
(p. 344). Second, the discrepancy between moral reasoning and moral
behavior in real-life situations can be accounted for by mediating factors
such as situational variables, concrete versus hypothetical moral dilemmas, ego strength, affect, role-taking ability, age, and the distinction
between moral and socially conventional behavior. Research endeavors
must, therefore, continue to address the question of the role these
mediating variables play in the moral reasoning/moral behavior chain.

It should be apparent from this discussion that the application of
Moral Education procedures to the reduction of aggressive behavior
involves the consideration of a myriad of factors. While these techniques
have proven to be effective for increasing moral reasoning stage, there
is at present only a modest amount of evidence indicating that these
effects are transferred to moral behavior in real-life situations. Moral
Education (and the enhanced levels of moral reasoning consequent to
its utilization) may have its greatest impact upon overt behavior when
account is taken of the array of artifactual and moderator variables
already discussed, and when Moral Education is employed as a contributing component in a larger intervention package, all of whose components are designed to interact and impact synergistically. As Zimmerman
(1986) has commented:

> It is maintained that it is necessary to possess both anger inhi-
> bition skills and alternative behaviors to aggression when elic-
> iting prosocial behaviors. However, if youngsters possess the
> ability to respond in a prosocial manner and if they have the
> skills necessary to inhibit or decrease impulsive anger and
> aggression, the question that remains is whether the delinquent
> youngster will choose to use these skills. To increase the prob-
> ability that the youngster will make this choice, it is argued that
> one must intervene on a cognitive-moral level. In other words,
> youngsters must also understand *why* they are engaging in a
> certain behavior. Moral Education is designed to impact on this
> level and . . . this method has proven to be effective in enhancing
> the sociomoral reasoning of aggressive youth. As with other
> techniques implemented in isolation, however, Moral Education
> does not consistently yield changes in actual behavior. Indeed,
> prosocial values by themselves may not be sufficient for the elic-
> itation of prosocial behavior. This discrepancy may in part
> emerge because the youngsters did not have in their behavioral
> repertoires alternative prosocial behaviors or the skills needed
> to successfully inhibit antisocial behavior. (p. 80)

In the case of ART, the synergism of the training components is hypoth-
esized to increase the likelihood that prosocial behavior will occur by

(1) explicitly teaching such behavior (Structured Learning component), (2) enhancing trainee ability to thwart competing anger arousal responses (Anger Control Training), and (3) maximizing the likelihood the individual will choose to enact his newly learned prosocial skills because the consequent heightened level of moral reasoning permits, encourages, or even impels an enhanced sense of fairness, justice, and concern for others (Moral Education).

Chapter 7

Trainer's Manual for Moral Education

Throughout history adults have been involved in teaching children what is the "right" or "wrong" action to take in a particular situation.* Adults have also tried to teach children why one "ought" to behave in a certain manner. Unfortunately, with changing values and rules for appropriate behavior in today's society, youth are faced with many situations that they do not know how to think about, respond to, or challenge. They are confronted with situations in which they question what values are worthwhile, how to apply values to specific situations, and how to behave when two values conflict with each other.

Moral Education through dilemma discussion groups is a method designed to teach adolescents how to think about moral issues, how to deal with moral situations that do not have clear-cut solutions, and how to use principles of fairness and justice in their interactions with others. Dilemma discussion groups attempt to achieve two major goals: (1) increasing the moral reasoning stage of the adolescent and (2) helping the adolescent use newly learned and more advanced reasoning skills in the real world.

In general, these goals are achieved through peer group discussions of different kinds of stimulating moral dilemmas and the reasoning underlying various behavioral choices in these moral situations. Thus, adolescents are exposed to different ways of thinking about moral issues. In these discussions, trainees are asked to explain the reasoning leading to the position they have chosen. In this way, group members are exposed to different stages of moral reasoning (i.e., different rationales underlying behavioral choices made by trainees operating at different levels of moral reasoning). Exposure to advanced (usually one stage

*This chapter follows, in general outline, Arbuthnot, J., & Faust, A. (1981). *Teaching moral reasoning: Theory and practice*. New York: Harper & Row, and Gibbs, J. C., Widaman, K. F., & Colby, A. (1982). *Social intelligence: Measuring the development of sociomoral reflection*. Englewood Cliffs, NJ: Prentice-Hall. The creative contribution of Ben Taylor to the development of this training manual is both very substantial and very much appreciated.

higher than the youngster's own reasoning stage) reasoning stages creates confusion called cognitive conflict, or disequilibrium, that may contribute to the trainee's attainment of a higher level of moral reasoning as a means of resolving the conflict. Exposure to more advanced reasoning stages also provides trainees with the opportunity to take on the role of another person (i.e., to put oneself in someone else's shoes). In sum, there are at least three basic principles involved in enhancing moral reasoning development that form the basis for the specific procedures used in dilemma discussion groups: (1) exposure to the next higher stage of moral reasoning, (2) inducement of confusion over genuine moral dilemmas, and (3) opportunity to take on the role of another person. Dilemma discussion groups can be applied to many moral issues, including the values of life, property, law, truth, affiliation, authority, contract, conscience, and punishment.

It is important to note what dilemma discussion groups are not. First, this method does not involve "indoctrination" or the teaching of any specific values or beliefs. The trainer should *never* attempt to force trainees to accept his personal values. Rather, this method is aimed at self-discovery and helping adolescents develop the effective problem-solving skills needed to arrive at their *own* solutions to moral conflicts they may be faced with in life. While trainers do not mandate what is good, they do attempt to encourage discussions from which trainees can discover for themselves what is good.

Second, it is important to stress that dilemma discussion groups do not simply provide opportunities to clarify values. In these groups, trainees are asked to defend the reasoning underlying their position in relation to how consistent their rationale is with principles of fairness and justice. As these rationales will vary, the trainer should not view one behavioral choice or reason as the only way to effectively think about a moral situation. In contrast, one aim of this method is to help adolescents develop flexible reasoning processes that can be adapted to the demands of their lives and the situations they are in.

Third, it is important to note that dilemma discussion groups are not a form of dynamic or behavioral therapy in which emotional conflicts are uncovered or specific behaviors are changed. Rather, these groups always remain focused on the discussion of moral issues by using specific, sequential procedures. This is not meant to imply that personally relevant moral issues cannot be discussed. It simply means that discussions should always focus on the examination of moral reasoning in relation to moral issues. Finally, dilemma discussion groups cannot be led successfully by all people. The next section addresses the knowledge and skills trainers need to run effective dilemma discussion groups.

PREPARING FOR MORAL EDUCATION

The assessment of moral reasoning stage and the structuring of group discussions are the major activities of the moral trainer. As such, the trainer must both lead, listen, and observe. Typically, one trainer finds it difficult to do all of these tasks successfully at the same time. Thus, it is highly recommended that each group be run by a team of two trainers—a trainer and a co-trainer.

Selecting Trainers

The running of effective dilemma discussion groups involves these trainer attributes:

1. Knowledge of the main features of moral development theory and moral discussion group techniques: background, assumptions, procedures, and goals
2. Knowledge of moral reasoning stage assessment (this involves the use of abstract reasoning abilities)
3. Ability to reason at least one stage above that of group members (+ 1 stage reasoning)
4. Ability to use a nondirective teaching style (i.e., ability to provide only a moderate amount of group structure)
5. Ability to maintain a "devil's advocate" position without leaving youngsters with the impression that there are specific ways to behave in moral situations or right/wrong answers to the dilemma being discussed
6. Ability to orient both group members and supporting staff to dilemma discussion groups (e.g., create the proper attitude)
7. Ability to create experiences that will promote the self-discovery of higher stage reasoning (e.g., ability to structure, initiate, and sustain group discussion)
8. Ability to effectively deal with group management problems

Preparing Trainers

In an ideal situation, trainer preparation is maximized when potential leaders initially participate in a dilemma discussion workshop. In this workshop, one or two experienced trainers demonstrate how moral stage assessments are made and how to run dilemma discussion groups. After this demonstration, beginning trainers practice co-training several groups with an experienced trainer, thus gaining several opportunities to practice what they have observed and to obtain feedback regarding their performance prior to running their own groups.

When a workshop is unavailable, the task of preparation rests solely with the trainer. Under these circumstances, it becomes even more important for the potential trainer to follow these sequential training steps:

1. Read Chapter 6.
2. Thoroughly read and study the trainer's manual (this chapter) and work through the stage assessment exercises presented in it.
3. Practice running dilemma discussion groups using friends, colleagues, or adolescents as group members before starting the real-life group.

While this may seem like a large task right now, in the long run it will make the role of a moral educator far easier and much more enjoyable. To enhance this preparation process, it will be helpful to review some of the major theoretical ideas discussed in Chapter 6 and to begin training in moral stage assessment.

Theoretical Review

Morality. The concept of morality cannot be easily defined. For the purpose of training it may be best to think about morality in terms of key words such as principles, justice, fairness, equality, and respect. It is also useful to think about morality in terms of what processes it involves. In this way, morality may be seen as involving

> those skills, values and abilities that comprise (1) thinking or reasoning (problem solving, decision making) in a rational way, while (2) showing an awareness of, and consideration for the needs, interests and feelings of others as well as oneself, and (3) behaving constructively, i.e., in ways that benefit both self and others, in the problematic or conflictual social-interpersonal situations which one encounters in one's daily interactions with other people. Morality, then, involves cognitive (thinking), affective (feeling), and behavioral (doing) aspects which are necessarily interrelated. (Edelman & Goldstein, 1981, p. 259)

Content versus structure of thought. The basis for dilemma discussion groups can be found in cognitive developmental theory. This theory focuses on cognition, particularly the way people over the course of their development think or reason about laws, rules, and principles. The content of moral cognitions involves *what* one is thinking or actually saying (i.e., opinions). In contrast, the structure of moral reasoning involves *how* one is thinking or the process of thinking (i.e., what underlies one's words). This distinction implies that while the content of an individual's reasoning may vary from situation to situation, the structure remains relatively constant over different moral dilemmas for a person at a given level of moral reasoning. For example, the structure of moral reasoning will be fairly similar for a person whether he is reasoning about the value of life or property. It also implies that while the content may be similar between lower and more advanced reasoners, the reasoning process will be different.

Moral situations. A moral situation involves a conflict in which at least two conflicting interests or values are evident. These situations often involve, but are not limited to, conflicts between responding to legal/societal norms or responding to the needs of others (e.g., stealing in order to save someone's life).

Moral issues. The concept of moral issues or moral norms relates to the distinction that has already been made between content versus structure of thought. Moral issues relate to the content of the individual's moral reasoning rather than how the person reasons (structure). More specifically, moral issues involve "the values the person is reasoning about" (Arbuthnot & Faust, 1981, p. 68). These moral issues include life, property, truth, affiliation, authority, law, contract, conscience, and punishment.

Moral stages. The cognitive developmental theory of moral reasoning proposes six stages of moral development (see Table 5 in Chapter 6). These six stages represent qualitatively different ways of thinking and reasoning about moral issues and emerge over an individual's life span. Movement through these stages is said to occur in a predictable and invariant sequence (i.e., movement from Stage 1 to Stage 2 to Stage 3, etc.), with later stages representing more complex and abstract ways of reasoning about moral issues. The theory also suggests that the moral structures of the earlier stage serve as the foundation for the development of the moral structure of the next stage (hierarchical integration). In addition, each stage is believed to reflect an organized way of thinking about moral issues (structured whole).

However, while movement through the stages occurs in an invariable sequence and hierarchical order, the theory also maintains that an individual does not reason at only one stage in all situations. Rather, people are seen as reasoning primarily at one stage (dominant stage) and secondarily at adjacent stages, either one stage below or above the predominant stage. This idea of primary and secondary stage reasoning has important implications for those running dilemma discussion groups because it suggests that trainers likely will see some variability in an individual's responses across different moral dilemmas (e.g, Stage 1 reasoning on one moral dilemma and Stage 2 on another). A corollary of this idea is that people can understand reasoning at or below their own stage but usually cannot understand reasoning that is more than one stage above their own reasoning stage. As will become more apparent as the discussion proceeds, this is why efforts are made to create debates between adjacent stage reasoners (e.g., Stage 1 reasoners debating Stage 2 reasoners) in dilemma discussion groups. Finally, the theory proposes that the qualitative changes that emerge in moral development reflect changes in the individual's thought structure (reasoning process changes). This moral advancement is induced by cognitive conflict.

Cognitive conflict. The concept of cognitive conflict is crucial to the understanding of how dilemma discussion groups work. Cognitive developmental theory proposes that through the child's interactions with others, he is increasingly exposed to situations in which moral values conflict and appropriate rules for behavior are unclear. Repeated exposure to these "value-conflictual" situations leads to cognitive conflict. In an effort to resolve this unclear and value-conflictual state, children experiment with alternative ways of reasoning. These alternative ways of reasoning are usually reflective of the next higher stage of moral judgment. Dilemma discussion groups create cognitive conflict for group members through discussions of value-conflictual situations; these discussions expose youngsters both to the limitations of their current reasoning process and to alternative ways of thinking about and dealing with the situations.

Assessment of Moral Reasoning Stage

Characteristics of the stages. In order to run effective dilemma discussion groups, it is important to know something about moral reasoning stage identification because, as will be discussed in detail later, this identification forms the basis for how the trainer will structure the actual group discussions. As such, it is one of the major activities of the moral trainer. Although the precise identification of all moral reasoning statements requires extensive training and practice, the beginning trainer can develop basic assessment skills with some practice and time.

The first step in becoming an effective assessor of moral reasoning is to become familiar with the characteristics of each of the moral reasoning stages (see Table 5 in Chapter 6). At this time, it will be helpful to discuss the most commonly seen stages in more detail. The discussion will focus primarily on the major characteristics of the first four moral reasoning stages in terms of both their moral and social perspective features. Before this is addressed, however, some clarification of the term social perspective is needed (see Table 6 in Chapter 6). Social perspective refers to a person's perception "of the relationship of self to others, or the self to society's rules and regulations [and] . . . involves one's thinking about human relationships and their place in society" (Arbuthnot & Faust, 1981, p. 121). Assessing the social perspective reflected in a statement can be more easily achieved than a direct assessment of an individual's moral reasoning stage because social perspective is often more clearly presented in the response. It can, therefore, provide good clues regarding the moral stage of the particular statement.

As Table 5 indicates, the major orientation of the Stage 1 reasoner is that of punishment and obedience. Adolescents at this stage determine what is right or wrong by focusing on the punishment, external threat, or physical consequences of a behavior (e.g., going to jail). They are not concerned with the emotional or psychological hurt their behavior may have on others. Behavior is seen as unacceptable if it leads to one's own punishment or if it results in physical harm to a high status person or that person's belongings. Acceptable behavior is that which adheres to concrete, externally defined rules, which avoids punishment, leads to reward, complies with power, or serves one's own interests when there are no external rules against it. As such, morality is seen as a number of clearly defined rules established by powerful people. These rules are not seen as having any relation to society. Indeed, the adolescent at this stage has no understanding of society, although he may have some conception of family. In addition, moral reasoning at this stage typically lacks any true sense of fairness and justice. Morality is, in effect, understood as an "eye for an eye, a tooth for a tooth." The value of life is often determined by the importance of the person, and one obeys simply to avoid punishment, not because it is for the social group's welfare. In sum, morality is determined by and learned from others, not oneself. The social perspective of youths at this stage is highly egocentric and narrow. While there is an awareness of oneself and of an outside world, there is no recognition that other people may have different feelings and thoughts than one's own. The concept of mutuality does not exist, as people act only in self-interest. Other people are seen only in terms of their ability to provide punishment or rewards, such that moral decisions tend to be based on concrete, physicalistic concerns.

The major orientation of the Stage 2 reasoner, as indicated in Table 5, is that of instrumental relativism (i.e., individualism, instrumental purpose, and exchange). Youths at this stage determine what is right by doing what meets their own needs or perhaps those of another person and by focusing on making equitable and fair exchanges or deals. In other words, while making sure that one's own needs are maximized, Stage 2 reasoners allow other people to satisfy their own needs as well. To do this, adolescents must be able to recognize that other people may have different needs from their own. Acceptable behavior for everyone, therefore, includes those actions that allow one to acquire wanted materials, status, services, or help. Although there is a "marketplace" quality to Stage 2 moral reasoning, it represents an advance over Stage 1 reasoning in that it is more internally defined (i.e., choices may allow one to meet personal needs), and there is less of a focus on the consequences of a behavior or physicalistic qualities. Youths at this stage also have developed a sense of the organization of social groups. This awareness of social organization is quite self-focused, however, in that it is determined by the exchange of egocentric interests between people (e.g., "You scratch my back and I'll scratch yours"). The intentions of others are not really considered to be important. As such, a good choice is evaluated in terms of whether it leads to a positive outcome for the person making the choice (i.e., the instrumental value of the behavior), rather than being determined by a sense of commitment and respect. Personal rights are highly determined by ownership: A person can do what he wants with his own belongings and with his life even if these choices are in conflict with the rights or needs of others. Rights are, therefore, determined by each individual, rather than by a group or societal consensus.

As already alluded to, the social perspective of the Stage 2 reasoner involves the recognition that one's personal views may differ from other people's positions and that these other people may also perceive situations differently from each other. Youths at this stage also recognize that people depend on each other to respond in an agreed-upon way. While mutuality is considered, it is typically understood in terms of one or at most a few people. In addition, if a few people's viewpoints are being considered, their ideas will tend to be looked at separately rather than as related or as part of a group. In other words, relationships are generally seen in dyadic terms, with moral reasoning reflecting individual rather than group concerns. These individual concerns are self-oriented; issues involving the group good and the good of the larger society are not considered. In sum, Stage 2 reasoning is primarily characterized by the idea that one will meet the needs of others only when doing so also meets one's own needs.

As Table 5 indicates, the major orientation of the Stage 3 reasoner is that of interpersonal concordance, or "good boy-nice girl" positions (i.e., mutual interpersonal expectations, relationships, and interpersonal conformity). Individuals at this stage determine what is right by following the "Golden Rule" principle of doing unto others what you would want them to do unto you. Acceptable behavior involves being nice, loyal, and trustworthy; having good intentions; conforming to group expectations; doing what will lead to approval; and behaving within role expectations. Stage 3 reasoners feel it is important to be concerned about others because they would want others to be concerned about them in a similar situation. As such, Stage 3 reasoners are concerned about establishing and maintaining good relationships with the people in their group network. This requires that the individual possess some sensitivity to the rights, feelings, and viewpoints of others, and an understanding of reciprocity and mutuality.

Stage 3 reasoners have developed the capacity for reciprocal perspective-taking, that is, the ability to view an action from another person's point of view. This capacity allows the Stage 3 reasoner to attend more closely to the intentions of others and the meaning of another's behavior. Thus, the particular actions enacted become secondary to the person's motivation. By focusing on intentions rather than actions, Stage 3 reasoners are able to excuse typically unacceptable behavior (e.g., to condone stealing something in order to save a loved one's life). For the Stage 3 reasoner, moral conflict is often resolved by looking for and using previously and fairly established group rules. The expectation is that others will recognize one's own needs if one follows group rules. While this requires the individual to perspective-take and to subordinate personal needs for the good of the social group and, as such, represents advance over Stage 2 reasoning, the morality of people at Stage 3 continues to be somewhat self-oriented.

This egocentrism takes the form of seeking to gain approval from legitimate authority figures: The goodness of a behavior thus is determined by whether it results in approval. As such, a rather conventional, stereotyped morality is evident in that what is good continues to be defined externally. Concerns about society beyond the immediate social group have not yet emerged. It may already be apparent that the social perspective of the Stage 3 reasoner involves an understanding of the "group good" and the ability to perspective-take. Genuine concern is evident in Stage 3 reasoners' interest in others. Relationships and group membership are important simply for the sake of these relationships and not because one needs another person to achieve a desired goal. Indeed, relationships are perceived as a mutual sharing between two or more people. The desire for mutuality necessitates that the Stage 3 reasoner consider the thoughts and feelings of other group members and place his individual needs behind those of the relationship or group (i.e., self-sacrifice). In other words, individuals will attempt to make choices that please everyone involved (i.e., will behave like a "good person" would).

The major orientation of the Stage 4 reasoner, indicated on Table 5, involves considerations about law and order, the social system, and conscience. Appropriate behavior for the Stage 4 reasoner is determined by the desire to maintain order and law in the larger society and by meeting one's obligations to society in an effort to prevent social disorder or to maintain self-respect and a good conscience. In effect, the individual behaves in a manner that facilitates the functioning of the entire society. The Stage 4 reasoner often uses a legal position to determine what is acceptable or unacceptable. However, unlike the Stage 1 reasoner, who may uphold law out of fear of punishment, or the Stage 3 reasoner, who is obedient because of the desire to conform to being good, the Stage 4 reasoner obeys because laws are made by society and must be upheld out of respect and fairness to all members of society. Just as rights are earned by society's members, laws are rules designed by elected members of society to assure that everyone's rights are maintained. As such, laws assure that society will function in an orderly, peaceful manner.

It is apparent that this orientation reflects an advance over Stage 3 reasoning in a number of ways. First, the Stage 4 reasoner recognizes that to guarantee equality, fairness, and order, society's rules must encompass all social groups, rather than just certain segments of the society. Second, individuals at Stage 4 also realize that loyalty, the intention to do the right thing, and small group relationships (Stage 3) are not enough to guarantee that laws and rights are upheld. Rather, Stage 4 reasoners maintain that strict standardization of the law is needed to maintain equality and order. The rigidity evident in the reasoning process of the early Stage 4 individual emerges in response to the belief that if subjective feelings and favoritism enter into the running of society chaos will ensue.

As the Stage 4 individual develops, however, he begins to question the underlying principles used in establishing laws. Contradictions between legal laws and moral laws and the injustice of some legal laws become increasingly evident to the more advanced Stage 4 reasoner. This awareness marks the movement to Stage 5 reasoning. (Stage 5 reasoning, which emphasizes law but involves a realization that most values are relative and a belief in some nonrelative values that must be upheld in any society, and Stage 6 reasoning, which emphasizes universal principles of justice, equality, and dignity over law, will not be addressed in detail in this manual. Judgments at these two levels are attained by relatively few individuals and, as such, are not likely to be evident in running dilemma discussion groups with youth. For more information on these two stages refer to Chapter 6.) The social perspective of the Stage 4 individual is characterized by the realization that all people, including oneself, are needed for the successful functioning of the larger society. It is this focus on the "social good" that differentiates Stage 4 from Stage 3 reasoners, whose focus is on the "group good." While dyadic or small group relationships are still seen as important, the social perspective evolves to encompass the meaning and impact these relationships, and people in general, have on the entire society. People are not seen only as sharing a relationship but as sharing a society.

Eliciting information about moral reasoning stage. Once a trainer is familiar with the characteristics of each stage, the second step in becoming an effective assessor of moral reasoning involves learning how to get the kind of information needed to make accurate stage assessments. Specifically, the trainer needs information that reveals the underlying reasons for a behavioral choice. Simple statements like "I'd steal the drug" will not give the trainer the rationale used to make the decision. When this situation occurs, the trainer must be prepared to ask questions that will reveal the "why" behind the action. Two key guidelines should always be followed when asking for elaborations of responses:

1. Ask open-ended questions (ones that encourage explanation, rather than simply a "yes" or "no") designed to reveal the reasons underlying the behavioral choice (e.g., "Could you tell me more about your reasons for making that choice?"; "In what way do you think that is the best action to take?"; "I'm not sure I understand your reasoning for that choice").
2. Listen actively and closely to the meaning of the youngster's statements and either mentally or verbally paraphrase or rephrase the statement to ensure complete comprehension of the response presented. If your paraphrase is inaccurate, ask the trainee for clarification with another open-ended question. An example of paraphrasing follows:

> Bill: John shouldn't report his friend to the police because friendship is based on mutual trust and respect. To report him to the police would be breaking an important rule of friendship.

> Trainer: The value of friendship is important to you. To report John would be like violating the rules of relationships. Does that capture what you were saying, Bill?

Paraphrasing requires some practice and should be done with friends, family, or colleagues before actually running a dilemma discussion group.

It is also helpful to know what to avoid when evaluating moral reasoning stages. The following list briefly describes conditions to avoid when identifying moral stage during group discussions:

1. Regardless of the trainee's response, do not express negative judgments. Instead, encourage further elaboration of the response when necessary (e.g., "I'd like to be able to fully understand your ideas"; "Tell me a little more about that").
2. Do not pretend to agree with the trainee's ideas as a means of encouraging more discussion. Express interest, not agreement.
3. Avoid asking too many questions, as this tends to elicit defensiveness from the trainee. Using open-ended questions, rather than closed-ended questions (questions requiring yes/no answers or short responses) often prevents this from occurring.
4. Avoid asking "why" questions repeatedly as they, too, tend to elicit defensiveness.

Practice exercises. Once a trainer is armed with the basic skills needed to be an effective moral reasoning assessor, practice in assessment is the next step. Two sets of practice exercises with answer keys follow. Referring to Tables 5 and 6 and to the earlier discussion of the stages in this chapter will help with the exercises. While these exercises provide initial practice, it is important to reiterate that expertise in this area requires a great deal of practice and time. The reader is, therefore, referred to Gibbs, Widaman, & Colby (1982), in which additional practice exercises are presented.

Exercise I—Heinz Dilemma

In Europe, a woman was near death from a special kind of cancer. There was one drug that the doctors thought might save her. It was a form of radium that a druggist in the same town had recently discovered. The drug was expensive to make, but the druggist wanted people to pay ten times what the drug cost him to make.

The sick woman's husband, Heinz, went to everyone he knew to borrow the money, but he could only get together about half of what the druggist wanted. Heinz told the druggist that his wife was dying and asked him to sell it cheaper or let him pay later. But the druggist said, "No. I discovered the drug and I'm going to make money from it." So the only way Heinz could get the drug would be to break into the druggist's store and steal it. *What should Heinz do?*

Assess what stage of moral reasoning the following responses reflect:

1. Heinz should steal the drug because it isn't really bad to take it. And his wife might be a really important person.

2. It's wrong to steal someone's property because there are laws that protect property. In this case he wouldn't really be wrong, though, because a human life is at stake. Life has important value that overrides things like property. And it's his wife's life. He has taken a vow to protect her and has a responsibility as her husband to save her. He should expect to pay the druggist back and maybe go to jail for awhile.

3. No, he shouldn't steal it. He couldn't be blamed if she died. It was the druggist who was mean and selfish. He should obey the law, because if people just made selfish decisions all the time, there would be chaos.

4. No, he shouldn't steal it. He might not care for his wife anyway. And he could always find a new one. What good would it do to save her if he was in jail, anyway! And the druggist is just trying to make some money. After all, that's what people are in business for.

5. Heinz probably doesn't really want to steal the drug but it's all right in this case because he needs it badly to save his wife's life. And he needs her and wants her to live. And the druggist deserves to have it stolen for trying to rip off his customers.

6. The law forbids stealing from another person. But at the same time, the law was not designed with circumstances such as these in

Note. John Gibbs/Keith Widaman, *SOCIAL INTELLIGENCE: Measuring the Development of Sociomoral Reflection,* © 1982, pp. 193-200. Exercises I and II adapted with permission of Prentice-Hall, Inc., Englewood Cliffs, NJ.

mind. Heinz would be justified in taking the drug, but would have to make real and social compensations for it. The law here is not doing a good job in protecting basic human rights. The value of life is far more important than the value of private property. So Heinz should feel no guilt in his act.

7. He should steal the drug. He was only doing what a good and loyal husband would do. He should care enough about her to want to do it and should feel guilty if he didn't. And while it isn't nice to take someone else's property, the druggist was being heartless and cruel.

8. No, he shouldn't take it. He'd be taking property of the druggist and probably harm his store. He'd get caught and be punished. And besides, some really important person might need the drug badly.

9. No, even though the druggist morally had no right to charge that much, legally he does. Heinz doesn't have a legal right to take someone else's legal property. We all have to respect the rights we guarantee by law to others. If not, society would break down.

10. He shouldn't steal it because he should think about his life and future, so he should not get involved with his wife's death.

11. He shouldn't steal it because he would be taking other people's things.

12. It isn't really right to steal even though the community probably wouldn't blame him for the theft. However, he has agreed to live by the standards of the community. So he must weigh whether such individual acts would ultimately result in the greatest good for all. By breaking into another's legal property, Heinz would be violating principles of trust which are part of the contract he has made with the community.

13. I guess he should steal it because it would benefit his wife and he was acting out of good conscience. But he still broke the law and should therefore be punished.

14. He shouldn't steal the drug because taking things from others is really mean. If Heinz took the drug it would not be right because the drug is the druggist's pride and joy, because he found something that can save lives.

15. No, because it's not yours and kids could be put in a detention home and adults could be put in jail.

Using the same dilemma, now determine the stage of the response to the question *" What should the judge do?"*

16. Heinz shouldn't be sent to jail because he saved a life. It is better to steal than to let someone die. The judge should help Heinz, put him on probation, and warn him never to break the law again, but to ask for help from the authorities.

17. He should be sent to jail because if the judge goes easy on him, then he'd have to go easy on everyone else and no one would get placed in jail.

18. Heinz should not be put in jail because the justice that would be served would be that of the individual. Individual rights rather than society's right would be served. If the judge feels that Heinz was forced to steal, the judge should be able to see the unfairness of the country's legal system and try to change it.

19. Heinz should be sent to jail because sooner or later everyone would feel justified to steal. Everybody would steal and say it was needed for this or that and the morals of society would soon break down.

20. He shouldn't be sent to jail because he was trying to be good and he's nice.

Exercise I Answer Key

1. Stage 1	6. Stage 5	11. Stage 1	16. Stage 3
2. Stage 4	7. Stage 3	12. Stage 5	17. Stage 2
3. Stage 3	8. Stage 1	13. Stage 3	18. Stage 5
4. Stage 2	9. Stage 4	14. Stage 3	19. Stage 4
5. Stage 2	10. Stage 2	15. Stage 1	20. Stage 1

Exercise II—The Broken Promise

In this exercise, try to stage the responses without the benefit of referring to a specific moral dilemma. [Some responses in this exercise are transitional responses in which a dominant level of reasoning is evident along with some reasoning at a higher level, for example, primary reasoning at Stage 3 with some Stage 4 reasoning indicated.]

1. Keeping a promise to a friend is important because it's important to be able to place your trust in others. But if someone told me something that he was doing, I wouldn't tell because it's none of my business to tell on him.

2. Letting one's children keep earned money is important because if the parents take the money, then the children will get mad at their parents and it might end up in an argument or fight.

3. Keeping promises to one's children is important because children have to mind their parents and it's stupid to tell your children that they could go and then turn around and say no.

4. Helping one's parents is very important because if you love your mother and you want to do what she wants you to do, then do it.

5. Keeping a promise to a friend is very important because it's important to keep a promise to a friend, also to anybody else one knows, not necessarily friends only, because our words reflect the kind of a person we are.

6. Letting one's children keep earned money is very important because it not only lets the children have fun but they may have worked hard for the money, and to hand it over to parents isn't fair. Not unless the parents were in poverty. Then you should help them out.

7. Keeping a promise to a friend is important because being loyal to a friend is important. You should regard their trust in you very highly because much is based on trust.

8. Letting one's children keep earned money is important because the children should learn values, and the action of a parent reflects very highly on the children. By earning the money the children have shown responsibility and if this money is taken away, so will the meaning of earning the money.

9. Helping one's parents is very important because even though it was Judy's money and her mother wasn't being fair when she changed her mind, you should still respect what someone says and still trust them and not hold a grudge just for one mistake.

10. Letting one's children keep earned money is important because otherwise you will be stealing your children's money.

Exercise II Answer Key

1. Stage 3; Stage 3/4*
2. Stage 1
3. Stage 1

4. Stage 2; Stage 2/3
5. Stage 4
6. Stage 2; Stage 2/3

7. Stage 3
8. Stage 4
9. Stage 1; Stage 1/2
10. Stage 1

---

*Stage 3/4: This representation denotes a transitional response in which the primary moral reasoning process is at Stage 3 with some Stage 4 reasoning evident.

Group Organization

Number of Trainees and Trainers

Dilemma discussion groups are ideally run with small groups of trainees. In the research conducted on this program, groups were made up
of 12 boys. As mentioned earlier, a trainer and a co-trainer should lead
the discussion groups.

Number of Sessions

In ideal situations, dilemma discussion groups are incorporated into the
ongoing activities at school, home, or the residential treatment setting.
However, in reality this rarely occurs and therefore some guidelines
must be established. This program recommends a 10-meeting curriculum to maximize motivation and interest throughout the course of the
group. However, it must be noted that when resources have been available, dilemma discussion groups have been conducted within school
settings for an entire academic year without producing boredom. So if
it is possible, continue to run the group for as long as necessary (i.e.,
until the trainees have reached an age-appropriate stage of moral
reasoning).

Length and Spacing of Sessions

Dilemma discussion classes are held for about 1 hour. However, as the
length of the class often depends on how verbal the trainees are and on
how interesting the dilemma is, sessions can range from 45 to 60 minutes. This variability raises a question: How many dilemmas should be
discussed in each class? During an hour-long class, a complete discussion of at least one dilemma (a thorough discussion of one dilemma can
take about 35-45 minutes) and the introduction and gathering of initial
opinions on a second dilemma should occur. Discussion groups should
be spaced a few days apart to encourage thinking about the dilemmas.

CONDUCTING DILEMMA DISCUSSION GROUPS

There are six general steps involved in running Moral Education
dilemma discussion groups.

   Step 1: Form small groups of trainees at two to three consecutive
   stages of moral reasoning.

   Step 2: Choose and prepare moral dilemma situations that will
   induce cognitive conflict and that are relevant to the
   trainees.

Step 3: Create the proper set by explaining to the trainees the rationale for dilemma discussion groups, what they will be doing, what the trainer's role is in the group, and what guidelines to follow for participation in the group discussion.

Step 4: Begin the discussion by presenting the dilemma, getting initial opinions and rationales from the trainees, and then creating a debate between the lowest reasoners and those one stage higher (noted as + 1 stage).

Step 5: Guide discussion through all the stages represented by group members (e.g., start with a debate between Stage 1 and Stage 2 reasoners, then structure a debate between Stage 2 and Stage 3 reasoners, and so on if more than three levels of reasoning are represented), creating cognitive conflict for as many trainees as possible. Then present a + 1 stage argument for the group to discuss (e.g., if the highest stage represented in the group is Stage 3, then present a Stage 4 argument).

Step 6: End discussion following the debate of the highest stage argument or when all the major issues and important differences of opinion have been addressed.

Before these six steps are discussed in detail, it will be helpful to define some of the terms that will be used throughout the remainder of this manual. In dilemma discussion groups, cognitive conflict can be generated in two ways. The two ways are the following:

1. "+ 1 SC"

   This type of conflict is read as "plus one stage conflict." It occurs when group members hold different positions on a dilemma (e.g., some trainees say "steal the drug" while others say "do not steal") *and* when these different behavioral choices are based on reasoning one stage apart (e.g., "pro" stealing Stage 1s and "con" stealing Stage 2s). This type of conflict means that trainees at the lower stage are exposed to reasoning one stage above their own (+ 1 reasoning). The exposure to + 1 SC elicits the awareness that one's own reasoning is not fully adequate and thus generates disequilibrium—the sense that one's view of the world has been shaken up.

2. "Non-PC"

   This type of conflict is read as "nonpreferred conflict." It is not as ideal as + 1 SC because it does not create as much disequilibrium and does not provide exposure to + 1 stage reasoning.

As such, Non-PC is less likely to enhance moral reasoning. Non-PC occurs when group members maintain different positions on a dilemma, *but* these positions are based on reasoning at the same stages (e.g., everyone is at Stage 1) or two or more stages apart (e.g., some trainees reason at Stage 1 while the rest reason at Stage 3).

Whenever possible, it is better to create a +1 SC discussion (detailed in Preferred Circumstances, Steps 4 and 5). If this is not possible (if statements are not provided that allow the trainer to structure a +1 SC discussion or if the trainer is unable to accurately assess reasoning stage), the next best alternative is to structure a Non-PC discussion (detailed in Nonpreferred Circumstances, Steps 4 and 5). With this terminology in mind, the discussion will now focus on describing each of the six steps involved in running dilemma discussion groups.

Step 1: Forming Groups Based on Initial Assessment of Stages

The first step in conducting dilemma discussion groups involves the formation of groups based on an initial assessment of moral reasoning stages. Before describing the conditions needed to form an ideal group it is important to stress that dilemma discussion groups can be conducted even if the ideal conditions do not exist because of institutional restrictions (e.g., preformed classrooms or counseling groups) or because a range of different stages of reasoning is simply not available. In these cases, the trainer simply takes a more active role in the moral discussion process. For example, if only one moral reasoning stage is represented in the group, the trainer will always need to provide the +1 reasoning arguments. In fact, in most dilemma discussion groups involving antisocial adolescents, the trainer will almost always be in the position of having to provide a +1 stage argument, at least some of the time. So remember that groups can be formed even if only one stage is represented in the group. If this happens, it simply means that the trainer will need to work under Non-PC conditions. If possible, however, it is best to form an *ideal* group.

To form an ideal group, three conditions should be met.

1. A range of consecutive moral reasoning stages must be represented by the trainees (e.g., Stages 1 and 2 or Stages 1, 2, and 3). Meeting this condition means that almost all group members (all but the highest stage reasoners) will be exposed to +1 stage reasoning. It also increases the chance that trainees will present different opinions.

Finally, meeting this condition keeps the discussion manageable in that the trainer does not have to be concerned about structuring debates across too many different stages. This would not only be difficult but would also be of little benefit to most of the trainees (remember that Stage 1 reasoners, for example, are unlikely to understand the reasoning of Stage 4 individuals because it is too advanced for them).

2. The number of trainees reasoning at a particular moral stage should be almost equally represented in the group (e.g., four Stage 2s, four Stage 3s, and four Stage 4s). Meeting this condition decreases the chances for peer rejection because it guarantees that there will be more than one group member at a particular stage. It is often difficult for one trainee to present an argument that the rest of the group is likely to disagree with because they are at a different stage.

3. Relatively small groups should be established, consisting of about 6 to 12 people (groups have, however, ranged from 20 to 30 individuals). Keeping the groups small increases the chance that everyone will have an opportunity to participate and decreases group management problems. A final note regarding group composition is that the ages of the trainees should not vary too widely.

In order to meet the first two of these conditions the trainer must be familiar with the procedures used for determining moral reasoning stage, previously described in the "Assessment of Moral Reasoning Stage" section. They will be briefly reviewed here:

1. Familiarize yourself with the characteristics of each of the six moral reasoning stages, particularly Stages 1 through 4.
2. Either administer a test to accurately identify moral reasoning stage (e.g., the Sociomoral Reflections Measure in Appendix A or the Moral Judgment Interviews of Arbuthnot & Faust, 1981) or conduct informal interviews about solutions to moral dilemmas as described earlier.

Following the assessment of moral reasoning stage, trainees should be assigned to groups based on the three conditions just described.

Step 2: Choosing and Preparing Dilemmas

Choosing Dilemmas

The second step in conducting dilemma discussion groups involves the selection of dilemmas for debate. Thirty stimulating dilemmas have been preselected for use when running dilemma discussion groups and are included at the end of this chapter. However, if the trainer opts to choose or develop his own dilemmas, three major goals need to be achieved:

1. Select dilemmas that will generate cognitive conflict for as many trainees as possible.
2. Select dilemmas that will create interesting and productive discussion.
3. Select dilemmas that clearly deal with moral issues (e.g., issues of life, property, affiliation, etc.).

When running groups with trainees who reason at two or three consecutive stages, it is at times difficult to select dilemmas because the issues that create disequilibrium for one stage of reasoners may not create cognitive conflict for trainees reasoning at another stage. Nevertheless, different stages ideally need to be represented in the group. To avoid this potential problem, several guidelines can be followed in choosing dilemmas for discussion.

1. Select or construct dilemmas that generate several issues and questions but that are open ended, so that the dilemma can be elaborated if issues at certain stages are not automatically raised or if no counterarguments from higher stage reasoners are provided. A lack of extensive, precise details helps maintain the open-ended quality of a dilemma so that when higher stage counterarguments are not generated spontaneously, elaborations can be added to create these higher stage arguments or new issues can emerge.

Example: Suppose that in response to the Heinz dilemma a Stage 2 reasoner argues that Heinz should steal the drug because he needs his wife. If Stage 3 reasoners do not spontaneously produce a counterargument, the trainer might elaborate the dilemma by adding information that may change the position of the Stage 2 and not the Stage 3 reasoner. Specifically, the trainer might change the sick person from a wife to a friend or stranger. This kind of elaboration is likely to create the material needed for the development of a counterargument, which is necessary for the structuring of a debate.

2. Choose dilemmas involving genuine moral conflict—situations in which at least two people have differing claims (e.g., Heinz wants to save his wife's life and the druggist wants to earn money) and in which one behavioral alternative or another must be chosen.

3. Select dilemmas that trainees will be able to understand given their intellectual abilities.

4. Select dilemmas that will most likely lead to different action alternatives for trainees reasoning at different stages. With experience

and some knowledge of group members, the trainer's ability to correctly anticipate probable responses will increase.

5. Choose interesting dilemmas by considering their relevance to the youngsters, the probability that the moral situation will actually occur in real life, the novelty of the issue, and the ability of the dilemma to stimulate challenging questions, disagreement, and cognitive conflict. It is important to stress that not all relevant issues are moral issues. For instance, many relevant dilemmas deal with controversial or personal rather than moral issues (e.g., premarital sex). It is recommended that controversial and personal issues not be selected for discussion unless it appears that the group needs to discuss these issues to maintain sustained interest in the program. If controversial issues are introduced into the group, it is best to wait until trainees have met for a period of time.

Preparing Dilemmas

After selecting a number of dilemmas to be discussed, the trainer, as in any teaching effort, must prepare the dilemmas prior to the beginning of each group. This preparation is designed to accomplish three goals:

1. To make the dilemmas useful in assessing the trainees' moral reasoning stage
2. To stimulate debates at different stages
3. To generate counterarguments at different stages, if necessary

This preparation is particularly important for the inexperienced trainer because it is very difficult to elaborate a dilemma or develop a counterargument when one is on the spot. In order to adequately prepare dilemmas the trainer should follow three general guidelines. The first guideline is to try to anticipate how trainees at a particular stage will respond to the dilemma by referring to the characteristics of each stage (see Tables 5 and 6). For example, using the Heinz dilemma one might anticipate that Stage 1 reasoners will be concerned about the consequences of their action. Heinz might not want to steal for his wife because he would end up in jail. On the other hand, maybe he would steal the drug because his wife would be angry if he did not. Stage 2 reasoners will be concerned about self-interests. In this view, Heinz might steal the drug because he needs his wife around to raise the children. However, he might not steal the drug because his wife never did anything for him. The trainer should be concerned with anticipating how the trainees will reason at a particular stage rather than with what behavioral alternative will be selected. This type of preparation will make it far easier to assess the actual responses made in the group when that time arrives.

The second guideline to attend to involves preparing elaborations of dilemmas for those instances when it is necessary to generate disagreements between trainees at different stages (see Example, p. 146). Third, it is important to prepare a counterargument for each of the stages represented in the group, as well as an argument that is one stage above the highest stage represented in the group. In addition, the trainer should be prepared to argue for at least two behavioral alternatives at each stage. Preparations of this kind are helpful in situations when arguments at certain stages are not verbalized automatically and when elaborations of the dilemma do not promote active discussion of counterpositions.

Using the Heinz dilemma, stage preparations might include:

Stage 1: Steal—His wife may be an important person.
Not Steal—You will be put in jail for it.

Stage 2: Steal—He needs her to clean and take care of the children.
Not steal—He does not like her anymore.

Stage 3: Steal—Nobody wants to see someone die.
Not steal—If he went to jail he would not be around to take care of his family, like a good husband would.

Stage 4: Steal—He would be saving the life of a human being. The value of life is more important in this instance than property.
Not steal—We have a contract with society to protect the rights of others, in this instance, property rights.

During an hour-long class, a complete discussion of at least one dilemma and the introduction and gathering of initial opinions on a second dilemma should occur. With less verbal trainees it is often possible to completely discuss two different dilemmas in one session. At times, it may even be necessary to introduce a third dilemma into a session, although this is not recommended because it is difficult to completely discuss three dilemmas in 1 hour. However, given that it is a possibility, the trainer must prepare three dilemmas for each class (i.e., anticipate stage responses, create elaborations, and develop counterarguments). It is certainly acceptable to not complete a discussion in one session. In fact it is sometimes desirable to leave the discussion incomplete in order to encourage trainees to think about the dilemma after the class. This additional time between classes can lead to further thoughts that were not initially recognized and can facilitate moral reasoning advance. Discussion of the dilemma can be resumed in the next class if desired by the trainees.

Prior to the first dilemma discussion group, the two trainers (remember it is helpful to have a trainer and co-trainer involved in these classes) should also determine what responsibilities each will have during the group. For example, one trainer may decide to take primary responsibility for asking the questions needed to get stage responses while the other person records and assesses the level of the responses. Since the latter person has assessed the responses, she may then decide to take on the primary responsibility of structuring the initial discussion while the other trainer handles later debates. These rules should not be rigidly adhered to, as the aim is to create a flexible, open, and nonjudgmental atmosphere. It is suggested only to prevent the new trainer from being overwhelmed with the many demands placed on her during these groups. So even if the trainer has decided to assess responses during a particular class, she can feel free to ask questions, guide the discussion, or perform any of the other tasks of a dilemma discussion group leader.

Step 3: Creating the Proper Set

With Step 3, the trainer is at last in the class getting ready to start the initial dilemma discussion group session. The group has been formed (Step 1) and the dilemmas have been selected and prepared (Step 2). Step 3, Creating the Proper Set (or appropriate expectations), marks the beginning of the actual class and is the first task the trainer undertakes in the initial meeting. It is a crucial step because it establishes the foundation for the structure of the group meetings. There are four general goals that need to be accomplished during this phase of the initial session. These goals, as well as the procedures to accomplish them, are presented next.

The first goal involves explaining the rationale and purpose of dilemma discussion groups and some of the theory on which the group is based. The following ideas should be included in the presentation.

1. The group will meet to discuss situations in which people have conflicting claims.
2. The goal of the discussion groups is to enhance everyone's ability to think or reason about these conflictual situations.
3. Although everyone may think he knows how to resolve these situations, almost everyone can develop further by experimenting with different ways of thinking about conflictual situations so he is better prepared when actually faced with a real conflictual problem.
4. As people mature, they develop different ways of thinking about these situations.

5. Discussion of conflictual situations seems to increase a person's ability to think about and solve these problems when they really happen.

When discussing the purpose and rationale of the group meetings, be sure to adjust the level of the presentation to the intellectual abilities of the trainees, to include all the major ideas about the rationale underlying dilemma discussion groups, and to limit the amount of time spent discussing the rationale (i.e., it should not be a formal academic presentation). In addition, when introducing the class to trainees, the word "moral" should be dropped as it can sometimes elicit confusion and defensiveness (this reaction is why the class is referred to as a dilemma discussion group rather than as Moral Education). Adjusting the level of the presentation to the trainees is applicable to all of the goals in Step 3.

The second goal is to discuss the trainees' role in the group and group procedures by explaining the format of the meetings. The following ideas should be included in the presentation.

1. Conflictual situations involving dilemmas will be presented by the trainer to all trainees.
2. These situations are not like math problems because there is never just one right answer to a situation.
3. After presentation of the situation, all trainees will have a chance to share their opinions and solutions.
4. Trainees' different viewpoints will then be discussed with each other. Group members will be expected to do most of the talking, which may be hard initially, but will likely become easier with time. The discussions will be something like a debate; to help everyone be actively involved the group will be sitting in a circle.

The third goal is to explain the trainer's role in the group.

1. There will be no evaluations of whether trainees' answers are right or wrong because there are no right or wrong answers.
2. The trainer's role is not to present the right solution to the situation because there is none and because this is a time for trainees to use and develop their own ways to think and reason about these problems.
3. Although most of the talking will be done by trainees the trainer's role is to help everyone focus on a few ideas at a time and to help the group talk in an orderly manner about the ideas brought up.

4. Although the trainer will not express personal ideas and solutions (this tends to interfere with the quality of the discussion), at times the trainer will play "devil's advocate" when important ideas have been missed.
5. The trainer will make sure that all trainees have a chance to share their opinions, if desired, and that respect for each other is always maintained.
6. The trainer will help trainees share their ideas clearly.

The fourth goal involves explaining ethical rules for group behavior and involvement.

1. It is important that everyone feel safe to share openly his ideas. To create this feeling, all group members must respect others' ideas. Respecting others' ideas does not mean always agreeing with them; it is fine to disagree because that is the best way to learn from each other. However, it is not okay to disagree by talking about unrelated issues, by not allowing someone to express an opinion, or by using personal insults. Trainees who disagree with others should stay on the subject, give everyone an equal chance to answer, argue in a fair way, and listen to what others have to say.
2. Respect trainees' freedom of belief: No one should feel he has to agree with any of the positions argued by anyone else, including the trainer. There are no punishments for disagreements—everyone should listen to each other and keep an open mind.
3. Respect trainees' freedom of choice to determine when to share their solution to each dilemma.
4. Respect the confidentiality of all responses made during the class, unless doing so is in some way dangerous to the individual or to others.

Sample Introductory Statement

A sample introductory statement to create the proper set follows: "I imagine you're wondering what this class is all about. In this class, we'll be talking about ways to resolve conflict situations—situations where there is more than one way to think and act. Together we will be discussing and thinking about how you choose which way is fairer. We're really going to be focusing on how come you came up with that solution to the problem, not just what your solution is. In other words, we'll be talking about the reasons you have for coming up with that solution. I know that everyone probably thinks he knows how to solve problems involving conflicts, but almost everybody can benefit by thinking about and experimenting with different ways to handle these situations. We feel that if you experiment with different ways to think about these situations now, you'll be better prepared to handle them in the future. You know that as people get older they naturally develop different ways of thinking about these situations. These classes often speed up this natural process by helping people develop new and better ways to think about the situations now. Better here does not mean right or wrong. There are no right or wrong answers to these situations. However, there are better or worse solutions in the sense of helping you learn how to get along better with people. For example, you can learn how to make better decisions so you won't be hassled by teachers, parents, and peers as much. Also, if you respond to them differently, they are likely to act differently with you. So the goal of the group is to increase everybody's ability to think about conflict situations so you might be able to avoid hassles in the future.

"We are going to start these classes by having somebody, either one of us or a group member, read a conflict situation out loud. Remember, these situations aren't like math problems because there's never one right answer to them. After reading the situation, everyone here will have a chance to share his opinions and solutions. In fact, that's going to be your major job in the group. That is, your job will be to discuss with each other your differences of opinion. In other words, unlike lots of other classes you've been in, you're expected to do most of the talking. This may be hard at first, but with time I hope it will become easier. The discussions will be something like a debate, and to help everyone be involved we'll be sitting in a circle.

"While your job is to do most of the talking in here, our job will be to help everyone focus on a few ideas at a time, to help the group talk in an orderly way about the ideas you bring up, to help everyone share his ideas in an understandable way, and to help make sure that everyone who wants to will have a chance to share his ideas. Sometimes we might take on a devil's advocate position when we think an important idea has been missed. By devil's advocate, I mean that we might take a different position than the group to add to the discussion. However, we wouldn't be giving you the right solution to the situation for two reasons. One, because there isn't a right solution and, two, because this is a time for you to be developing and experimenting with your own ways to think about these problems. For the same reasons, we won't be sharing our personal opinions about how to think about the problem. Remember, you're not getting a grade in here, so we're not going to be judging your answers.

"A couple of other points. While we want this to be a place that's open, flexible, and safe for all to share their ideas, there will be some rules that we're going to follow very strictly. One rule is that all group members will be expected to respect the other members' ideas. Our job is to make sure that respect is maintained. This doesn't mean that you can't disagree with each other. In fact, it's fine to disagree because that's the best way to learn from each other. But it's not okay to disagree by insulting others, changing the subject, or not letting someone express an opinion even if it's different from your own. It's okay to disagree by giving everyone a fair chance to answer, arguing in a fair way, staying on the subject, and listening to each other. In other words, we don't want anyone to feel they have to agree with anyone else in the group, including us. Just keep an open mind. There are no punishments for disagreements. I also want to mention that we expect all group members to respect each other's privacy. This means that if personal things are discussed in here, it shouldn't be discussed with others unless that person wants you to. Respecting each other's privacy doesn't mean that you can't continue to discuss the conflict problem outside the group. In fact, feel free to do this; it can often be helpful.

"Does anyone have any questions about what I just said?" *(Answer questions.)* "Okay, then let's get started as that's the best way to understand all this."

Foundation for Later Steps

Remember that some kind of an introductory statement *must* be discussed in the initial meeting. Unless any confusion about these points emerges in later sessions, Step 3 does not need to be repeated during later classes. Thus, the importance of addressing these issues early in the training cannot be overstated. It is ethically important because trainees have the right to know what is involved in the activity they are undertaking. Furthermore, it is useful because trainees often demonstrate greater interest when procedures are explained.

The procedures the trainer will follow when conducting Steps 4, 5, and 6 depend on what type of circumstances or conflict unfold in the group. Recall that two ways of generating cognitive conflict can emerge in dilemma discussion groups: + 1 SC, or preferred circumstances (when trainees at a lower stage are exposed to reasoning one stage above their own), and Non-PC, or nonpreferred circumstances (when trainees have different solutions to a dilemma but these positions are based on reasoning at the same stage, or two or more stages apart). While preferred circumstances may evolve naturally, in work with antisocial youth the trainer is more than likely going to be in the position of having to create + 1 SC himself or work under Non-PC. As the different procedures followed under these two circumstances can be confusing, the discussion will initially focus on conducting Steps 4, 5, and 6 under preferred circumstances (+ 1 SC). Subsequently, procedures to follow for conducting Steps 4, 5, and 6 under nonpreferred circumstances will be addressed. In each of these separate discussions, general issues will be addressed first, then specific procedures for each situation.

Preferred Circumstances
Step 4: Initiating Discussion

Remember that in the first group meeting, the trainer will initially spend some time creating a proper set (Step 3 is not repeated in subsequent sessions unless necessary). This should not take longer than 10 to 15 minutes. Immediately following this introduction, the trainer initiates a discussion of a dilemma. The overall goal when initiating discussion is to set up a debate between group members who have expressed the lowest reasoning stage on a dilemma and disagreeing trainees reasoning one stage above the lowest stage.

A discussion begins when the trainer reads a dilemma to the group (if desired one of the trainees can be selected to read the dilemma). It is often helpful to provide written copies of the dilemma for trainees to follow while someone reads it out loud. The trainer should then make sure the dilemma is fully understood by (1) either summarizing it himself or asking group members to summarize the main points (these points and the characters and their roles can even be written on the board), (2) encouraging questions, and (3) clarifying misperceptions about the dilemma. Following this summarizing process, the trainer should provide a few minutes for trainees to think about the dilemma and formulate a solution to the dilemma problem (e.g., "In a minute everyone will have a chance to give his opinion of the problem, but let us take a few minutes to quietly think about it first"). If desired, the trainer can have trainees write down their response. It is important to reiterate that in these dilemmas a moral problem is presented in which trainees must decide between two behavioral choices (e.g., stealing versus not stealing). The trainees should also be thinking about why they have chosen a particular behavioral alternative.

After the thinking period, the trainer should go around the circle, having each trainee express an opinion about the dilemma and his reasons for choosing a particular solution (if desired the different values presented by trainees can be written on the board to aid retention and focus discussion). It is often helpful to start with a verbal trainee or one who appears to want to speak. Inform trainees that they can pass if they want to and that they can express their opinions later if desired. The trainer will need to recall these initial statements for the subsequent discussion. As such, it is often helpful to take short summary notes of the initial opinions of trainees. This is easily accomplished by rephrasing out loud the trainee's response, and, if the paraphrase is accurate, recording the major idea in the response. If possible also record, but *do not* say aloud, the stage of the response. If the major meaning of the statement is not accurately rephrased, the trainer should continue to ask "probe" questions. Probe questions are designed to get at the reasoning underlying the solution (e.g., "How come you think that is the fairest solution?"). The trainer should ask probe questions until he either understands the meaning of the response and, if possible, the stage of the response, or until the trainee begins to perceive the questioning as threatening.

After getting everyone's initial opinion of the dilemma, the trainer's next task depends on what type of conflict has been presented. Under preferred circumstances the following conditions will be evident:

1. Trainees will maintain different positions (behavioral alternatives) on a dilemma, which are based on different moral reasoning stages.
2. Trainees reasoning at different stages will have argued for different solutions.
3. The trainer has successfully identified the moral reasoning stage for most of the trainees' responses.

Under these circumstances, the trainer would first structure a debate between trainees reasoning at the two lowest stages who have different positions. Trainees reasoning at other stages would not initially be included in the discussion (they would, however, be asked to listen to the debate). When initiating the discussion, the trainer simply brings the attention of the group to the differing viewpoints (both solution and reasoning) by concisely restating the positions and by asking trainees at the lowest stage to debate their differences with the + 1 stage reasoners. The trainer can choose any of the trainees to begin the discussion (it is helpful to pick someone who has presented a clear and complete argument) by asking him to repeat or elaborate on his response. Subsequently, a + 1 stage reasoner with a different solution is asked to respond.

For example, the trainer may initiate a discussion to the Heinz dilemma by saying: "I've heard several different viewpoints about this situation. We'll start with two of these positions. Dave, Lee, and Steve don't think Heinz should steal the drug because he'll end up in jail [Stage 1 response]. On the other hand, Tom, Joe, and Fred think Heinz should steal the drug because he needs his wife around to take care of the children [Stage 2 response]. Dave, how about sharing your opinion again, and then, Tom, you explain to Dave and the others how come you disagree with them. The rest of you can feel free to jump in and support Dave or Tom or add any other ideas."

In summary, initiating a discussion under preferred circumstances involves getting initial opinions, determining that the opinions differ across solution and stage for a subset of the group, and setting up a discussion between lowest and + 1 stage reasoners who hold opposite opinions. It is also important to note that the process for initiating a discussion (i.e., read and summarize the dilemma, go around the circle to get opinions, set up the initial discussion) is repeated every time a new dilemma is introduced into the group. Indeed, following the initial session, the trainer will begin every other session with this procedure unless a dilemma from the prior session is being carried over into the subsequent one.

Preferred Circumstances
Step 5: Guiding Discussion

After an initial discussion between the lowest and + 1 stage reasoners has been structured, the trainer is now ready to move on to Step 5, guiding the discussion. This applies not only to the initial discussion but to all subsequent debates. To effectively guide a dilemma discussion, the trainer must be able to get as many trainees as possible to experience + 1 SC. The experience of + 1 SC is achieved by (1) exposing trainees to + 1 stage reasoning and (2) exposing trainees to additional factors that promote disequilibrium. The major factor needed to elicit disequilibrium involves helping lower stage reasoners realize that their reasoning does not completely help to resolve the dilemma. In other words, it is absolutely essential that during the + 1 SC discussion trainees become aware that their reasoning is inadequate to resolve the dilemma. This fact clearly does not imply that they are inferior people and therefore it should be explained in a way that does not elicit defensiveness. It is this awareness of inadequacy that creates disequilibrium, which in combination with + 1 stage reasoning stimulates moral development. Therefore, the overall goal when guiding the initial discussion and all subsequent discussions is to have the lower stage reasoners realize the inadequacies and limitations of their reasoning.

In the previous section, it was stated that the presence of + 1 stage reasoning is a condition for structuring + 1 SC. This means that when the trainer moves to guide the discussion under preferred circumstances, he already knows that + 1 stage reasoning is evident. The question now becomes one of determining how to maximize opportunities for lower stage reasoners to become aware of the inadequacy of their reasoning. There are at least three ways that the awareness of inadequate reasoning or disequilibrium can emerge.

1. Lower stage reasoners come to realize that + 1 stage reasoners are able to resolve specific aspects of the dilemma that they were unable to resolve and that initially appeared to be unresolvable.
2. The + 1 stage reasoners may directly point out the limitations, flaws, or contradictions of the lower stage reasoners' rationale, or the + 1 stage reasoners may ask questions that the lower stage reasoners cannot answer.
3. General exposure to + 1 stage reasoning, even without discussion, can create disequilibrium.

Ideally, at least one of these three circumstances will emerge over the course of the + 1 SC discussion without the assistance of the trainer. However, even under the best of circumstances the + 1 stage reasoners will be able to accomplish this goal without the trainer's assistance only about 50 percent of the time.

When lower stage reasoners do not recognize the limitations of their reasoning and the greater adequacy of + 1 stage reasoning, the trainer should first attempt to determine the cause of the difficulty. The second step depends on what has been identified as the cause of the problem. The problem may be due to negative attitudes toward participation, defensiveness, closed-mindedness, or the lack of clarity of the + 1 stage reasoners' arguments. If the + 1 stage reasoners present a clear argument and the lower stage reasoners continue to reject the higher stage position, the trainer might first ask the lower stage reasoners to explain why they have dismissed the higher stage response. If they have rejected the argument because it is beyond their understanding, then perhaps some error in assessment has been made and the trainer will need to make the appropriate adjustments to continue to guide the debate (e.g., altering assessment of stages and restructuring the debate). If they have rejected the argument because of defensiveness or closed-mindedness, the trainer might intervene by asking trainees to try to think about these problems without letting their emotions interfere with their reasoning. Trainees should try to understand, but not necessarily accept, the other trainee's opinion before rejecting it. It can be helpful to ask the lower stage reasoners to rephrase another's opinion to enhance active listening. The trainer can also simply encourage trainees to think about the arguments over the week before making a final decision. Of course, the trainer should not continue to challenge the position of lower stage reasoners to an irritating level as this will only increase defensiveness. If these interventions fail, the trainer simply goes on to other trainees and continues to guide the discussion by either structuring another debate or by having a general discussion of the major issues presented.

If lack of clarity of the + 1 argument is behind the rejection, the trainer should first have other + 1 stage reasoners try to present the argument in a more precise manner. If this is unsuccessful, the trainer should next try to clarify the + 1 argument by rephrasing the position to help the + 1 reasoners continue the discussion. If this intervention fails, it will be necessary for the trainer to play devil's advocate by arguing for the prior + 1 position or a new + 1 position. The following methods can be helpful to the trainer when playing the devil's advocate role to create awareness of inadequacy (i.e., disequilibrium):

1. Point out the contradictions or flaws in the lower stage argument by asking questions and/or suggesting hypothetical situations. Of course, what contradiction is pointed out depends on the response (opinion and reasoning stage) given.

Example: Using the Heinz dilemma, suppose a trainee states that everyone, including Heinz, should look out for himself. The trainer might ask the trainee what Heinz should do if he (the trainee) needed the drug to live and it was in Heinz's best interest not to steal it. More than likely the trainee will say Heinz should steal the drug to save his life. The trainer might then respond to this contradiction and the flaws in the argument by saying "In one situation, you said that Heinz should look out for himself, but then you said if it was your life at stake, Heinz should steal it. It sounds like you said two different things. What do you think?" If the trainee does not see the contradiction, the trainer might make a more direct statement—"Are you saying that you would not want Heinz to steal the drug because it is not in his best interest even though you might die without the drug and that is not in your best interest?"

2. Present unresolvable questions to the trainee. What questions you propose again depends on the opinion and reasoning stage of the trainee.

Example: Using the Heinz dilemma, suppose an argument is presented in which the solution is based on how much Heinz likes his wife or the druggist. The trainer could then propose that both the wife and the druggist are equally liked and ask, "Now how would you decide which choice to make?"

3. Point out the injustice of the decision from the perspective of another person in the dilemma (imaginary role playing), or ask trainees to imagine that an equal probability exists that they could be any person in the dilemma and, on that basis, to now try to arrive at a fair solution. These role playing techniques are effective in creating awareness of inadequacy because by taking another's perspective the injustice of a solution is somewhat easier to recognize.

Example: In imaginary role playing, the trainer might say, "Tom, you said that Heinz should not steal the drug for his wife. Now, pretend you are Heinz's wife. How would you feel about your husband's refusal to steal the drug because he does not want to go to jail when you will die without it?" In ideal role taking, the trainer might say, "Everybody pretend there is an equal chance you might be Heinz, his wife, the druggist, or the judge. Now, try to fairly solve the situation."

4. Add hypothetical information to the dilemma or point out any overlooked details that might increase awareness of inadequacy. What information or details are specified will again depend on the response of the trainee.

Example: Suppose a trainee states that Heinz should not steal the drug because he would be put in jail. The trainer might point out that judges often consider the motive of the person when deciding what sentence they will give.

5. Clarify how + 1 reasoning can solve problems that lower stage reasoning cannot resolve. What clarification is used will depend on the solution and reasoning stage of the response.

Example: Consider once again the situation of what Heinz should do if he likes his wife and the druggist equally. The trainer might explain that while both people are equally liked, being married involves a special kind of commitment, a vow, and different responsibilities than someone has toward a friend. So in Heinz's position it might be fairer to uphold his vow as a husband because it would be a decision based on both contract and friendship. By doing this, the trainer has just demonstrated how Stage 3 reasoning can be used to resolve a situation that Stage 2 reasoners may have found to be unresolvable.

6. Present a dilemma that is somewhat similar to the one being discussed, but which differs in such a way that the reasoning used in the first dilemma would not be adequate for resolving the second dilemma. Then demonstrate the use of + 1 reasoning for the new situation.

Example: Using the Heinz dilemma as the first situation, the trainer might say, "Suppose there are two men, Tom and Dick, who work in a laboratory. It so happens that both of them are very close to discovering a cure for cancer. In fact, Tom has half the information that is needed to discover the cure, while Dick has the other half. Tom wants to collaborate with Dick, so that together they can discover the cure. Dick does not want to collaborate with Tom because he wants all the credit for himself. Now Tom has to decide whether to steal this information from Dick. In the Heinz dilemma some of you argued that Heinz should steal because that is what a good person would do (Stage 3 reasoner). Does this apply in this situation as well?" This analogous situation will often result in Stage 3 reasoners realizing that their solution is inadequate. The trainer might then explain that Tom could resolve the dilemma by using rules made by society that involve property rights of all people, including scientists. In this case, the rules involve respecting Dick's right to publish or share his information when he wants to (+ 1 stage reasoning).

It is important to note that these six methods for playing devil's advocate are not mutually exclusive and can be used simultaneously if the opportunity arises.

The discussion should continue until the lower stage reasoners have realized that their arguments cannot resolve the dilemma and that the + 1 stage argument is more adequate, or until all major issues have been discussed and it is obvious that the lower stage reasoners will not change their rationale. The initial discussion usually takes between 10 to 20 minutes. It is important to keep in mind that it is always better to end a discussion somewhat sooner than later if the trainer is unsure of how long to let it continue. This decreases the chance that group members who are not involved in the debate will become bored or that defensiveness or hostility will emerge between the debaters.

Following the initial discussion, the trainer initiates a debate between the previous + 1 stage reasoners and trainees arguing from the next highest stage and making an opposite behavioral solution (e.g., if the initial Heinz discussion is between Stage 1s against stealing and Stage 2s in favor of it, the next debate will be between Stage 2s in favor of stealing and Stage 3s against this action). Using the Heinz dilemma, the trainer might introduce the second discussion by saying: "The important differences in opinion between those who think Heinz should not steal the drug because of the negative consequences and those who think Heinz should steal the drug because of needing his wife to help around the house have just been discussed. Some other ideas were mentioned before that we need to get back to. Joe, Bruce, and Barry said that Heinz should not steal the drug but gave a reason we have not talked about yet. If I remember it right, all three of you said that you have to consider how the druggist would feel having someone steal his property.

Did I remember it correctly? Joe, could you explain to the people who feel that Heinz should steal the drug why you think you have a fairer way of dealing with the problem?"

During the second discussion, the trainer's task again involves encouraging trainees to debate their differences, ensuring continued attention on the topic, ensuring respectful treatment of trainees by each other, and, if necessary, taking on the role of devil's advocate by using any of the aforementioned methods. In this debate, the previous + 1 stage reasoners are provided with opportunities to discover the limitations of their reasoning and the greater adequacy of higher stage reasoning. The trainer ends this debate when lower stage reasoners recognize the inadequacy of their reasoning or when all major issues have been discussed. Once again, the trainer reviews what was argued and initiates a debate between the most recent + 1 stage reasoners and those at the next highest stage (e.g., if Stage 2s and Stage 3s have just debated, the Stage 3s and Stage 4s will debate next). For example, the trainer might say, "If I remember correctly the three of you said. . . . Can you explain to the people who have just argued why you think you have a fairer solution?" Continue using these procedures until trainees at the next to the highest stage have debated those at the highest stage. In this way, the trainer proceeds, stage by stage, from the lowest to the highest stage argument presented in the group. When the highest stage argument presented by any trainee is reached, the trainer then presents a + 1 and opposing argument in order to point out to the highest stage reasoners the inadequacy of their argument. If available, the trainer should use one of his previously prepared arguments (e.g., if the highest stage argument presented in the group is a pro-stealing Stage 4 position, the trainer would present a previously prepared Stage 5 position against stealing). The procedures for guiding a discussion under preferred circumstances are repeated for all sessions, regardless of whether it is the first or a subsequent meeting.

Preferred Circumstances
Step 6: Ending Discussion

In the sixth and final step of one moral discussion, the major task required of the trainer involves determining when it is appropriate to end the discussion. Under preferred circumstances, the discussion of a particular dilemma is stopped when the group debate has progressed sequentially up the stages and the trainer's + 1 stage argument has been discussed. In addition, the discussion is stopped when all trainees have had the chance to address all relevant issues regarding the dilemma.

All trainees, it is hoped, have experienced disequilibrium through exposure to +1 stage reasoning and have realized that their current reasoning stage is inadequate.

It is important to stress that a discussion should not be stopped simply when interest decreases slightly, particularly if the group has not yet sequentially progressed up the stages, including the trainer's +1 stage argument, or if the group has not completed discussing all the relevant issues in the dilemma. When interest decreases, the trainer should point out a missed issue or ask a stimulating question to again activate the discussion. A discussion should be stopped either when it is no longer productive (i.e., when interventions to stimulate discussion are repeatedly ineffectual) or when progression through the stages or discussion of major disagreements has been achieved. The trainer should also remember that to maintain interest it is always better to end a discussion somewhat early rather than too late.

The trainer can end the discussion of a particular dilemma by summarizing the major issues addressed in the debates and by relating the discussion to situations the trainees may have experienced or may experience in the future. Dilemma discussion meetings can be ended by following any one of several procedures. One method involves having trainees write down the single best argument they heard during the discussion and then reading it out loud. A second procedure involves having trainees tell the person sitting next to them something helpful he had said during the discussion. And finally, the trainer could ask several trainees to say something about what was better during the current week's discussion than the prior week's debate. When the discussion of one dilemma has ended, the trainer either stops the meeting or initiates discussion of the next dilemma. In the latter case, the same procedures are followed except that it is of course unnecessary to repeat Steps 1 through 3.

As previously mentioned, it is always preferable to try to create +1 SC and thereby work under preferred circumstances. Since doing this is not always possible, it is important that the trainer develop the skills necessary to work under nonpreferred circumstances (Non-PC). The next several sections address the methods that can be used when working under Non-PC.

Nonpreferred Circumstances
Step 4: Initiating Discussion

Initiating discussion under nonpreferred circumstances (Non-PC) begins just as it does under preferred circumstances. To review, each session begins with the reading of a dilemma, followed by a summary of the major points of the dilemma, and a thinking period for formulating a solution. The trainer then goes around the circle, getting opinions and rationales about the dilemma, rephrasing statements and writing down their gist, or asking probe questions prior to evaluating the reasoning level evidenced by the statements. If a + 1 SC condition is not evident the trainer proceeds by using Non-PC techniques. Whenever possible, the technique used to resolve the problem should be designed to try to elicit a + 1 SC situation. The four types of Non-PC situations and techniques to use in them follow.

Type 1

In this type of Non-PC situation, all group members agree on the solution to the dilemma with different stages represented (e.g., everyone states that Heinz should steal but for reasons that are indicative of different stages of reasoning. In this situation, the trainer should present one of the prepared elaborations, particularly one that will lead to different solutions on the part of specific stage reasoners (e.g., Stage 1 reasoners will maintain their position while Stage 2 reasoners will change their opinion).

It is important to note that what elaborations are used will depend on what solutions have been offered and what stages are represented. In other words, the trainer needs to be able to anticipate what effect the elaboration will have on different stage reasoning. For example, if Stage 1 reasoners say Heinz should steal the drug because his wife is an important person and Stage 2 reasoners say Heinz should steal it because he needs his wife around to take care of the children, one might elaborate the dilemma by adding the information that Heinz does not love his wife anymore and that he has a girlfriend whom he wants to marry. With this elaboration Stage 2 reasoners will likely change their position because if Heinz's wife dies, he would be free to marry his girlfriend, who would then take care of the children. Stage 1 reasoners would not be likely to change their position, so it would be a useful elaboration because it would create + 1 SC in this case. However, this elaboration would be unlikely to affect Stage 3 or Stage 4 reasoners because the issues raised by the elaboration would not be very relevant to them. As such, a different elaboration would need to be developed. This is why it is important to prepare for group discussions by anticipating responses and preparing potentially useful elaborations.

If elaborations do not yield the desired + 1 SC, the trainer can present an opposing position (+ 1 SC) to begin the discussion. This argument should be directed toward trainees presenting the lower stage arguments.

Type 2

A Type 2 Non-PC situation occurs when opinions given on a dilemma do not divide evenly along stage lines (e.g., some of the Stage 1 and Stage 2 reasoners select one solution, while other Stage 1 and Stage 2 reasoners choose another position).

In this situation, two different paths can be taken. One path involves having trainees who disagree within the same stage debate their differences (e.g., Stage 1s for and against stealing) and then have the Stage 2 trainees with opposing views debate their differences among themselves. If it is possible to structure +1 SC after this debate, proceed along those lines.

The second path involves having trainees one stage apart and holding different opinions discuss their differences (e.g., first have pro-stealing Stage 1s versus Stage 2s against stealing, then have Stage 1s against stealing versus pro-stealing Stage 2s). Two situations of +1 SC will automatically develop when using this alternative. A general group discussion can then follow these two initial debates.

Type 3

When initial responses cannot be accurately assessed for stage by the trainer, a Type 3 situation exists. In this situation, have any two groups of trainees with differing opinions discuss their differences, thus creating Non-PC. Further discussion may enable the trainer to carry out stage identification so that +1 SC can then be structured at an appropriate time. If stage identification is still not possible, Non-PC structure can still be helpful. This situation frequently occurs for the beginning trainer and, as such, will be discussed in more detail in the section on guiding the discussion.

Type 4

Type 4 Non-PC situations occur when few or no trainees participate in the discussion. The type of intervention depends on the reasons underlying the problem. If the trainees cannot state initial opinions because the dilemma is puzzling, the trainer should encourage discussion of the questions or clarify the confusion. Typically confusion is related to conflicts between different values (e.g., life versus law). The group can discuss which values should be considered more important and which are less important. Then the discussion of the dilemma can be stopped or elaborations can be provided to help structure a +1 debate. If this is not possible, the trainer should either conduct a general discussion of the major issues or enter the devil's advocate role.

If trainees are inhibited or too frightened to speak in the group, the trainer should provide both gentle and sensitive encouragement to facilitate participation or should again explain the role of group members (i.e., that they should be doing most of the talking). If encouragement is unsuccessful, the trainer can implement a different format for starting the discussion. For example, trainees can be asked to write down, rather than verbalize, their initial opinions (without names). The papers can be given either to the trainer or to other members to read. The discussion can then systematically address all of the major arguments presented. Another method involves breaking the larger group into smaller groups of three or four members. Each group then develops a position on a dilemma which they present together when the larger group again meets (presenting as a group is often less threatening to trainees). If the problem is due to boredom, other interventions may be used. These are presented in the section that addresses managing problem behaviors in the group.

Role Playing in Nonpreferred Circumstances

These four situations cover the major Non-PC conditions the trainer is likely to encounter. It is important to stress that, as with the assessment of stages, expertise at identifying how to structure a discussion emerges over time and with practice. So the trainer should not get discouraged if he misses a structuring opportunity when he is first learning the procedures involved.

Before moving on to Step 5, one other solution to a Non-PC situation should be mentioned. This solution involves the use of role playing. The best way to describe the use of role playing is through an example. Using the Heinz dilemma, the trainer could assign different roles to several of the group members. One trainee could play the role of Heinz, another the druggist, still another the wife, and, if desired, the judge could be brought into the situation. Having trainees act out different roles can sometimes lead to changes in opinion or reasoning, particularly when they are assigned to roles that require them to take on the perspective of a person they had not previously considered and to role play a $+1$ stage argument. For example, one might assign a Stage 1 reasoner who has decided that Heinz should not steal the drug because he would end up in jail to the role of the wife. In this role, the trainee might be able to begin to understand the wife's position of not wanting to die and may, as a result, begin to think about the dilemma differently. When using role playing, it is important to remember that the role play itself is not likely to produce changes in reasoning stage as it simply focuses on what the trainee would do. This means that following the role play a group discussion of the issues that emerged during the role play should be conducted (i.e., the discussion focuses on the "why" issues). The discussion may elicit different initial opinions, allowing a + 1 SC debate to be structured. It is also important to note that role playing can also be used under preferred circumstances. Indeed, it can sometimes be a nice change in format from the typical procedure and can help to maintain interest in the group.

Nonpreferred Circumstances
Step 5: Guiding Discussion

Many of the guidelines described for initiating discussion under Non-PC and guiding the discussion under preferred circumstances (i.e., creating disequilibrium, especially the devil's advocate role) are also relevant when the trainer is actually guiding a Non-PC discussion. When + 1 SC is not initially evident, the trainer should attempt to create it by following one of the procedures described in the last section and then guiding the discussion according to the guidelines for preferred circumstances. There are, however, several situations in which the trainer may be unable to achieve this goal. These circumstances and the methods used to deal with them when guiding the discussion will now be addressed.

When initial arguments do not create + 1 SC and when trainees at different stages present the same behavioral choice (Type 1 situation), or trainees at the same stage offer different behavioral choices (Type 2 situation), the trainer intervenes by structuring a Non-PC discussion as described in the section on initiating discussion under nonpreferred circumstances. Briefly, the trainer could have trainees systematically discuss the major differences of opinion, he could provide elaborations of the dilemma to generate conflict across the stages, or he could introduce major points that participants have missed. A devil's advocate position could also be adopted. Again, if a + 1 SC condition emerges as a result of these interventions, the trainer should try to structure the appropriate debate. And finally, if possible, the trainer could structure two different + 1 SC debates as described under the Type 2 situation. After the discussion, the trainer should provide a + 1 stage argument relative to the highest stage represented in the group. The stage of this argument should be changed if it appears to be too low or high for the highest stage reasoners.

When the trainer is unable to identify the stages and cannot structure + 1 SC (Type 3 situation), Non-PC can be structured in two ways. One way is to rank order the initial responses in terms of their seeming complexity or sophistication. Then the trainer can ask trainees with the least complex rationale to debate those with the next simplest and opposing view. For example, a statement like "Heinz should not steal the drug because it is not nice" is much simpler than the response "Heinz should steal the drug because he has an obligation to his wife to help and protect her." These two groups of trainees can debate each other. The trainer then proceeds systematically up this rank ordered hierarchy of responses until all the major issues have been raised and all trainees with different viewpoints have had a chance to discuss their opinion (this mirrors guiding the discussion under preferred circumstances except that the trainer is not aware of the precise stage). The discussion should focus on two or three opposing positions at a time so as to avoid confusion.

When all the major issues in the group have been discussed, the trainer should then point out any important ideas that were missed, or he can present a + 1 stage argument (i.e., the trainer can place himself in the role of devil's advocate by using any of the methods described in guiding the discussion under preferred circumstances). What + 1 stage argument is presented is based on the most complex argument provided by the group. This will naturally involve some guesswork, since the trainer may still be unable to accurately identify the stages represented in the group. The trainer should closely observe the reactions of trainees to determine if his guess is accurate. If the + 1 argument induces conflict for those presenting the most complex argument, it is likely to have been a correct estimation of stage. The argument level is probably inaccurate if it is not understood at all or if it is unstimulating for the assumed highest stage reasoners. It is important to note that if over the course of the discussion the trainer can accurately identify stages, he should attempt to structure a + 1 SC debate instead of continuing with the Non-PC debate.

The second and less preferred method for guiding discussion when the trainer cannot identify stages involves having any two groups of trainees with differing opinions debate each other. Again, the trainer tries to structure + 1 SC if the opportunity arises.

Nonpreferred Circumstances
Step 6: Ending Discussion

Under nonpreferred circumstances, the trainer stops discussion when all important, differing positions have been addressed, when trainees have had the chance to discuss any additional issues they see as important, and when the trainer has specified and encouraged discussion of any missed points and/or has proposed and discussed an estimated + 1 stage argument. The trainer can end the discussion of a particular dilemma or the entire dilemma discussion group meeting by following any one of the procedures previously described in the section on ending discussions in preferred circumstances.

As mentioned before, it is important that a discussion not be stopped simply when interest decreases slightly, particularly if the group has not yet sequentially progressed up the stages, including the trainer's + 1 stage argument, or if the group has not completed discussing all the relevant issues in the dilemma. When interest decreases, the trainer should point out a missed issue or ask a stimulating question to again activate the discussion. A discussion should be stopped either when it is no longer productive (i.e., when interventions to stimulate discussion are repeatedly ineffectual) or when progression through the stages or discussion of major disagreements has been achieved. The trainer should also remember that to maintain interest it is always better to end a discussion somewhat early rather than too late. When the discussion of one dilemma has ended, the trainer either stops the meeting or initiates discussion of the next dilemma. The same procedures are followed as with the first dilemma except that it is of course unnecessary to repeat Steps 1 through 3.

Changes following the First Group Discussion

The behavior of trainees at times changes over the course of the program. As the group progresses, trainees sometimes begin to take on more and more responsibility for keeping the discussion active. The trainer should of course encourage this type of behavior and provide less guidance to trainees. For example, after a couple of meetings, older trainees rarely need to have it repeatedly explained that after reading the dilemma everyone will have a chance to share his opinions about the situation. Toward the end of the dilemma discussion program, it is also possible to have trainees bring in their own moral dilemma situations. If this is done, however, the trainer should make sure that the situations actually deal with moral conflicts and issues. To guarantee this, the trainer should ask trainees to submit their dilemmas a couple of weeks before they are actually to be used. This will give the trainer enough time to review the dilemma and prepare it for discussion. While these types of changes can be made over the course of the program, the trainer, however, must always maintain the role of assessing stages, initiating discussions, structuring and guiding debates, and managing group behavior problems.

Transfer of Training: Homework Assignments

To facilitate opportunities for trainees to use what they have learned in the dilemma discussion group in real-life settings (i.e., transfer of training), the trainer can assign homework. In the area of moral reasoning, homework assignments simply involve handing out a dilemma at the end of one class and asking trainees to think about it and write down their opinions and rationales in preparation for the next week's class. As part of this assignment, trainees could be instructed to ask several different people (e.g., parents, teachers, employers, peers) what their position and reasoning is on the dilemma. Trainees are asked to use, but not necessarily agree with, this input in their own thinking about the dilemma. Some dilemmas are particularly appropriate to use as homework assignments. For example, in a shoplifting dilemma, trainees could be instructed to go out and ask a store manager how she would feel if she learned a customer witnessed a shoplifting incident but did not report it to her. As the ultimate goal of dilemma discussion groups is to prepare trainees for real-life conflict situations, it is strongly recommended that homework assignments be used whenever possible.

Alternative Format for Dilemma Discussion Groups

As mentioned previously, it takes some time and practice to assess moral reasoning stages. This is complicated further because the trainer is responsible not only for stage assessment but also for initiating, guiding, and ending discussions and for managing group behavior problems. Because this is a lot for a new trainer to do, even with two trainers in the room, an alternative method has been established. In this method, there is less emphasis on specific stage assessment during the group. It also facilitates the development of group cohesion and permits general discussion during the debate. However, this alternative method is not the preferred format because it is less likely to create disequilibrium and the corresponding awareness of the inadequacy of lower stage reasoning to resolve the dilemma (i.e., there is the risk that there will be no exposure to + 1 stage reasoning). Therefore, this method should only be used if the trainer is having difficulty assessing stage responses or if there is continually little variation in the reasoning stages of trainees (e.g., the dominant reasoning stage of the entire group is Stage 2). The sequential steps to follow when using this format are as follows.

1. As in the preferred format, perform Steps 1 and 2 (i.e., forming groups and choosing and preparing dilemmas) prior to begin-

ning the moral discussion group (of course, less attention needs to be directed toward stage assessment).

2. In the initial session, Step 3 (i.e., creating the proper set) should be performed. It does not need to be repeated in subsequent sessions unless necessary.

3. Hand out copies of the moral dilemma.

4. Read the dilemma out loud or have a trainee read it.

5. Summarize the major points of the dilemma or have a trainee summarize them. Clarify any misperceptions or answer any questions that emerge about the dilemma.

6. Get initial opinions (both solution and reasoning) from the trainees by going around the circle. If necessary, when getting the initial opinions ask probe questions or rephrase responses to assure accurate understanding of the statement and, if at all possible, to assess reasoning stage. It is not necessary to elaborate on the dilemma or initiate a debate with the trainee at this time. This step should take no more than 15 to 20 minutes.

7. After gathering the initial opinions, ask for a hand vote from the trainees regarding their behavioral choice (e.g., steal versus not steal).

8. Divide the larger group into two smaller groups. This division is based on which behavioral alternative has been selected (e.g., one group would be comprised of *all* trainees who voted to steal; the other group would be comprised of *all* trainees who voted against stealing). If the larger group cannot be divided into two fairly equal sized groups, attempt to elaborate the dilemma in such a way so as to get a more even split.

9. Separate the two smaller groups by having each group go to opposite sides of the room. One trainer should be with one of the groups, while the co-trainer should be with the other group. A trainer is needed for both of the groups in order to guide the small group discussion.

10. Both trainers help their group develop a *best* reason for their position by having the trainees discuss and debate among themselves the reasons underlying their decision. To do this, follow many of the same procedures used in guiding a discussion. This step should take about 10 to 15 minutes.

11. As part of the small group discussion, have each group elect a spokesperson who will subsequently present the group's decision.

12. Have the elected spokesperson of each group present the group decision and rationale to the other group. Summarize the major

ideas and reasoning presented by the spokesperson on a black-board or large piece of paper. Any ideas that were discussed during the smaller group discussion but are overlooked during the spokesperson's presentation can be raised by any group member or the trainers.

13. Following the spokesperson's presentation, guide the two groups in a debate. At this time, any group member is free to contribute to the discussion. Again, follow the procedures already described for guiding a group discussion. It is also important to remember to focus the debate on a couple of issues at a time to prevent chaos and to increase the probability that trainees will come to realize the inadequacy of their reasoning. If necessary, adopt the devil's advocate role to facilitate the discussion.

14. Allow the two groups to debate each other until either the groups are converging on a solution and rationale or until all major issues have been addressed and the discussion is no longer providing opportunities for exposure to the limitations of current reasoning. If the two groups are not converging on a decision and rationale, end the debate by following any one of the several procedures previously described.

15. If desired, assign homework assignments.

16. Repeat Steps 3 through 15 in all subsequent sessions.

MANAGING PROBLEM BEHAVIORS IN THE DILEMMA DISCUSSION GROUP

As in any teaching effort, a number of group management problems may emerge during the dilemma discussion group. In this section, we will discuss the kinds of problems specific to these groups and provide some guidelines for dealing with them. It is important to stress, however, that these guidelines should not be implemented rigidly. Trainers should rely on their own judgment of the situation, as well as their knowledge of the trainee, in deciding what intervention will be most helpful.

Insensitive Participation

At times the intensity of a moral discussion can escalate quickly, often leading to personal attacks or insults on one or a group of individuals. Although the ideal way to prevent such provocation and insensitive participation is by following Step 3, Creating the Proper Set, these initial guidelines may be forgotten by trainees during the course of a heated debate. Nevertheless, as this type of behavior violates one of the basic ethical guidelines for group participation, the trainer must be prepared to intervene quickly. If disrespect for another group member is expressed, the trainer should immediately adopt a directive stance (in contrast to the relatively nondirective role typically maintained) by first asking group members to stop the discussion. An explanation of why the discussion was stopped and a reminder to trainees of the guidelines for discussion should then be presented in a sensitive manner without attacking the attacker. A word of caution: The trainer should not confuse an active discussion with a personal attack. If the discussion remains focused on moral issues it is probably an acceptable debate. If, however, the debate begins to address the personal aspects of a group member, then it is probably a personal attack. It is also important to remember that repeated confrontation of a trainee's opinion, not his person, should also be stopped as it often alienates the trainee. The trainer should always act conservatively and stop the discussion if it is unclear which situation is occurring.

Overactive Participation

While the overactive participant can be an asset to the group during initial and stagnant classes, there are times when his activity can be disruptive to group functioning. There are usually two kinds of overactive participants. The first is attentive and offers relevant and stimulating statements, but talks so much that other members, particularly the less verbal ones, have little opportunity to speak. The second type of overactive participant is typically egocentric, always wanting the conversation to focus on his ideas. This type of participant often interrupts other group members by raising irrelevant issues, is unable to attend to the arguments of other group members because of poor listening skills, or manifests complete disregard for others' opinions.

One of several interventions may be implemented in a group with an overactive participant. They include:

1. Encourage the less verbal trainees to speak more frequently (discussed in detail in the next section).
2. Discourage the overactive trainee from talking so often by
    a. Having all willing trainees present positions at the beginning of the discussion (this diverts attention from the overactive participant).
    b. Quickly asking other trainees for their positions as soon as the overactive individual is finished speaking.
    c. Quickly summarizing the overactive trainee's response and then encouraging other trainees to speak (this interrupts long verbalizations).

    d. Setting firm limits (e.g., "Joe, thank you. I think we understand your position on this dilemma. Now, let's hear from other group members"; "Your idea doesn't seem to relate to the issue on the floor. Let's stay with the current issue for a while, and we'll try to return to your idea later").

    e. Meeting with the overactive participant individually to explain the effect of his behavior on the group and to try to understand the motivation underlying his behavior. If possible, try to positively frame your explanation (e.g., "I appreciate your interest and help but . . ."; "I welcome your ideas but . . ."; or "Your ideas are important but . . .").

When intervening in these situations, the trainer should always begin with less direct and confrontational methods (2a, 2b, and 2c). If these strategies are unsuccessful, more directive methods may be necessary (2d and 2e).

Underactive Participation

Unlike the quiet participant, who will at times offer an opinion, the underactive participant rarely, if ever, speaks during the class. It is important to note that if there are only a few trainees who choose not to be active, this will not be disruptive to the group as long as they maintain interest in the discussion. In other words, interest rather than active verbal involvement is important for a gain in moral reasoning. In addition, although hostility may develop if many trainees are quiet, most active groups can usually accept several quiet members. If hostility develops, however, the trainer should again point out that while participation is encouraged, people have the right not to speak during the class if they so choose.

    Typically, there are three reasons for underparticipation: anxiety when speaking in groups, inability to understand group discussions (the group is too advanced), or boredom. In order to intervene in the first two of these situations, the trainer must be able to differentiate interested from uninterested listeners. The interested listener can usually be identified by noting his posture and facial expression (e.g., eye contact with the speaker, alert expression, facing speaker, leaning forward, etc.). The uninterested listener is usually restless, bored, and cannot follow the group discussion. He may fidget in his seat and bring up irrelevant issues when he does speak.

    Once the trainer has identified underactive participants as interested listeners, she may assume that it is probably discomfort when speaking in groups, shyness, or lack of confidence that is making it dif-

ficult for the trainees to speak. In this situation, the trainer should try to
encourage the trainees to become active in the following ways:

1. Begin the discussion by moving around the circle.
2. Ask other trainees to express a position first.
3. Express interest in hearing the opinions of quiet trainees.
4. Directly ask, but don't demand, specific trainees to share an idea.
5. Provide empathic encouragement by letting the quiet trainees know you understand their feelings about participating.
6. Increase the structure of the group by spending more time gathering initial opinions.
7. Reduce the threat to the trainees by making such statements as "Take your time"; "Give it a try"; "I'll help you with it."
8. If absolutely necessary, add more active trainees to the group (this often disrupts group functioning and is therefore not highly recommended).

If the group appears to be too morally or cognitively advanced for
a trainee, the trainer should initially try to simplify the trainee's task.
This can be achieved by simply asking him what he would do in the
moral situation rather than also asking him to explain the reasons
behind the decision, or by asking him which arguments seem to make
the most sense to him (e.g., the trainee can simply say "this group's" or
"John's"). If these interventions are not successful, and the trainer sen-
ses that the trainee is overwhelmed by the group's activity, it may be
necessary to remove him from the group to prevent further embarrassment and threats to self-esteem. Of course, this should be handled in a
private meeting with considerable discretion.

Negative Attitudes

At times, trainees have or develop negative attitudes about dilemma discussion groups. When negative attitudes occur, they typically take the
form of silence, disinterest, or more hostile kinds of statements (e.g.,
"This is a waste of time") and can be damaging to the group process.
One of three reasons often underlies these attitudes. The first possibility
may be related to the trainee's more general personality style—hostile
and negativistic toward almost everything in his life. The negativistic
person will tend to begin the group with a negative mind set. While it
is often difficult to successfully intervene with the characteristically
negativistic youngster, the trainer can try to generate interest by meeting alone with him and talking about the difficulty. Sometimes assigning
the negativistic trainee to a special role in the group can effectively

decrease the intensity of his negative attitudes (e.g., keeping a record of meetings; writing the major issues in a dilemma on the board).

Negative attitudes can also develop from actual or misperceived rejection or criticism from the group. The nature of the intervention by the trainer will of course depend on whether the perception is real or imagined. If the trainee's perception of the situation is accurate, the trainer should intervene by first stopping the group and then providing an explanation of why this action was taken. Meet with the disrespectful group member privately if the offensive behavior continues. If the trainee has inaccurately perceived a statement from another group member as a personal affront (this can often be identified by noting any changes in behavior—movement from being verbal to being quiet or sulking), the trainer should meet with the trainee alone, explaining that his peers did not mean to intentionally insult him and that his presence in the group is desired. The trainer also can have the trainee speak with the perceived offender under his guidance.

A third possibility emerges when the significant people in the trainee's life (e.g., parents, guardians) have expressed negative attitudes about moral issues being explored and discussed outside of the home. Under this circumstance the trainer can attempt to intervene by meeting with the appropriate adults in an effort to understand their attitudes and clarify any misperceptions they might have about dilemma discussion groups.

Boredom and Stagnation

Boredom among trainees can be easily identified, as the trainer's prompts and encouragement often result in silence or complete passivity. Usually boredom results from overly methodical, routinized methods of dilemma group discussion, the selection of inappropriate dilemmas, a homogeneous group (no diverse stages are represented), wide variation in moral reasoning levels of trainees, or problematic leadership styles.

Overly methodical, routinized classes may result from repeatedly using the same type of group format and dilemmas that are too similar in the issues and conflicts they present. In addition, the fact that the classes will usually be held in the same room, with the same trainees, and with the trainer responding in the same manner may also contribute to the trainee's sense of repetitiveness. In this situation, the trainer should alter procedures by using different formats (e.g., role playing, discussing actual historical events like Watergate or the Middle East conflict). Typically, this situation does not occur when conducting short-term groups (6 to 12 weeks). However, if the trainer is running groups for longer time periods these changes may be necessary to maintain sustained interest. If it appears that the trainer's choice of dilemmas is eliciting boredom, the trainer simply needs to choose different dilemmas to reduce bordom, ones relevant to the type of trainees in the group.

If a group is comprised of trainees who reason at the same dominant moral stage, and this is causing boredom, the trainer can try to add members who reason at different dominant stages. Since this is not always possible, it may be necessary for the trainer to take a more active role in the group. As described earlier, this role should be one of devil's advocate in which + 1 stage arguments are provided to the group. The trainer can also try to elaborate the dilemma to elicit different stage responses.

The trainer should be highly sensitive to those situations in which a trainee exhibits significantly lower moral reasoning levels than the remaining group members. When this situation occurs, the person whose reasoning is far lower than that of the other group members is often left feeling frustrated and inadequate. His statements are frequently ignored by other trainees. The best way to prevent this situation from occurring is to accurately assess reasoning stage prior to starting the group. However, as inaccurate assessments sometimes occur, the trainer needs to be aware of some alternative interventions. If at all possible, the trainee should be moved to another group which is more in line with his ability. When this is not feasible, the trainee should be supported and encouraged, and the trainer should make sure his statements are not ignored or overly criticized. If significant negative feelings emerge, however, the trainer should consider asking the trainee to leave the group. Once again, this should only be done with discretion and sensitivity. If an individual is functioning considerably above other group members, he should be moved into a higher level group. When this is not feasible, the trainer should spend some of the group time providing + 1 stage arguments to challenge his reasoning and stimulate interest.

Problematic Leadership Styles

Two types of problematic leadership styles can occur. The first involves overly directive, structured leadership, in which the trainer dominates discussions and creates rigid rules for behavior. Trainers can identify an overly directive style by noting how long they talk (more than 25 percent of the time is too much), by determining if they are trying to directly teach the stages (describing the characteristics of each stage), and by deciding if they are using more closed- or open-ended questions. By speaking less often and encouraging more discussion among trainees, by discontinuing trying to teach the stages, and by asking open-ended questions more frequently, the trainer should be able to successfully decrease directiveness and provide a moderate degree of structure.

The second problematic leadership style involves a highly nondirective, unstructured approach. This style is easily identified by simply observing the level of disorder present in the group. If unimportant issues are addressed, if the discussion jumps around from one issue to another, and if there are numerous interruptions, the group is usually in need of more structure. By adopting a more active stance in guiding the debate, by preventing sudden changes in the issues being addressed, and by helping the group attend to relevant issues, the trainer should be able to effectively increase structure. In taking a more active role, the trainer should remember not to talk to each trainee on an individual basis. Rather, the trainer's active role should involve encouraging group members to talk to each other, not just to him or the co-trainer.

As the assessment of one's own effectiveness can be difficult, it is helpful to have the two trainers alternate as trainer or co-trainer in order to give each one experience with each role. For example, one trainer can direct the initial discussion around the circle, while the other records responses and helps in the tasks of stage assessment, initiating discussion, and guiding discussion. The recorder can then structure the group for the second discussion and the other trainer can lead the discussion. The co-trainer, while of course participating in the discussion, can, for example, take on the role of encouraging less active members to participate or detecting the emergence of boredom or negative attitudes. Following the class, the trainers can provide constructive feedback to each other. For instance, they can serve as observers of each other's leadership style, they can share ideas, they can offer each other support and encouragement, and their skills can enable them to complement one another. Given trainers who work well together, the advantages of having two trainers in a class cannot be overemphasized. It is, therefore, highly recommended, especially for beginning trainers.

Leadership of moral dilemma groups requires preparation, skill, and flexibility. Their successful management will often be a challenge to the trainers, but their potential value in enhanced moral reasoning ability for the trainees is considerable. The present chapter has sought to provide in detail the procedures necessary to lead moral dilemma groups. The dilemmas used in the groups during ART are provided in the remainder of this chapter.

The Used Car

A salesman who did a great deal of traveling traded in his car every 2 years. In 2 years of driving he would average about 80,000 to 100,000 miles. By the time he was ready to sell the car, the car's motor and transmission were almost completely gone. Before he advertised, he would put the mileage back to about 30,000 miles, fill up the motor and transmission with heavy oil, and clean the car so that it looked almost like new. The body of the car was in excellent condition and only a trained mechanic would be able to detect what had been done to the car.

When the car was advertised a young couple, just married, came to look at the car. The couple told him that they did not have much money and that they would buy it if he sold it for $50.00 less.

The salesman's son knew what the father had done to the car and felt that the father was cheating these people. He tried to convince his father not to do it, but the father would not listen. The son felt he should really warn the people, but if he did that he knew that his father would be furious and he did not know what the father would do.

1. Refer to the first paragraph. Do you believe that it is okay for a person to turn back the mileage, etc., before selling a used car? Why or why not?

2. Refer to the second paragraph. Does it matter whether someone rich or poor comes to buy the car? Why? What if the man was selling it to some friends of the son?

3. What should the salesman's son do in the above situation? Why?

4. What do you think might happen between the son and the father if the son told these people the truth? Why?

5. Does a person have more responsibility for the behavior of a member of his family than he does for a stranger? Why or why not?

6. If he were working for a used car salesman who tried to cheat someone, would that make it any different? Would a person be responsible for the cheating if he knew about it and didn't speak up? Why or why not?

7. Which is more important—to be a loyal son or a truthful person? Why?

8. What should the law be in a situation like this? What should happen to the father? Should the son be considered an accomplice?

Note. The moral dilemmas in this section were reprinted with permission from Blatt, M., Colby, A., & Speicher, B. (1974). *Hypothetical dilemmas for use in moral discussions.* Cambridge, MA: Moral Education and Research Foundation, Harvard University.

The Dope Pusher

The narcotics problem in this country has reached alarming proportions. Hundreds of people die each month and thousands of young lives are ruined. All of these drugs are illegal in this country. The drugs are brought in and distributed by an organized crime group. These groups of organized crime are very hard to crack. The people who work for these groups do not talk when they are caught. So far, the government has not been able to find enough legal evidence to jail these people.

A dope pusher had been caught in a high school. He was questioned by the police as to the source of his supplies, but he refused to cooperate. Some people say that we should get the information in any way we can; if they do not talk voluntarily, they should be forced to talk by some method. These people claim that if we did that, we could eliminate these criminals and save many lives.

1. Would you approve of it or give the police the right to keep people in jail until they agreed to talk or to question them at great length in order to find out information that would help control the organized drug traffic? Would you approve of torturing them in some way?

2. Is it morally justifiable to control one evil by using evil means? Why or why not?

3. Suppose 50 pushers are caught in 1 week. The police department does not know how much information each of these pushers has. Should they torture all of them and take a chance on torturing an individual who does not have any information that would help crack the ring? Why or why not?

4. Some people feel that they could not torture another person. Why do you think they feel that way?

Riots in Public Places

During the middle and late 1960s there were numerous riots in a large number of American cities. In almost all of the riots, there was a great deal of looting (mass stealing from stores). During a riot in Chicago, Mayor Daley issued orders to the police to shoot rioters and looters. The police were ordered not to shoot to kill but rather to cripple or maim the rioters and looters.

1. A policeman who was ordered to a riot area saw a group of teen-agers looting. He was in conflict within himself about whether or not to shoot. What should the policeman do? Why?

2. Would your decision be the same if you were the owner of the store? Would your decision be the same if you were the teenage looter?

3. Try to come to a solution that all three people (the policeman, the store owner, and the looter) could agree upon.

4. Suppose this policeman followed orders and killed a looter by mistake. Was this right or wrong? Why? Should he be punished? Why?

The Passenger Ship

A passenger ship sank in the middle of the Atlantic. There was a great deal of panic on the ship as it became known that the ship was sinking. People were rushing into the lifeboats. The ship finally sank, and most of the people managed to get into the lifeboats.

One of the lifeboats was very overcrowded. It became evident that the boat would sink unless a number of people on it would get off. One of the passengers suggested that they take ropes and have people dragged behind the boat. However, it was winter and a person would be paralyzed if he stayed in the water for more than 10 minutes. People came up with many suggestions in order to avoid making the decision about who should live and who should die. But nobody came up with a solution that would save all the lives in the boat. After some discussion, two general opinions emerged. Some people believed that they should leave themselves to chance. What will happen will happen. They felt that it was wrong to make a decision to kill people. They might all die or all might be saved. Another opinion was that they should draw lots as to who should stay in the boat and who should be thrown overboard.

1. Which of these two alternatives would you see as the more justified and why? Do you have any other suggestion?

2. Do you think it is justifiable to kill a few people in order to save many?

3. Would a lottery be a fair way to make the decision? Why or why not?

4. If they decided to have a lottery but two people refused to participate, should they be allowed to abstain and stay in the boat? Why or why not?

5. Do you think there is any way to decide whose lives are the most valuable? Why or why not?

The Case of Charles Manson

Do circumstances change a person's responsibility for his actions?

Charles Manson was born an illegitimate child. His first years of life were extremely difficult. His mother was irresponsible, and Charles was neglected. Finally, when he was 5, his mother disappeared and left Charles behind. No one knew where she went. The neighbors reported to the police that Charles had been abandoned. The police put Charles in the permanent custody of his relatives when his mother did not come back for several months.

When Charles started school he soon became known as a trouble-maker. The teachers began throwing him out of their classes. His relatives had a hard time with Charles and could not handle him. Besides, they had children of their own and really did not care for Charles.

It was not long before Charles was brought to the attention of the police. He was caught stealing, vandalizing, and so on. After a number of offenses, he was sent by a juvenile court judge to a reform school. He spent approximately 8 years in the reform school. During those 8 years, he ran away a number of times, committed some offenses while he was out, and was finally sent back to the reform school. He was released from the reform school when he became of legal age.

At the age of 28 he became a leader of a mystical group. He and a number of members of this group were convicted of a multiple murder which included Sharon Tate, an actress, and several of her friends in her secluded California home.

1. Can or should you hold Charles Manson responsible for his behavior? Could you place the blame of a person's actions on the conditions or circumstances of his life?

2. Could Charles claim that the responsibility for his actions rests with society? The judge, who is a representative of society, sent him into the reform school. The reform school did not do its job. What do you think about this argument?

3. How should he be punished:
    a. If you consider him responsible for his actions?
    b. If you don't consider him responsible?

4. Why do you feel he *should* or *should not* be punished?

5. Should he get the death sentence? Why?

6. Do you think that Charles was insane, and if so should that make a difference in his punishment? Why?

7. What, in general, is the purpose of putting someone in prison?

8. If you disagree with the idea of putting people into prisons, what do you think would be a just solution? Why?

LSD

Doug, who is a high school senior, is a chemistry whiz and has a chemistry laboratory in his house. He has been taking drugs like LSD, which he used to buy. One day he thought, "Why spend all that money; I could make them myself." He asked the chemistry teacher what the formula for LSD was. The teacher asked him why he wanted to know. Doug told him the truth. The teacher knew the possible harm that can come from taking drugs and wondered what to do.

1. Can a person do whatever he wants in his house? Is his home his castle? What should the limits be on a person's individual rights?

2. If Doug had no intention of selling his drugs, can he make them for himself? If he intended to sell them, would that make a difference? Give your reasons.

3. If the police heard that Doug was producing LSD in his laboratory, but knew that he used the drugs for himself, should they interfere?

4. What should the teacher do? Why?

5. If the teacher tells Doug what the LSD formula is and the school administration finds out, should the teacher be fired? Why or why not?

6. If the teacher doesn't tell Doug but suspects that he will get the information somewhere else, should he tell Doug's parents or the police? Why or why not?

7. If Doug makes LSD at home and is caught, should he be punished? If so, how and why? If not, why not?

Shoplifting

Mrs. Jackson was doing her grocery shopping one weekend in the big supermarket near her house. As she walked into one of the back aisles, she saw a young man putting some cans of food into his coat pocket. She wondered whether or not to turn the young man in to the store manager.

1. Should she report him to the manager or let him get away with shoplifting the food? Why? Is there something else that she might do?

2. If she tells him to put it back and he refuses, should she turn him in? Why?

3. If she knows that shoplifters are always prosecuted by that store and often end up going to jail, should that make a difference in her decision? Why?

4. What if the man who was stealing looked very poor?

5. If she were an employee of the store, should that make a difference? Why?

6. Suppose she knew that the manager of the store was a selfish man who exploited his customers because his was the only store in the neighborhood. Should that make a difference? Why?

7. What should the penalty for shoplifting be? Why?

8. Should the amount of punishment depend on how badly the man needs the food? Why?

9. In what way could the young man's shoplifting affect Mrs. Jackson?

The Booby Trap

A farmer's house was repeatedly broken into. Each time he reported the robbery to the police, but the police could not catch the thieves. So the farmer came up with his own device. He rigged up a gun to go off in case someone opened the door. He and his family had a way of getting into the house without triggering the gun.

Eventually the robber came in and was shot in the leg. The bullet went through his thigh and he was limping. The doctor told him that he would have a limp for the rest of his life. Therefore, the robber sued the farmer for damages.

1. Do you think that a person has a right to use any means to protect his own property?
2. If this case got to court, what do you think would be the judge's verdict?
3. What do you think the verdict should be?
4. Should booby traps like the one the farmer set up be against the law? Why or why not?
5. Should the law allow people to shoot prowlers? Why or why not?
6. Should the law allow people to kill prowlers? Why or why not?

Plagiarism

There was one course in college that was known to be very difficult. It was an elective (not required) course in which the professor assigned five papers during the semester.

A senior in college took this course and wrote the first four papers. When the time came to hand in the fifth paper, he had many other things to do in order to graduate. One of his friends had taken the course 2 years previously and still had his papers. He asked this friend for one of the papers. He rewrote some parts of it and handed it in, believing that the teacher would never remember a paper that had been written that long ago, especially since many people take the course. However, the professor recognized the paper and the name of the student who had originally written it.

1. What should the teacher do? Why?

2. Suppose the set punishment for plagiarism is expulsion from school. Should the professor consider the fact that the student is a senior and is about to graduate? Why or why not?

3. Is expulsion from school a fair punishment for plagiarism? Why? If not, what is a fair punishment? Why?

4. Is the student who lent the paper guilty in some way? Why? Should he be punished? Why?

The Toy Revolver

Henry, a young man in his early 20s, wanted to get married but he did not have any money. He thought of a way of making money quickly. He bought a toy revolver that really looked like a real gun. He went to a distant section of town and tried to hold up a grocery store. The store owner was an old man who, when he saw the gun aimed at him, became frightened, had a heart attack, and died. Henry was caught and tried for murder.

1. Do you think Henry was guilty of murder? Why or why not?

2. When he was brought before the judge, what sentence should the judge give him? Why?

3. Should Henry get the same sentence as someone who used a real gun to rob and accidentally killed someone? What if the man with the real gun did not kill anyone, should he be given a longer or shorter sentence than Henry?

4. Henry seemed really shocked and upset about the old man's death and said that he had learned not to rob anyone again. Should he be let off without a jail sentence or should he be made to go to jail? Why?

The Robin Hood Case

A man invented a way to win at cards without ever losing. He often plays cards with a rich old gentleman, who is very stingy with his money. The young man knows he will be cheating at cards, but he could use the money he won usefully in helping the poor people in the neighborhood. He knows he can't get any of the old man's money any other way, because the old man is leaving it to his children who are already very wealthy.

1. Is this all right? Why or why not?
2. What if he were keeping the money? He needs it because he is very poor. What if he were not very poor but not as rich as the old man, would it be all right to keep the money in that case? Why should (shouldn't) these things make a difference?
3. Should it matter whether he's cheating a nice old guy or a mean guy? Why?
4. Is this better or worse than stealing from the old man? Why?
5. What should the law be?
6. Should he be punished differently if he gave the money away than if he kept it?
7. Does this end (helping the poor) justify the means? Do good ends ever justify bad means? (Give examples.)

Drugs

One day Joe discovered that his older brother was selling dope. He knew that selling drugs is illegal and also that drugs are bad for people, that they ruin people's lives.

1. What should Joe do?
2. Does it, or should it, make a difference to Joe that it is his brother who sells the dope?
3. Would it make a difference if it were Joe's best friend? Why?
4. Which of the two problems is central: whether the dope is illegal or that it is hurting people?
5. Joe tried to stop his brother, but his brother got very angry and told him that if he got him into trouble eventually the brother would get revenge. What do you think of that?
6. Does it make any difference what kind of drugs he's selling? What if it's marijuana? What if it's heroin?
7. Should it be against the law to sell marijuana?
8. Should it be against the law to smoke marijuana?
9. What punishment should someone get if convicted of selling marijuana? What punishment for selling heroin?

The Secluded Country Road

A couple was walking on a secluded country road. Suddenly, two young boys on a motorcycle pulled up. They looked like members of a motorcycle gang, and appeared to be very tough. They told the boy, "Go, and leave the girl to us. Nothing will happen to you if you leave but if you refuse we will kill you."

1. What should the boy do, stay and fight and at least attempt to protect the girl? This would mean that he is taking a chance of being killed. Or should he leave as he was told to do?

2. Is there a point at which a person's honor is more important than his life?

3. What if the girl was not a girlfriend but simply someone he knew only slightly?

4. Suppose while he was trying to decide what to do he became firmly convinced that the two boys would physically harm the girl if he left. Before, he thought that they were just talking tough, but now he is convinced that they are serious and will probably harm the girl if he leaves. Does this change his responsibility?

New York versus Gerald Young

Mr. Young, a middle-aged man, was walking down a street in New York City in the middle of an October afternoon when he saw two older men struggling with a boy of about 18 years. The boy was crying and struggling to get free from the men, but they were holding onto him. Mr. Young, naturally believing that the boy was being attacked by these men, ran to his rescue and began fighting with the men. One of the men he threw on the ground and fell on by accident. The man, obviously in great pain, drew a gun on Young and announced that Young was under arrest for interfering with an arrest and assaulting a policeman. Unknown to Young, these men were plainclothes policemen who had been chasing this boy because he had just held up an old man. Young was arrested even though he had no way of knowing that these men were policemen or that the boy had been involved in a crime. Young had no previous record and was a regularly employed factory worker and supporter of a wife and three children.

1. Do you think that Young should have interfered in this incident? Was it any of his business? Does a man like Young act at his own risk when he intervenes to try to help a stranger?

2. Is a person responsible for injuring another if he is acting in self-defense? Is the defense of another the same or different from self-defense in regard to injuring the attacker?

3. Would you call this an accident? Did Young hit the man by accident? Is there a difference between what happened in this case and a case of an accident? Should the law treat this case differently than one involving an accident?

4. Young may have acted with noble intentions, but policemen have very difficult jobs and often risk their lives to try to prevent crime. Plainclothes policemen have it even harder because people do not even know that they are acting as policemen. Would you think that our society, through its laws, should do everything to protect policemen from incidents like this? (It turned out in this case that the policeman whom Young threw on the ground broke his leg as a result of the fight.) Should men like Young be found guilty in order to protect policemen? If yes, why? If no, then why not?

5. Young was brought to trial on two counts (offenses): for interfering with a lawful arrest and for injuring a policeman. How do you think the court should judge each of these offenses? Are they the same or different? Why?

The majority of the New York Supreme Court ruled that Young could not be held responsible for interfering with the arrest because he simply did not know that the boy was being arrested. They also felt that he should not be held responsible for injuring the policeman for he thought (even though he was mistaken) that he was actually rescuing the boy from attackers. A man should not be held responsible for an honest and reasonable error in judgment if he had intended to do what was right. If the law held men like Young responsible, no one would ever be willing to risk helping a stranger in need because he might be making a mistake in judgment. The law should encourage people to help one another in times of trouble, not discourage it. Therefore, the majority of the court found Young innocent on both offenses. However, one judge dissented from (disagreed with) the majority ruling. He believed that the society's first responsibility was to protect its policemen, who protect all of us from crime. If the court let Young go free, it would be encouraging people to interfere with the policemen's work. Therefore, Young should be held responsible at least for injuring the policeman.

1. With which of these two opinions do you agree? Why?

2. Would it have made any difference if the boy were Young's son? Would it have made any difference if he were a son of Young's friend? Why?

3. What if Young knew the two men were policemen but thought the boy was innocent and that the policemen were just picking on him? Should he interfere in that case?

4. Suppose he did intervene and could prove the boy's innocence, should the court hold him responsible for interfering with an arrest and assaulting a policeman? Why?

Saving a Life

A soldier, while on a patrol mission in Vietnam, stepped on a land mine and lost both his arms and legs. In addition, he was blinded. Thanks to advanced medical knowledge and fast treatment, the doctors were able to save his life. Had he not received quick attention, he would have died from his battle wounds.

1. Do you think that the doctors made the right decision when they preserved his life? Why?

2. If you were the soldier, which would you choose: to live or to die? Why?

3. Should doctors automatically decide in all circumstances to try to preserve life? Why or why not?

4. Is it conceivable that some people would have rather died than lived, but later on they are not resolved enough psychologically to kill themselves?

The Kidney Transplant

Patty Barnes was near death at Massachusetts General Hospital. Although she was only 25 years old, both kidneys were irreparably diseased and she needed an immediate kidney transplant in order to survive. The hospital had been trying to find a suitable donor for some time but had not been able to locate anyone for the donation. Just at the point where her doctor was ready to give up, he found the perfect tissue match in a man who had just been killed in a car crash. However, the man had not given his consent for the donation of his kidney.

1. Should the doctor transplant the dead man's kidney into Patty Barnes in order to save her life? Why or why not?

2. The doctor knows that it is illegal to transplant any organ, even from a dead man, without his consent before he died. Should that enter into the doctor's decision? Why or why not?

3. The doctor decides to ask the dead man's wife for permission to perform the transplant. What should she do? Why?

4. Suppose she knows that he was opposed to the idea of donating his organs and even stipulated in his will that an autopsy was not to be performed upon his death. What should she do in that case? Why?

5. Suppose the wife really feels it would be wrong to let Patty die. Then what should she do? Why?

6. Should the law allow other people to refuse to donate a person's organs after the person died? Why or why not?

7. Do you feel it is a moral obligation to allow organs to be used after your death? Why or why not?

The Bomb Shelter

One day the air-raid sirens began to sound. Everyone realized that a hydrogen bomb was going to be dropped on the city by the enemy, and that the only way to survive was to be in a bomb shelter. Not everyone had bomb shelters, but those who did ran quickly to them. Since Mr. and Mrs. Jones had built a shelter, they immediately went to it. They had enough air inside to last for exactly 5 days. They knew that after 5 days the fallout would have diminished to the point where they could safely leave the shelter. If they left before that, they would die. There was enough air for the Joneses only. Their next-door neighbors had not built a shelter and were trying to get in. The Joneses knew that they would not have enough air if they let the neighbors in and that they would all die if their neighbors came inside, so they refused to let them in.

The neighbors were trying to break the door down in order to get in. Mr. Jones took out his rifle and told them to go away or else he would shoot. They would not go away. He either had to shoot them or let them come into the shelter.

1. What variables are involved in the conflict? What is the moral issue involved in this problem?

2. What should Mr. Jones do? Give your reasons.

3. Is killing in the case of self-defense the same or different from murder? Yes or no, and why?

4. If there were some chance that they could all live (if the Joneses let their neighbors in) should they accept the risk to their own lives and do it? Why or why not?

Misrepresentation

Two young college students met in their freshman year. The girl was an orphan on scholarship at the college but told her boyfriend a fantastic story, which she made up. She said her parents were in the Orient and her father was a wealthy businessman who believed that children should not be given any money even though he was controlling a large amount of money in trust for her. The boy came from a poor family but he had ambitions of going into business and becoming rich. He believed his girl-friend's story and saw her as a good prospect. The girl was a very lonely person and desperately wanted to get married. The couple got married 6 months after they met. One week after the wedding the boy found out that the story was a fantasy. She told him the truth about her life. The boy was extremely angry and sued for divorce. He claimed that he had been cheated and humiliated.

1. Should he get a divorce on these grounds?
2. What do you think are legitimate grounds for divorce?
3. Should people who intend to get married ever keep secrets from each other? If so, what kinds of things and why? If not, why not?
4. Should a married couple try to stay together and make it work out even when they do not really love each other? Why or why not?
5. What is your conception of an ideal marriage?

Lt. Berg

During World War II, Poland was under German occupation. In a small village, a German soldier was killed at night, but the Germans could not find out how it had happened. The people of the village either refused to inform them or they just did not know. So orders came from Berlin to kill all the population of the village, including the women and children. Lieutenant Berg, the German officer in charge of the soldiers in the village, called his superior and argued that they should not kill the women and children, just the men. The high command in Berlin disagreed but after a long argument between Lieutenant Berg and the command, the orders were changed. The Germans killed all the men and let the women and children live.

After the war, Lieutenant Berg became a Catholic priest. Twenty years later he was identified as the lieutenant who killed all the men in the village. He was accused of mass murder of civilians and brought to trial. He admitted that he had carried out the order to kill all the men in that Polish village, even though he had known that there was no evidence to indicate that they were guilty. He told the court that he had spared the lives of the women and children.

1. Should Father Berg be tried at all? Yes or no, and why?
2. Should the court consider the fact that he did save some people and give him a smaller sentence? Yes or no, and why?
3. Does it, or should it, make a difference to the court that he has become a priest after the war?
4. Lieutenant Berg argued that they should save the women and children. Are the lives of women and children more important than the lives of men?
5. Suppose that the German high command refused to change the order, and Lieutenant Berg knows that if he does not execute all the people in the village, he himself will be shot for disobeying orders. Should he sacrifice his own life?
6. What would you do if you were a soldier in wartime and you were given an order by a superior to kill civilians in a village because some of the civilians were known to be working with the enemy but that it was impossible to know which civilians were actually working with the enemy?

Perjury

John Henderson discovers that his brother Bill has been selling heroin to young people for some time. Bill has been accused of this crime and is on trial. His brother, John, has been called as a witness. He knows that if he tells the truth Bill will go to jail for a long time. If he lies, he will be guilty of perjury. However, if he lies there is a good chance that Bill will probably go free.

1. What should John do? Why?

2. What if Bill were not his brother but a good friend? Should that make a difference? Why?

3. Suppose Bill's crime had been less serious, such as driving without a license or turning in false fire alarms, should that make a difference? Why?

4. John decides to lie under oath to protect his brother, but he is turned in by another witness. Should John be punished? What should his punishment be? Why?

5. Should a family member be allowed to refuse to testify in court? What about a good friend? Why? Give the best reasons you can think of on both sides of the question.

The Doctor's Responsibility

Dr. Katzen was sitting at home watching a football game on television when he heard a huge crash outside his house. When he went outside to see what had happened, he saw that a bad traffic accident had taken place. The driver of one of the cars was lying face down and appeared to be unconscious. Dr. Katzen feared that if the man were not treated soon, he might die. However, he was also aware of the fact that treating someone in such a situation could easily lead to a lawsuit.

1. Should Dr. Katzen come to the aid of the injured man? Why or why not?

2. If the injured man were not really in danger of dying, but if he were in great pain, should Dr. Katzen help him? Why or why not?

3. If Dr. Katzen knew that a lawsuit could possibly lead to his losing his license to practice, how should that influence his decision?

4. Do you think it is fair that doctors can be sued for coming to someone's aid? Why or why not?

5. If Dr. Katzen treated the victim who later recovered and refused to pay the medical bills on the grounds that he never asked for treatment, should he be forced to pay? Was it right for Dr. Katzen to charge him at all? Why or why not?

The Noisy Child

During World War II, a group of people were trying to run away from the German Gestapo who were trailing them. One of the women in the group had an infant who was ill. It was not known what was wrong with the child but it cried continuously. All of the people were hiding together in a small attic of a large house. One of the men in the group suggested that they kill the infant because it made a great deal of noise. Otherwise, the Germans might discover them and kill them all.

1. What should the mother of the infant do and why?

2. Is it justified to kill one person if it will increase the chance of saving a lot of people?

3. Suppose they killed the baby and the Germans never came into the house, are they guilty of murder?

4. Do you consider this kind of killing murder or self-defense? Why?

The Stolen Car

James is 18 years old. One day, he and a friend stole a car and planned to paint it, change the license plate, and generally fix it up so they wouldn't be caught. James tells his older brother, Bill, about their plan and asks him not to tell anyone about it. Bill wonders what he should do.

1. What should Bill do? Why?

2. Bill tells James to return the car but James refuses. What should Bill do now? Should he tell their father? Why?

3. If Bill decides to tell their father, what should the father do? Why?

4. Suppose Bill knew the people from whom James had stolen the car. Should that make a difference in his decision? Why?

5. According to the law, a citizen is required to report any crimes he may know about. What do you think the purpose of this law is?

6. Should the law require you to turn in a relative? Why?

7. What about turning in a friend? Why?

8. Should decisions about whether to turn someone in be left up to the judgment of the individual? Why or why not?

9. Can you think of a good reason why a decision to turn someone in should not be left up to an individual?

10. Suppose the crime committed by James and his friend was considered to be a felony under the law. Would you consider Bill (and their father if he knows) to be an accessory? Why or why not?

Discrimination

In some neighborhoods there is an unwritten agreement between people not to sell or rent their homes to certain groups of people, such as Jewish or black people. One of the people in such a neighborhood decided to sell his home. He put an advertisement in the paper. A black person responded to the advertisement and wanted to buy the house.

When the neighbors heard that a black person wanted to buy the house they were alarmed because they knew that if that family bought the house a lot of people would want to move out of the neighborhood, with the result that the value of the houses would drop. In order to prevent this transaction, the neighbors got together and tried to prevent the owner from selling to the black family.

1. What should the owner of the house do? Why?

2. What would be the right thing to do? Why?

3. If the people in the neighborhood had evidence that the value of their houses really would go down, should they be able to legally prevent a man from selling a house to a black family? Why or why not?

4. If the man selling the house decided not to sell it to the black family, should he legally be forced to (since the black family had come first and could pay what he asked)? Why or why not?

5. Should there be a law prohibiting this kind of discrimination? Why or why not?

6. How could the people in the neighborhood keep their property values high without discriminating against people on racial or religious grounds?

Defense of Other Persons

Mrs. Ethel Spartels lived with her husband just outside Melbourne, Ohio. One Saturday late in October her husband's brother, George Spartels, dropped by to visit the Spartels in their new home. After showing George about the house, Mrs. Spartels went about her housework while her husband and his brother sat by the television in the front room. Shortly, Mrs. Spartels heard the two men begin to argue. She tried not to interfere but suddenly she was forced to run to the living room door as the two men had started fighting. She saw them involved in a violent fight: Harry, her husband, was on the front room floor covering his face and George was bending over him, kicking and stomping on him.

Panic-stricken, Mrs. Spartels raced down the hall to the bedroom and took her husband's revolver from the dresser drawer. She ran back to the front room and opened fire on her husband's brother. She fired a total of five shots, two of which struck George: one in the chest and the other in the throat. George fell to the floor, falling on top of the unconscious body of her husband.

When the police arrived, the two men were taken to the hospital. Mrs. Spartels was arrested by the police for wounding her husband's brother with the intent to commit murder.

1. Did Mrs. Spartels do the right thing in defending her husband?
2. Should she have done it even if she didn't love her husband?
3. Suppose it was a friend she was defending? Suppose it was a stranger?
4. What should the law be about a situation like this? Why?
5. Should the law be different if it is a relative than if it is a stranger? Why?
6. What restrictions should there be on a person's right to defend someone else?
7. What could happen if there were no restrictions?
8. Should you be required to prove that the person you are defending was really in grave danger? How could you do that?
9. Why do you suppose people are so reluctant to defend a stranger they see being mugged on the street? What should someone do in that case? What should the law be in such a case? Would your opinion be the same if you were the one being mugged? What if it was one of your relatives (mother, sister, brother, father, etc.) being mugged on the street?

Judge Sholl:
I have been thinking over the proper way to direct the jury...
I have been giving some thought to the question of lawful

excuse. . . . My present intention is to direct them that it is a lawful excuse for killing another human being if the accused honestly believes on reasonable grounds that another person is in imminent danger of death or dangerous injury from a third person and that the action taken by the accused is absolutely necessary for the preservation of that person from suffering death or dangerous injury at the hands of such third person. Now, I have not been able to find a great deal of authority for that. There are some authorities dealing with the question of self-defense and the question of provocation, which purport to limit the right to intervene to the case of a close relative. There are, however, other authorities which say that, to prevent a violent felony, even a stranger may, in a sufficiently extreme case, kill the malefactor.

The direction I have outlined seems to go beyond some of the authorities, and yet there is support for it in other books that I have looked at, and it does seem to me to be commonsense. . . . It would be very dangerous to lay down the doctrine that if a person saw a felony about to be committed, and if, although it might be prevented in a number of ways other than by taking life, that person elected to take life, he or she would then be entitled to say that it was a lawful homicide. I think that would be a most dangerous doctrine, but I think that, if qualified by the expression . . . "absolutely necessary" for the preservation of that person from death or dangerous injury, the doctrine does not go beyond what public policy ought to sanction. . . .

The law in many American jurisdictions does not follow what seemed to Judge Sholl to be "commonsense." The statutes of many states have adopted common law rulings which restrict the right to use deadly force in defense of others to those within a narrow circle, typically including close relations and servant or master.

Lying in Order to Help Someone

After high school, Mike got a job as a plumbing apprentice in a large plumbing company. He worked under an experienced person who taught him how to become a tradesman. One day Mike's boss made a mistake which would cost the company about $400 and blamed the mistake on Mike so that the owner would be angry at Mike instead of him. The next day Mike got fired from the job.

Mike told his parents what happened and tried to get another job. But it was difficult finding one and after 2 weeks of looking he still had no results. One day when he came home, his parents told him that the owner of the company had called and asked him to come back to work. Mike believed the story and returned. What actually happened was that Mike's father called the owner, apologized for Mike (about something that Mike had never done), and pleaded with him to take Mike back.

1. The parents lied to Mike. Do you think that lying, in this case, was a justified act? Give your reasons.

2. If Mike found out the truth about how he was allowed to take back his old job, how would he feel? Why would he feel that way?

3. Is lying in the attempt to help another person different from lying in order to help yourself? Why or why not?

4. Was it right for the parents to call the company owner and lie to him? Why or why not?

Rockefeller's Suggestion

Nelson Rockefeller, while Governor of New York, issued a statement proposing a solution to the drug problem. According to his plan, anyone convicted of selling heroin more than once would receive a mandatory life sentence with no chance of parole. Rockefeller felt that although a few people who sell drugs would suffer from such a law, so many lives would be saved and so much crime would be prevented that it would more than compensate for the few people suffering.

1. Do you agree or disagree with Rockefeller? Why?
2. If you disagree with this plan, what would you propose as a solution to the drug problem?
3. In general, is it justifiable to be unfair to a small minority of people if it leads to much greater good for the majority?
4. What should the punishment be for selling heroin? Why?
5. Many heroin addicts must sell drugs in order to pay for the drugs they need. If they sell only to people already addicted and do not try to influence people to start using drugs, should they be given a lighter sentence than someone trying to involve non-drug-users in taking heroin? Why or why not?

The Desert

Two people had to cross a desert. When they started, both had equal amounts of food and water. When they were in the middle of the desert, one person's water bag broke and all his water ran out. They both knew that if they shared the water they probably would die of thirst. If one had the water, that person would survive.

1. What should they do? Give your reasons.
2. If one person gets the water, who should have it? Why?
3. Suppose when they started out on this trip they decided to take so much water for both of them but each person carried one half. Should that make a difference as to how they should go about deciding who should live and who should die? Why or why not?
4. If you were confronted with the choice that either you or another person had to die, how and what would you decide? Why?
5. Suppose the two people are husband and wife, should or would that change the issue?

Suppose the two men were driving through a desert and they each bring with them canteens of water for drinking. Their trip is supposed to last for only a few days and so they have both brought only enough water for that time. One of the two, however, drinks almost all of his water as the two go on, while the other is less thirsty and drinks less. Late one afternoon their car breaks down, leaving them stranded. This is a desert where few people ever pass through and therefore they will have to walk to their destination, which could take a long time. Only the man who did not drink much has enough water to last that period of time. If he keeps his water for himself, he will be able to make it alive, but if he shares his water with the other, they will probably both die of thirst.

1. Should the first man share his water even if it will probably mean death for both, or should he save himself? Why?
2. Is this situation very different from the one described in the first paragraph? Why or why not?

The Threat

Three young robbers broke into the apartment of a young married couple. The robbers had guns and told the couple not to move or make a sound; if they did, they would be shot. The man and his wife both obeyed their orders. After the robbers gathered all the valuable possessions, they started to molest the woman in front of her husband. They told her that if she resisted, screamed, or did not cooperate, they would kill her husband. They had a can of gasoline with them and threatened to set him on fire if she did not cooperate.

It was evident that the three rough guys meant it and that there was a good chance they would do what they threatened.

    1. What, in your opinion, is the central problem in this dilemma?

    2. What should the wife do; what would you do in her place? Why?

    3. What should the husband do? What would you do in his place? Why?

Drunken Driving

In the past 6 months three persons had been killed by drunken drivers in a particular district of a city. The mayor and the police chief, as a result of this, ordered the police to crack down on drivers who had been drinking. One night a policeman stopped a car and found that the driver had been drinking heavily. The policeman saw that the driver was an old friend from school. He knew that his friend's wife was very sick and that his friend was under a severe strain. The family spent almost all of their money on doctor bills. If he arrested the driver for drunken driving the man might lose his job and the family would go deeper into debt. His friend said that he was sorry and that it would not happen again. The policeman is faced with a conflict. His duty is to arrest the drunken driver or the policeman himself could be fired. He stopped his friend once before for drunken driving and took him home. This time he does not know what to do.

1. Should the policeman's actions be dictated by his feelings of friendship or duty? Why do you feel that way?
2. What is meant by professional responsibility?
3. What would be the best or most important reason for the policeman to report his friend?
4. What would be the best or most important reason for the policeman *not* to report his friend?

Chapter 8

Program Description and Evaluation

We conducted two major evaluation projects to examine the efficacy of ART on a number of criteria. This chapter will present these projects in detail. We will describe the experimental settings, our general research plan, and specific experimental design; the ART curriculum employed; all aspects of both programs' preparation and implementation; and the results of each evaluation.

ANNSVILLE YOUTH CENTER PROJECT

Annsville Youth Center is a New York State Division for Youth residential facility for boys ages 14 to 17 who have committed such crimes as assault, burglary, auto theft, robbery, possession of stolen property, criminal trespass, and drug use. At the time our evaluation was conducted, 60 adolescents were in residence at Annsville, and 50 employees in all categories constituted its staff. The residents' median age was 15. Their ethnic background was 50 percent black, 40 percent Caucasian, 9 percent Hispanic, and 1 percent Native American. Approximately half the youths came from New York City, the other half from mostly urban areas all over New York State. Annsville is situated in a rural area of New York State and occupies 10 acres of a 100-acre reserve formerly used as a state forestry camp.

Our study plan at Annsville, in a broad sense, involved first pretesting the population of 60 boys (5 units of 12 boys each) on those qualities ART was designed to change, randomly assigning units to experimental and appropriate control conditions, and posttesting to discern change. We then internally replicated the test for efficacy by providing ART to adolescents who had been in our (first phase) control groups to see if they too changed on the several outcome measures. This overall evaluation sequence, as is described later in this chapter, was subsequently replicated in its entirety at a second New York State Division for Youth facility, in this second instance involving a maximum security center for youth incarcerated for such crimes as murder, manslaughter, rape, sodomy, arson, armed robbery, and aggravated assault.

Preparation

At Annsville, the evaluation of ART began with a multifaceted preparation phase consisting of ART curriculum development; staff orientation and training; resident structuring, motivation, and pretesting; and related activities. We will now describe in greater detail the substance of this preparation phase.

Curriculum Development

Table 7 presents an overview of the ART lessons employed for the Annsville and the subsequent replication project. A 10-week-long curriculum, consisting of 10 Structured Learning skills, 10 weekly sequenced lesson plans for Anger Control Training, and 10 sets of three moral dilemmas each for Moral Education was used. The skills, lesson plans, and dilemmas chosen from existing sources or developed by us in collaboration with Annsville staff, were coordinated with one another as much as possible. In almost any given week, the contents and character of the Structured Learning skill taught "fit with" the anger control situations role played and the dilemmas debated. In the real worlds of institution and community, in which we hoped the youths would apply ART, its three components each had to play an interlocking part. Thus, our goal from the start was to frame and implement each part of the program in coordination with each other part. Our aspiration in selecting the 10 Structured Learning skills was to obtain a set of skills in which participating youths were likely to be deficient but that they were likely to be motivated to learn because of the skills' intrinsic utility in the real world. We chose both skills for dealing effectively with unpleasant events (numbers 1, 3, 4, 5, 7, 8, and 10) and skills for effectively initiating positive events (numbers 2, 6, and 9). Note that for the research purpose of standardization of skills taught across all the Structured Learning groups participating in this evaluation project, we (investigators, facility administration, and staff) chose the particular skill curriculum. In practice, that is, in the use of ART under nonresearch circumstances, we very strongly recommend that the youths themselves have a major role in sharing the responsibility for selecting the skills to be taught, such participation having very positive potential implications for residents' motivation. In any event, for the Annsville evaluation, the 10 skills in Table 7 were selected. These skills and their behavioral steps are adapted from Goldstein et al. (1980) *Skillstreaming the Adolescent: A Structured Learning Approach to Teaching Prosocial Skills.*

The 10-lesson plan sequence for Anger Control Training, with some moderate modifications by us, is derived from that constructed by Feindler and her associates, as described in Chapter 4 (Feindler, 1979; Fein-

Table 7. Overview of Aggression Replacement Training

Week	Structured Learning	Anger Control Training	Moral Education
1	*Expressing a Complaint* 1. Define what the problem is and who is responsible for it. 2. Decide how the problem might be solved. 3. Tell that person what the problem is and how it might be solved. 4. Ask for a response. 5. Show that you understand his/her feelings. 6. Come to agreement on the steps to be taken by each of you.	*Introduction* 1. Rationale: Presentation and discussion 2. Rules: Presentation and discussion 3. Training procedures: Presentation and discussion 4. Initial history taking regarding *antecedent provocations—behavioral response—consequences* (A-B-C)	1. The Used Car 2. The Dope Pusher 3. Riots in Public Places
2	*Responding to the Feelings of Others (Empathy)* 1. Observe the other person's words and actions. 2. Decide what the other person might be feeling and how strong the feelings are. 3. Decide whether it would be helpful to let the other person know you understand his/her feelings. 4. Tell the other person, in a warm and sincere manner, how you think he/she is feeling.	*Cues and Anger Reducers 1, 2, and 3* 1. Hassle Log: Purposes and mechanics 2. Anger self-assessment: Physiological cues 3. Anger reducers: • Reducer 1. Deep breathing • Reducer 2. Backward counting • Reducer 3. Pleasant imagery 4. Role play: Cues + anger reducers	1. The Passenger Ship 2. The Case of Charles Manson 3. LSD

Table 7. (cont.)

Week	Structured Learning	Anger Control Training	Moral Education

3	*Preparing for a Stressful Conversation*
	1. Imagine yourself in the stressful situation.
	2. Think about how you will feel and why you will feel that way.
	3. Imagine the other person in the stressful situation. Think about how that person will feel and why.
	4. Imagine yourself telling the other person what you want to say.
	5. Imagine what he/she will say.
	6. Repeat the above steps using as many approaches as you can think of.
	7. Choose the best approach.
		Triggers
		1. Identification of provoking stimuli
		    ● External triggers (from others)
		    ● Internal triggers (from self)
		2. Role play: Triggers + cues + anger reducer(s)
			1. Shoplifting
			2. The Booby Trap
			3. Plagiarism

4	*Responding to Anger* 1. Listen openly to what the other person has to say. 2. Show that you understand what the other person is feeling. 3. Ask the other person to explain anything you don't understand. 4. Show that you understand *why* the other person feels angry. 5. If it is appropriate, express your thoughts and feelings about the situation.	*Reminders (Anger Reducer 4)* 1. Introduction to self-instruction training 2. Modeling use of reminders under pressure 3. Role play: Triggers + cues + reminders + anger reducer(s)	1. The Toy Revolver 2. The Robin Hood Case 3. Drugs

214

5	**Keeping Out of Fights**
	1. Stop and think about why you want to fight.
	2. Decide what you want to happen in the long run.
	3. Think about other ways to handle the situation besides fighting.
	4. Decide on the best way to handle the situation and do it.
		Self-Evaluation
		1. Self-evaluation of postconflict reminders
		  ● Self-rewarding techniques
		  ● Self-coaching techniques
		2. Role play: Triggers + cues + reminders + anger reducer(s) + self-evaluation
			1. The Secluded Country Road
			2. New York versus Gerald Young
			3. Saving a Life

6	**Helping Others**
	1. Decide if the other person might need and want your help.
	2. Think of the ways you could be helpful.
	3. Ask the other person if he/she needs and wants your help.
	4. Help the other person.
		Thinking Ahead (Anger Reducer 5)
		1. Estimating future negative consequences for current acting out
		  ● Short-term versus long-term consequences
		  ● Most to least consequences
		  ● Internal, external, and social consequences
		2. Role play: "If-then" thinking ahead
		3. Role play: Triggers + cues + reminders + anger reducer(s) + self-evaluation
			1. The Kidney Transplant
			2. The Bomb Shelter
			3. Misrepresentation

7	**Dealing with an Accusation** 1. Think about what the other person has accused you of. 2. Think about why the person might have accused you.	**The Angry Behavior Cycle** 1. Identification of own anger-provoking behavior 2. Modification of own anger-provoking behavior	1. Lt. Berg 2. Perjury 3. The Doctor's Responsibility

215

Table 7. (cont.)

Week	Structured Learning	Anger Control Training	Moral Education
	Dealing with an Accusation (cont.) 3. Think about ways to answer the person's accusations. 4. Choose the best way and do it.	*The Angry Behavior Cycle (cont.)* 3. Role play: Triggers + cues + reminders + anger reducer(s) + self-evaluation	
8	*Dealing with Group Pressure* 1. Think about what the other people want you to do and why. 2. Decide what you want to do. 3. Decide how to tell the other people what you want to do. 4. Tell the group what you have decided.	*Rehearsal of Full Sequence* 1. Introduction of using new behaviors (skills) in place of aggression 2. Role play: Triggers + cues + reminders + anger reducer(s) + SL skill + self-evaluation	1. The Noisy Child 2. The Stolen Car 3. Discrimination
9	*Expressing Affection* 1. Decide if you have good feelings about the other person. 2. Decide whether the other person would like to know about your feelings.	*Rehearsal of Full Sequence* 1. Role play: Triggers + cues + reminders + anger reducer(s) + SL skill + self-evaluation	1. Defense of Other Persons 2. Lying in Order to Help Someone 3. Rockefeller's Suggestion

3. Decide how you might best express your feelings.
4. Choose the right time and place to express your feelings.
5. Express affection in a warm and caring manner.

Responding to Failure
1. Decide if you have failed.
2. Think about both the personal reasons and the circumstances that have caused you to fail.
3. Decide how you might do things differently if you tried again.
4. Decide if you want to try again.
5. If it is appropriate, try again, using your revised approach.

| 10 | *Overall Review*
1. Recap of anger control techniques
2. Role play: Triggers + cues + reminders + anger reducer(s) + SL skill + self-evaluation | 1. The Desert
2. The Threat
3. Drunken Driving |

217

dler & Fremouw, 1983; Feindler, Marriott, & Iwata, 1984). Chief among the changes we made in the contents and progression of her procedures was the addition of a skill learned that week or previously in the Structured Learning class to Anger Control Training Lessons 8 through 10, as the new, added last link in the chain of "triggers + cues + reminders + anger reducers + self-evaluation" that constitutes, for Feindler, Anger Control Training.

The thirty moral dilemmas selected are derived from a larger pool of such materials presented in Blatt, Colby, and Speicher's (1974) *Hypothetical Dilemmas for Use in Moral Discussions*. We sought in making these selections to choose contents of relevance and interest to the youths we were seeking to teach, that is, contents pertinent to their daily lives and experiences. Note, therefore, such dilemma themes as discrimination, defending someone else, lying, use of guns, shoplifting, one's rights vis à vis the police, drug pushing, honesty in school, family loyalty, and so forth. If desired, additional or alternate dilemmas from Blatt, Colby, and Speicher (1974) can be chosen for use in the program.

Staff Training

The process of preparing staff for effective participation in the Annsville project consisted, as far as the investigators' roles were concerned, of two phases: (1) general orientation meetings for the entire staff and (2) training workshops for those staff members designated to conduct the initial 10-week sequences of Structured Learning, Anger Control Training, and Moral Education. Before describing these investigator-led orientation meetings and training workshops, it should be stressed that a crucial series of other activities—initiated and implemented by the facility's administration—were also part of this preparatory phase. These several steps, as well as the policies, roles, and behaviors of Annsville's administration during the implementation and maintenance phases of this project are presented in concrete detail in Chapter 10, the Administrator's Manual for ART. We have developed this manual and included it in this book because we feel there is much of substance we have learned regarding a facility administration's exceedingly important role in creating and executing quality action research.

A series of orientation meetings, accommodating Annsville's three-shift staff schedule, was held to provide information to staff about the forthcoming ART project and staff roles in it and to provide opportunities for questions. All facility staff—from counselors to cooks, managers to maintenance men—participated. In a lecture-discussion format, all details of the rationale and structure of the planned project were communicated and their implications for staff concerns explored. These concerns included an array of resident-oriented matters, such as motivation, reading levels, likely resistance, and optimal groupings; program-oriented implications, such as scheduling, implications for and connections with already ongoing Annsville programs, and required materials; and possible personal implications of the project for staff, including role expansion, role clarification, working hours, and implications for other ongoing responsibilities. At the suggestion of the facility director, facility administration left for part of each of these meetings, so that staff might have full and free opportunity to examine concerns with an outside project investigator. We feel that this series of orientation meetings was immensely useful in helping the ART project get off to an informed, participatory, and enthusiastic start.

The staff orientation meetings just described were scheduled so that the last one was held 3 weeks before the facility's first ART class. During the following week, all Annsville youth participated in the project's pretesting (described in the next section), and *all* staff—now informed about the component procedures of ART—were asked to choose which of the three procedures they preferred to learn. Our goal here was both to permit preferences to be expressed—to which we in fact responded—and to make clear that all facility staff were expected to be part of the ART project and become competent in at least one of the interventions that constitute ART.

Following resident pretesting, that is, during the week immediately preceding the beginning of the ART classes, three 2-day training workshops, one for each component procedure of ART, were conducted by the project investigators. Approximately half of the Annsville staff participated in one of these three trainer preparation workshops.* Though the *contents* of the workshops differed from one another, the *procedures* of all three were both didactic (reading the appropriate Trainer's Manual and supplementary materials, lectures by the workshop leader) and experiential (role playing, group exercises). As an illustration of our approach to training, an outline of contents and procedures and a schedule for the Structured Learning workshop is presented in Table 8.

Resident Structuring and Pretesting

Our preparation phase interactions with the 60 Annsville residents had two related goals: provision of information, or structuring, and enhancement of motivation for participation. We began with a poster campaign,

---

*Following the first 10-week sequence of ART, a second series of such workshops was held. The two series resulted in *all* Annsville staff being trained in one (or more) of the ART procedures.

posters hung in the halls, dining room, and elsewhere. Some posters were intentionally general—"Something Big is Coming"—while others aimed to give an initial (and we hoped enticing) sense of what was coming—"Join the Angerbusters." (The Angerbuster "gang" we sought to form is described more fully later.) Specific information about the nature, goals, formats, scheduling, and other details of Structured Learning, Anger Control Training, and Moral Education was communicated and explored in give-and-take unit meetings held daily by each 12-resi-

Table 8. Structured Learning Workshop

Day One

9:00 - 9:15	Introductions
9:15 - 10:15	Lecture: "Background of Structured Learning"
10:15 - 10:30	Break
10:30 - 11:30	Lecture: "Preparing for Structured Learning"
	1. Trainee selection and grouping
	2. Trainee motivation—external motivators
	3. Trainee motivation—internal motivators
	4. Structured Learning materials
	5. Preparing modeling displays
11:30 - 12:00	Group Exercise: Preparing Modeling Displays
12:00 - 1:15	Lunch
1:15 - 1:45	Lecture: "The Opening Session: Structuring Procedures and Rules"
1:45 - 2:45	Role Play: The Opening Session
2:45 - 3:00	Break
3:00 - 3:30	Lecture: "The Typical Session: Modeling, Role Play, Feedback"
3:30 - 5:00	Role Play: The Typical Session

Day Two

9:00 - 9:30	Review
9:30 - 10:00	Role play: The Typical Session
10:00 - 10:30	Lecture: "Resistance in the Structured Learning Group"
10:30 - 10:45	Break
10:45 - 12:00	Role Play: Dealing with Resistance
12:00 - 1:15	Lunch
1:15 - 2:15	Role Play: Dealing with Resistance
2:15 - 2:45	Lecture: "Transfer of Training"
2:45 - 3:00	Break
3:00 - 3:30	Group Exercise: Problems in Application
3:30 - 5:00	Group Discussion: Problems in Application

dent unit and its counselor and, on a less planned basis, also in individual meetings. In general, the youths' response to such structuring varied all the way from enthusiastic to resistive, with a "wait-and-see" attitude most typical.

We believe participant motivation to be as crucial to the success of ART as the didactic lessons themselves. Therefore we took a number of steps as early as this preparation phase to seek to enhance desire to participate. The major motivator, in the long run, for the success of ART or any intervention is that the intervention seem to its recipient to be likely to "work." "Work" in the case of ART means that the prosocial skills, anger-reducing techniques, and moral reasoning training "pay off," that is, seem utilitarian to the youth by increasing his effectiveness and life satisfaction. Thus, in all group and individual structuring sessions, great emphasis was placed on the real-world rewards that were likely to follow from enhanced skill competence and anger control ability. But extrinsic motivators can also serve a substantial role in the motivation of delinquent youth. We informed residents about the Structured Learning homework reward system which would be utilized: When at least five members of a Structured Learning group had completed two homework assignments, the group would be allowed to leave the facility under supervision for an evening of movies or pizza.

Our second major approach to the provision of external motivators sought to capitalize upon the immense responsiveness of youth to peer pressure. Since residents wind up in places like Annsville partially as a result of *antisocial* peer pressure, could we, we wondered, "capture" this mechanism and enhance resident motivation to participate via *prosocial* peer pressure. This thinking lay behind our creation of the "prosocial gang" we called the Angerbusters. The Angerbusters (which, incidentally, is what most of the residents came to call ART) began with the poster campaign described earlier and became concretized by the ART classes themselves and, symbolically, by a logo and T-shirt (see Figure 4) we developed. The T-shirt and status as an Angerbuster had to be earned, and the only way it could be earned was by successful participation in and completion of the 10-week ART sequence. At the close of this sequence as part of our maintenance phase, we held a graduation ceremony in which the 24 residents who had received ART during the first sequence were given, along with elaborate praise, an Angerbuster T-shirt. Our experience with the Angerbusters was a positive one. We offer it here as an illustration of the need in programs like ART both to mobilize peer pressure in constructive directions and to supplement intrinsic motivators with external rewards, be they T-shirts, tokens, privileges, or otherwise.

Figure 4. Angerbuster's Logo

Assignment to evaluation conditions. The five 12-resident units that comprised the Annsville census were randomly assigned to three evaluation conditions. Two units were assigned to Aggression Replacement Training (Condition 1). The 24 youths, in groups of 6 (*all* groups came from within, never across, units) for Structured Learning and Anger Control Training and 12 for Moral Education, met for the 30 classes over 10 weeks as described in the Aggression Replacement Training curriculum (Table 7). Two other units, also comprised of a total of 24 residents, were assigned to a Brief Instructions Control Group (Condition 2). This condition was designed to control for the effects of trainee motivation. That is, a youth's level of prosocial skill deficiency may change in positive, competency-displaying directions not (or not only) because a deficiency in the *ability* to understand and use a given skill has been corrected by skills training, but also because circumstances may increase his *motivation* to use an infrequently employed skill he may already (without training) possess in part or in whole. Being part of a study or being tested for a skill's presence, especially by a tester one may like and wish to please, are examples of motivational enhancement of skill performance other than by training. Thus, pre/post changes in a more skilled direction ought not be attributed to ART unless such changes can be shown to exceed that associated with simple motivational enhancement. The 24 adolescents assigned to the Brief Instructions Control Group were pretested, participated only in usual facility activities, not ART, and then were posttested 10 weeks later at the same time as those who had received ART. Just prior to their posttesting, however, Condition 2 adolescents were provided with test instructions designed to enhance their display of skilled behavior, that is, instructions about the nature, value, and utility of the skills involved, and especially the desirability of reflecting these skills in their posttest responses. We have used such brief instruction control procedures successfully in related investigations involving aggressive youth and adults (Goldstein, 1981).

The grossest, yet by no means the least important, intervention evaluation question is whether the intervention is superior in its effects to no intervention at all. Condition 3, the No Treatment Control Group, was designed to answer this question. The 12 youths assigned to this condition received pre- and posttesting only, with no intervening ART or motivational instructions.

The evaluation testing sequence. The testing sequence employed to evaluate the effectiveness of ART is presented in Figure 5. Three categories of situations, each increasingly removed from those used in the ART training itself, are reflected in these pre- and posttest batteries. The Situations Tests (Direct, Minimal Generalization, and Extended Generalization) are each comprised of a series of descriptions of stimulus situations that might occur in the resident's real world, in response to which one of the 10 Structured Learning skills in the ART curriculum would be, in our judgment, an optimal response. The resident is presented with each situation in turn and is asked to indicate exactly what he would do if he were in and had to respond to that situation. The Direct Situations Test (see Appendix A1), given both pre and post, consists of 40 such situations (4 for each of the 10 skills taught) described in an audiotape presentation. (The modeling displays developed and enacted by the Structured Learning trainers during the 10-week ART sequence portrayed these very same stimulus situations.)

Figure 5. Evaluation Testing Sequence

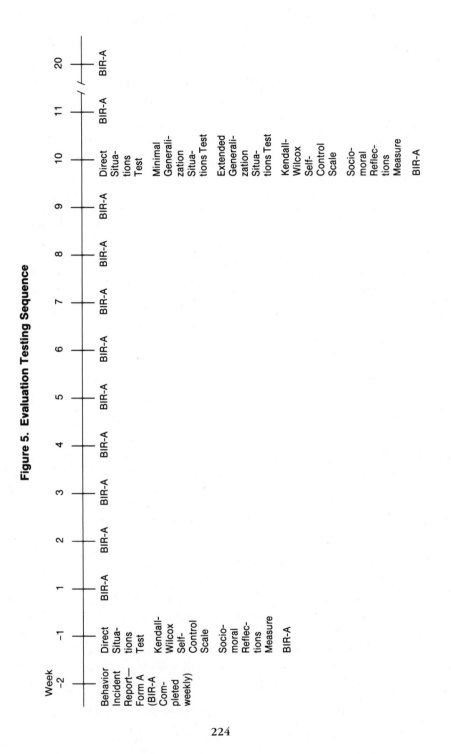

After listening to each situation, the youth tells a tester (sitting at a table with him) what his response would be to that situation. The number of correct behavioral steps described in response to these 40 situations on the pretraining Direct Situations Test is our operational measure of the youth's pre-ART level of psychological skills competence. As Figure 5 indicates, this measure was repeated for all 60 adolescents at the 10th-week posttesting. The difference between posttest and pretest scores on this measure is our evaluation criterion of skill *acquisition*. Skill *transfer*, operationalized here as the ability to use the skills in response to situations never posed before (unlike those used in the modeling displays and Direct Situations Test), was defined in two ways. The Minimal Generalization Situations Test (Appendix A2) consisted of four new situations per skill, situations not previously practiced by the youth. These situations, given as a posttest only, were also presented by audiotape to the residents while a tester recorded their responses verbatim. The Extended Generalization Situations Test—"extended" here meaning somewhat closer to real-life circumstances (see Appendix A3)—consisted of yet two more posttest situations per skill. These 20 situations, however, were presented in a more face-to-face, confrontational (not audiotaped) manner by each youth's tester. In total, therefore, the Direct Situations Test administered pre-ART consisted of 40 items, and the combined Situations Tests administered post were made of 100 situations: 40 Direct, 40 Minimal Generalization, and 20 Extended Generalization.

It is perhaps useful here, in the middle of our presentation of project measures, to stress that in our view all study measures are measures of the effectiveness of ART as a whole, not just of one of its components. The situations tests just described sound like measures designed to reflect changes in skill competency (they are) as a result of the part of the program explicitly designed to teach such skills—Structured Learning. We believe, however, that this view of the potential impact of a multimodal intervention such as ART is too simplistic. True, trainees may behave in a more skilled manner because they have been taught to do so. But trainees may also behave in a more skilled manner, as we described in considerable detail in Chapter 4, because they have diminished their level of anger arousal and are freer to use the skill or, as Chapter 6 proposes, because they have advanced their level of moral reasoning and elect to use the skill. We take a similar view with regard to our other outcome measures. As Figure 5 reveals, each youth's counselor rated him on both a pre and post basis on a standardized measure of impulsivity, the Kendall-Wilcox Self-Control Scale (see Appendix A4). Changes in scores may indeed reflect mostly gains derived in the

Anger Control Training classes, but surely ought not to be conceptualized as independent of the other components of ART. Being more prosocially skilled and viewing oneself that way and utilizing a more advanced level of moral reasoning can each be conceived of as helping lower one's level of impulsivity.

A third project measure was the Sociomoral Reflections Measure (see Appendix A5) developed by Gibbs, Widaman, and Colby (1982). It consists of two moral dilemmas very much like those employed in the Moral Education component of ART and a series of probe questions for each. This measure is designed to ascertain an estimate of the respondent's level of moral reasoning. As was true for the Situations Tests, the Sociomoral Reflections Measure was administered by an individual tester who recorded the resident's responses verbatim.

Finally, as noted on Figure 5, each week a staff member closely familiar with each participating youth completed a Behavior Incident Report (Form A) on him (see Appendix A6). This Report is an 18-item checklist in which the staff member can indicate whether during the week just ended the youth had engaged in such undesirable behaviors as instigating arguments or fights, harrassing others, cursing, fighting, throwing articles, requiring restraint, or other forms of acting out. Completion of this report on a weekly basis began 2 weeks before the ART program started, for base rate purposes, and continued for the next 20 weeks: 10 to reflect the first sequence of ART, and 10 subsequent weeks during which the 36 control group residents (Conditions 2 and 3) received their ART sessions. The Behavior Incident Report—Form A, perhaps the measure most clearly reflective of all three ART components combined, was thus administered in the Annsville project for 22 consecutive weeks. The administration of the pretest evaluation test battery completed the preparation phase of the Annsville ART project.

Implementation

Immediately following the two preparatory weeks devoted, respectively, to resident testing and staff training, the ART curriculum, as specified in Table 7, was implemented for the planned 10-week period. Scheduling, materials, personnel, and related administrative concerns associated with this implementation phase are discussed in the Administrator's Manual for ART (Chapter 10). In the present section, we wish to focus on the two implementation phase issues most germane to our roles as trainers and evaluators of ART—trainer *supervision* and steps taken to maximize *transfer* of ART-instigated gains.

Supervision

Twenty Annsville staff members conducted the 10-week curriculum. Working in pairs, they led the four Structured Learning groups and the four Anger Control Training groups, and conducted the two weekly 12-resident Moral Education meetings. Each week of the program, several of these sessions were observed by the ART supervisors, and each week separate supervisory meetings were held with the three categories of trainers.* These meetings provided many opportunities for corrective feedback, continued instruction, reformulation of group-specific tactics, preparation of plans and procedures for the next session, rewarding of progress, encouragement of enhanced coordination within trainer pairs, and learning by (not only from) the supervisors. Unanticipated concerns and challenges arose and were puzzled through and dealt with in a collaborative, ad hoc manner. Some issues discussed, for example, were the role of diverse resident reading levels, procedures for sustaining trainer and resident motivation, unexpected resistances, coordination of ART plans with other events occurring in the facility, readjusting optimal homework levels, resident-resident or staff-resident conflicts, and the relationship of ART to ongoing academic and counseling programs.

Clearly, this series of supervisory sessions was a valuable and reciprocal learning experience. Trainers were given the opportunity to make concrete through direct experience and feedback what they had learned in training workshops and the ART Trainer's Manuals. Supervisors, in turn, were given a very valuable and often challenging sequence of opportunities to reflect upon aspects of ART, correct oversights, elaborate procedural matters, and, in general, improve ART's form and substance, enhancing its prescriptive value for incarcerated youth.

Transfer and Maintenance

The crucial and highly interrelated goals of encouraging gains arising from an intervention to generalize across settings (transfer) and across time (maintenance) must be sought not only after the intervention is completed, but also *during* its implementation. A number of the specific procedures and materials constituting the three interventions that comprise ART are designed for transfer- and maintenance-enhancing pur-

---

*To aid in the integration of the three components of ART into a larger gestalt, such supervisory meetings were held on a joint basis—all three types of trainers together—during the replication of this evaluation project at a second Division for Youth facility, as discussed later in this chapter.

poses. These include the regular reliance on homework in Structured Learning, of role playing real-life hassles in Anger Control Training, and on the use of personally relevant dilemmas in Moral Education as well as other features of these interventions described in full in their respective Trainer's Manuals. Beyond these trainer-initiated steps, however, the project's supervisors were also able to facilitate a number of events whose goal was the enhancement of transfer and maintenance of ART-instigated gains. These largely staff-directed events will now be described.

While many potential avenues for transfer and maintenance enhancement now exist (see in particular Epps, Thompson, & Lane, 1985; Goldstein & Kanfer, 1979; Karoly & Steffen, 1980), our emphasis was placed upon (1) making and keeping staff (both those actually doing the training and, especially, those not doing training but interacting daily with the boys in the facility) as aware as possible of the specific ART skills being taught or goals being sought each week and (2) teaching staff how, where, and why to reward such competencies and goal attainments when they observed them. We started small. First, a discussion of these opportunities was incorporated into the preparation phase orientation lecture/discussions held with all Annsville staff. Second, each week we posted the name and steps of the Structured Learning "Skill of the Week" (the one being taught that week) over the desk on which the frequently visited log book was kept in the facility's staff log room. A series of memos was also sent to all facility staff. One memo sent in conjunction with the Skill of the Week posting read as follows:

> Dear Annsville staff member,
>
>   As each of you is aware, the Division for Youth in collaboration with the Syracuse University Center for Research on Aggression has recently begun at Annsville a new program, Aggression Replacement Training (ART). Participating residents (right now, Teams 1 and 4; next year, all other teams) attend three classes each week: (1) Structured Learning for prosocial skills training, (2) Anger Control Training, and (3) Moral Education. To maximize the success of this effort, however, it is vital that the youngsters who are involved be connected to program goals and procedures not only during the three in-class hours per week, but as often as possible during other times and activities each and every day.
>
>   You can help make this pioneering program a success, and your help would be immensely appreciated. During the ART classes, residents are learning new ways of behaving that will make them better citizens, at Annsville and after discharge. But new learning is fragile learning. New, constructive ways of

behaving *must* meet with success (be rewarded, be reinforced, work as well or better than old, aggressive ways of behaving) if they are to last. We will post in the log room the specific new skill we are teaching each week. *Please*, remember it, look for it, and when a resident behaves towards you, or towards others, in the skilled manner, try to reward his effort in some appropriate way. Perhaps you can provide a simple "well done" or other brief expression of praise or approval. Or, if the skill involves his expressing something to which you feel you can respond in ways that satisfy his request, need, complaint, etc., please by all means do so. If the resident handles situations in which he or others would usually get angry by using anger-reducing methods instead (e.g., deep breathing, counting backwards from 10, walking away from it, etc.) please let him know, however briefly you wish, that he deserves praise for such behavior.

Thank you very much for your assistance. Together, we can make ART an important success.

Sincerely,
Arnold P. Goldstein, Ph.D.

Approximately halfway through the 10-week ART program, that is, after sufficient new skills, anger reducers, and altered moral reasoning perspectives had been communicated to participating residents, we prepared and provided to all facility staff a more comprehensive and explicitly instructional document designed to aid their motivation and effectiveness as transfer and maintenance enhancers. This document, The Transfer Coach (see Appendix B), discusses the central importance of such staff activity, describes the resident behaviors to be responsive to, and defines and urges a series of specific staff coaching behaviors—prompting, encouraging, reassuring, and rewarding. It is our impression that this manual was a particularly useful aid to transfer and maintenance enhancement.

As indicated in Figure 5, each week staff members completed a Behavior Incident Report—Form A—for every Annsville resident. We came to view this event as an unintended but welcome addition to our transfer-relevant procedures as we increasingly realized that in addition to its intended evaluation function, it served the purpose of regularly focusing staff attention on the presence and absence of undesirable behaviors in residents' actions. Because filling out a Behavior Incident Report made staff more aware of behaviors, we changed the content of the BIR in our replication study to include not only 15 of the 18 original (Annsville version) items describing negative, acting-out behaviors, but also 15 positive, prosocial behaviors derivable from ART participation (see BIR, Forms A and B, Appendix A6, A7). Thus, the staff's attention was drawn to the particular constructive resident behaviors we wished them to reward, encourage, and otherwise help transfer and maintain.

A final transfer and maintenance procedure that we wish to single out for special emphasis (it is also considered in Chapter 3, The Trainer's Manual for Structured Learning) is the Homework Report required of each trainee each week. The homework assignment each week for all trainees was to enact in real life (in this case, in Annsville or while on a home visit) the Structured Learning skill role played successfully by the youth in that week's Structured Learning class. Every Structured Learning class began with a brief discussion of homework successes and failures and collection of Homework Reports. More detail on how we recommend these assignments and reports be used is provided in Chapter 3. We mention homework at this point in our discussion both to highlight our estimation of its very considerable potential value as a transfer and maintenance enhancer and to share our experiences of a serious difficulty we had in its utilization and how we corrected this difficulty.

To maximize resident motivation to complete each week's homework assignment, we established an extrinsic reward arrangement in which an evening out of the facility for pizza or movies was provided for every two homeworks completed, providing that at least five members of the group had completed the homeworks. Two things went wrong with this apparently insufficiently pretested arrangement. The rewards provided were too great for the tasks required—we soon owed a huge pizza debt. And too many of the boys were fabricating, not actually doing, their homework and submitting to us phony Homework Reports. To correct this situation, the pizza-reward system was discontinued after the 10th week of the ART program; the pizza debt was paid off; and we changed the homework procedure such that all assignments had to be conducted with a staff member or, if with another resident, with a staff member observing, who was required to observe and initial the Homework Report to signify its completion.

These several trainer-oriented and resident-oriented attempts to enhance transfer and maintenance, combined with the similarly oriented techniques built into the ART components themselves, are a valuable beginning—but only a beginning—toward this central intervention goal.

Results

Project data were analyzed by means of a series of 1×3 analyses of covariance, controlling for initial status on each variable examined. Table 9 presents the outcome of these analyses for the 10 Structured

Learning skills. Table 10 reflects the effect of ART intervention on changes in actual acting-out behavior (recorded on weekly Behavior Incident Reports—Form A) and the effect on rated impulsiveness (from the Kendall-Wilcox Self-Control Scale).

**Table 9. ART Effects (*F* Values) upon
Structured Learning Skills (Annsville)**

Comparison of Trainees versus Controls

Skill	Acquisition	Minimal Transfer	Extended Transfer
1. Expressing a Complaint	15.04*	16.61*	9.99*
2. Responding to the Feelings of Others	.13	.97	.25
3. Stressful Conversation	7.97*	6.93*	1.89
4. Responding to Anger	10.00*	2.89	5.07*
5. Keeping Out of Fights	13.01*	1.67	.34
6. Helping Others	.42	.66	.37
7. Accusation	1.11	.03	1.16
8. Group Pressure	16.73*	14.85*	5.47*
9. Expressing Affection	.04	.06	1.76
10. Responding to Failure	.74	1.71	.05

*Difference significant at .01 or less.

**Table 10. ART Effects (*F* Values) upon Acting-Out Behavior
and Rated Impulsiveness (Annsville)**

Measure	Comparison of Trainees versus Controls
Behavior Incidents	
Acting out: Change in Number	11.51**
Acting out: Change in Intensity	9.34*
Kendall-Wilcox Scale	
Rated Impulsiveness	10.67*

*Difference significant at .05 or less.
**Difference significant at .01 or less.

As can be seen from Tables 9 and 10, residents completing ART, in comparison to those experiencing either a motivation-enhancing but no-training experience or no-training alone experience, change significantly more on all study outcome criteria. They both acquire and transfer (minimal and extended) Structured Learning *skills* to a degree significantly beyond that acquired and transferred by controls. ART trainees also change significantly more in their overt, in-the-facility *behavior*. In terms of both number of acting-out incidents and the *intensity* of those that do occur (mild, moderate, severe), ART trainees perform significantly better than controls. This outcome also emerged, as Table 10 indicates, for pre- versus postratings by facility staff of trainees' *impulsiveness*.

The Sociomoral Reflections Measure results failed to yield a significant between-conditions difference ($F = .02, p > .05$). Participation in Moral Education sessions by this sample did not substantially alter *moral reasoning* level.

Two additional results of the Annsville project are of interest. The first constitutes a successful replication of an important segment of the evaluation results just presented. Following completion of the project's posttesting, in week 11, new ART groups were constituted for the 36 residents on the three control group units. These sessions duplicated in all major respects (curriculum, length, group size, materials, etc.) the first phase ART sessions. Our goal in this second phase was an own-control test of the efficacy of ART. Particular attention was paid to discerning possible reductions in acting-out behaviors by comparing the BIRs (Form A) for the 36 adolescents while in ART (weeks 11-20) with their BIRs when they served as control group members (weeks 1-10). Both of the statistical comparisons conducted to test for replication effects yielded positive results. Specifically, both the number ($t = 2.51$) and the severity ($t = 2.37$) of behavioral incidents showed significant reductions from phase 1 to phase 2.

All of the study findings presented thus far bear upon the effectiveness of ART in altering one or another *within-facility* resident behavior. Our final investigative result, in contrast, concerns the trainees' post-release, *within-community* behaviors and attitudes. As Chapter 9 will make clear in detail, we believe that effective and satisfying long-term community adjustment for delinquent youths *requires* intervention within the community. It is simply asking too much of a within-facility intervention to sustain improvements in the face of real-life demands when the intervention is not present.

In spite of our pessimism regarding such "inoculation effects," we did wish to learn whether ART affected trainees' in-community behavior—even in the short run—or whether the changes obtained were limited to institutional behaviors. Approximately 3 months after the respective releases from Annsville of 17 youths who had received ART and 37 who had not, the Division for Youth Service team persons* responsible for these youths were contacted by a regional office supervisor. By means of telephone interviews, the supervisor inquired of the youth service team worker into the home, family, school, work, peer, and legal postrelease adjustment of the 54 youths. At the time the interviews were conducted, neither the supervisor nor workers knew which youths had and had not received ART. For each youth, the supervisor and worker rated adjustment level in the five areas of inquiry. The straightforward and rather simple rating scale developed for this purpose, the Community Adjustment Rating Scale, appears in Appendix A8. As Table 11 indicates, in three of the five areas rated, as well as in overall community adjustment (total average rating across all five areas), the ART trainees were rated significantly higher than were youths who had not received ART.

MACCORMICK YOUTH CENTER

Our second evaluation of the efficacy of ART was conducted at Mac-Cormick Youth Center, a New York State Division for Youth secure facility for male juvenile delinquents between ages 13 and 21. In essence, this evaluation project sought both to replicate the exact procedures and

Table 11. Postrelease Community Adjustment Comparisons of ART and Non-ART Youths

Adjustment Area	Mean Rating ART Youths	Mean Rating Non-ART Youths	t value
Home and Family	1.60	.94	2.19*
School	1.14	.88	.82
Work	1.40	1.31	.26
Peer	1.67	1.07	2.16*
Legal	1.71	1.05	2.09*
Overall	1.56	1.02	2.48*

*Difference significant at .05 or less.

---

*Functionally, these staff persons hold aftercare responsibilities analogous to parole officers in adult corrections.

findings of the Annsville project and to extend them to youth incarcerated for substantially more serious felonies. There were 51 residents at MacCormick at the time the evaluation was conducted. Their median age was 18 years, 8 months. Their ethnic background was black (30), Hispanic (18), Oriental (2), and white (1). The crimes for which they were incarcerated included murder, manslaughter, rape, sodomy, attempted murder, assault, and robbery. In contrast to Annsville, whose 60 residents live in a single dormitory in a facility with a total (all shifts) staff of 50, MacCormick's physical layout consists of four wings housing an average of 12 residents per wing in single, locked rooms. MacCormick Youth Center has a staff of 130 and, as is true of Annsville, is located in a heavily wooded, sparsely populated area in upstate New York.

In all its procedural and experimental particulars, the MacCormick evaluation project replicated the effort at Annsville. It employed the same preparatory activities, materials, curriculum, testing, staff training, resident training, supervision, and data analysis procedures. Table 12 provides a fuller sense of the timing and sequencing of activities that constituted this replication project.

Table 12. ART Replication Project: Training and Evaluation Sequence

Date	Activity
Summer 1985	Staff and resident preparation/ motivation Materials preparation
Sept. 16–20, 1985	Staff orientation (one or more meetings) Resident orientation Resident pretesting (1 week)
Sept. 23–28, 1985	Staff training (three 2-day workshops for selected staff)
Sept. 30–Dec. 6, 1985	Resident ART training[a] (10 weeks) Staff supervision (10 weeks)
Dec. 9–Dec. 13, 1985	Resident posttesting (1 week)
Jan. 6–March 14, 1986	Resident ART training[b] (10 weeks)
Jan. 6–March 28, 1986	Data analysis

[a]First half of facility residents.
[b]Second half of facility residents.

Results

Replication project data were analyzed by means of a series of 1 × 3 analyses of covariance, controlling for initial status on each variable examined. Table 13 presents the results of these analyses for the 10 Structured Learning skills in the ART curriculum employed in this evaluation.

Table 14 presents the effect of ART on changes from base rate to intervention period on acting-out and prosocial behaviors (recorded on weekly Behavior Incident Reports—Form B, Appendix A7) and the effect on rated impulsiveness (from the Kendall-Wilcox Self-Control Scale—Appendix A4).

As Table 13 indicates, on 5 of the 10 Structured Learning skills significant acquisition and/or transfer results emerge. These findings, as well as the particular skills for which significant results were obtained, essentially replicate the Annsville Structured Learning results (four of the skills showing significant results are the same in both studies). In contrast to the Annsville results, however, the MacCormick data yielded a significant ($F = 14.73; p < .01$) F value on the Sociomoral Reflections

Table 13. ART Effects (F Values) upon Structured Learning Skills (MacCormick)

Comparison of Trainees versus Controls

Skill	Acquisition	Minimal Transfer	Extended Transfer
1. Expressing a Complaint	4.48*	5.28**	3.14*
2. Responding to the Feelings of Others	.07	.15	.64
3. Stressful Conversation	.98	.20	.47
4. Responding to Anger	2.26	7.09**	3.25*
5. Keeping Out of Fights	5.48**	1.70	2.99
6. Helping Others	.18	1.11	1.04
7. Accusation	5.98**	2.13	.22
8. Group Pressure	3.45*	6.89**	7.28**
9. Expressing Affection	1.27	2.93	.04
10. Responding to Failure	2.85	2.02	1.74

*Difference significant at .05 or less.
**Difference significant at .02 or less.

Table 14. ART Effects (*F* Values) upon Acting-Out and Prosocial Behavior and Rated Impulsiveness (MacCormick)

Measure	Comparison of Trainees versus Controls
Behavior Incidents	
Acting out: Change in Number	.69
Acting out: Change in Intensity	.53*
Prosocial Behaviors	8.64*
Kendall-Wilcox Scale	
Rated Impulsiveness	1.28*

*Difference significant at .01 or less.

Measure. At MacCormick, but not at Annsville, trainees in Moral Education sessions increased significantly in moral reasoning stage over the 10-week intervention period. We can only speculate about the sources of this discrepancy in findings. Different Moral Education group leaders in the two settings, sequence effects, and, especially, personality, aggression-proneness, and demographic differences between the participating residents in the two facilities (e.g., Annsville's mean age was 15 years, MacCormick's 18 years, 8 months) are each reasonable explanatory hypotheses.

Regarding overt, in-facility behavior, Table 14 reveals that residents who received ART, in comparison with those who did not, increased significantly over their base rate levels in the constructive, prosocial behaviors they utilized (e.g., offering or accepting criticism appropriately, employing self-control when provoked). In contrast to the Annsville findings, however, MacCormick youth receiving ART did not differ from controls in either the number or intensity of acting-out behaviors or their rated levels of impulsiveness. These latter findings appear to be largely explained by the substantial differences in potential for such behaviors between the two facilities. As noted earlier, Annsville is not a locked facility. Its 60 residents live in one dormitory, in contrast to the locked, single-room arrangement at MacCormick. MacCormick's staff is twice the size of Annsville's, and the facility operates under a considerably tighter system of sanctions and controls than does Annsville. Thus, the opportunity for acting-out or impulsive behaviors is lower *across all conditions* at MacCormick as compared to Annsville; a "floor effect" seems to be operating, which makes the possibility of decreases in acting-out as a result of ART participation at MacCormick numerically a good bit more difficult than at Annsville. At Annsville, such behaviors were contextually more possible at base rate, and thus could (and did) decrease over the intervention period. At MacCormick, all residents' base rates were low and probably for these contextual reasons (e.g., sanctions, controls, rich staffing, etc.), remained low. Their use of pro-social behaviors, in regard to which no floor or ceiling effect influences are relevant, did increase differentially as a function of ART.

The findings of the two investigations we have reported reveal ART to be a multimodal, habilitation intervention of considerable potency with incarcerated juvenile delinquents. It enhances prosocial skill competency and overt prosocial behavior and, in one of the two samples studied, it reduces the level of rated impulsiveness and both decreases (where possible) the frequency and intensity of acting-out behaviors and may enhance the participants' levels of moral reasoning. Furthermore, some moderately substantial evidence provided independently reveals it to lead to valuable changes in community functioning. In all, it is clearly an intervention deserving of both continued application and continued rigorous evaluation.

Chapter 9

Future Directions

We have demonstrated the effectiveness of ART on an array of delinquency-relevant criteria on two samples of incarcerated youth and have also shown replication effects on wait-list control youths subsequently given ART. In addition, initial evidence has emerged that youths receiving ART, in contrast to those not receiving it, will, on a postrelease basis, be rated as better adjusted on an array of significant community functioning dimensions. These several demonstrations of effectiveness, beyond their direct implications for the further study, use, and dissemination of ART itself, provide strong encouragement for not only the construction-design experimental strategy but also the affective-behavioral-cognitive multimodal treatment strategy that ART operationally implements. Our major conclusions from these investigations, therefore, are that (1) *within an institutional context*, ART is significantly promotive of higher levels of prosocial skills competency, higher levels of sociomoral reasoning, and lower levels of both impulsiveness and other varieties of acting-out behavior and (2) *within a community context*, beginning and tentative evidence points to a carryover of ART received while incarcerated to effective functioning in real-world settings.

Two recommendations for action follow from these conclusions. The first concerns utilization of ART for modifying within-institution behaviors. While certainly not the first behaviorally oriented intervention to show reliable within-institution effects, ART does so in a substantial manner and thus may be recommended for institutional management purposes. Second, within-institution change is not only valuable as a desired end in itself, but, importantly, is a "foot in the door" in the generalization-to-community-functioning process. Our studies show that prosocial alternatives to aggressive behavior can successfully be added to the repertoires of incarcerated youth and that such behaviors will transfer and maintain, at least on a short-term basis, to community functioning. It is a vital question, but nevertheless a separate question, whether such behaviors will transfer to and maintain on a longer term, enduring basis in postincarceration settings. We thus come to the first and clearly the most consequential future direction for the further development and evaluation of ART.

IMPLEMENTATION IN THE COMMUNITY

Although our own results demonstrate a positive carryover of ART-induced gains into community functioning, we have long been suspicious of the durability of such "inoculation effects" (Goldstein & Kanfer, 1979). The notion that treatment or training provided a client in a cloistered context (e.g., therapist's office, mental hospital, delinquency facility) can bring about positive changes in the individual that are so powerful that they override the antisocial or anti-mental-health influences present in the posttraining environment to which the client returns is, in our view, both naive and erroneous. The environment that an adolescent returns to is usually the very context in which he resided before incarceration, an environment—then and now—strongly and effectively promotive of the very behaviors and attitudes that ART or other interventions seek to change. We are pleased that our community follow-up showed positive effects, but our strong prediction is that later inquiry into the presence or absence of such maintenance of effects, for example, a year after release, would not show differences between ART and non-ART youths. Negative interpersonal, environmental, and other community influences are often simply too powerful.This is not to say that there is not very much that may be positive and promotive of effective community functioning in the environments to which many of the youths we have studied return. Such community settings can and do at times provide prosocial models, reward for prosocial behavior, and examples of other youths leading effective, satisfying prosocial lives. Nevertheless, such prosocial community settings often do not exist, and it is for the adolescents subject to negative community influences that our in-community training is predicted to be relevant and beneficial.

It follows, therefore, that if one wishes to accomplish enduring, positive changes in community contexts, the intervention provided must also occur *in the community*. This is certainly not a new suggestion, as numerous community corrections and diversion programs already exist. What is relatively new, however, is the availability of a multimodal intervention with sufficient potential for effecting substantial changes when offered on a within-community basis.

We are currently initiating and evaluating, again under the sponsorship of the New York State Division for Youth and the Division of Criminal Justice Services, just such an in-community program. ART is being provided to a sample of delinquent youth for a 1-year period, beginning on a while-incarcerated basis approximately 6 months before their anticipated release from a delinquency facility and continuing for 6 months on a postrelease, within-community basis. The effectiveness of this combined within-facility and within-community intervention effort is being compared to within-facility ART only, within-community ART only, and a no-intervention condition. In addition, to capitalize even more fully on potentially prosocial community influences, the parents or significant others of a subsample of youths receiving ART are also being trained in ART in separate parallel sessions for behaviors reciprocal to what is being taught the youths (following Kifer, Lewis, Green, & Phillips, 1974; Serna, Schumaker, Hazel, & Sheldon, in press). Given the demonstrated potency of ART offered on a within-facility basis, plus the evidence showing short-term carryover of effects into community functioning, we are guardedly optimistic regarding its impact when provided on *both* a preparatory basis (within-facility) *and* an *in vivo* basis (within-community). Evidence to be obtained over the 2-year term of this ongoing project will indicate whether or not such optimism is warranted.

CURRICULUM DEVELOPMENT

Our overall perspective underlying ART is psychoeducational. We do not see ourselves as therapists offering psychotherapy to patients or counselors providing counseling to clients. Instead, in both spirit and operation, our self-definition is of teachers or trainers conducting training with trainees. As noted in Chapter 1, Structured Learning was our first training offering. In developing ART, two additional, course-length training programs were added—Anger Control Training and Moral Education. We hope that our sense of experimentation and ongoing development has been made clear. In our view, *no* human services interventions—be they psychoeducational, psychotherapeutic, or otherwise—are ever complete or final. Efforts to alter human behavior or attitudes in the direction of enhanced effectiveness and satisfaction, ideally, are perpetually undergoing revision in both evolutionary and revolutionary ways as empirical evidence and relevant practitioner experience accumulate.

Thus ART, regardless of how well it performs, is at best to be considered merely a stop along the way in the never complete, open-ended challenge of human services intervention. The three course-length interventions that constitute ART are but the initial offerings in what we hope will eventually be a comprehensive curriculum of diverse offerings of demonstrated utility for delinquent youth. We ourselves are already well along in developing and evaluating additional psychoeducational courses for delinquents. One systematically teaches empathy (Goldstein & Michaels, 1985); the other teaches problem-solving skills (Grant, 1986). Our choice of the former grew from evidence revealing that responding to another individual in an empathic manner and temporarily assuming the individual's perspective decreases or inhibits one's potential for acting aggressively toward the other (Feshbach, 1982; Feshbach & Feshbach, 1969). Stated otherwise, empathy and aggression are incompatible interpersonal responses; hence learning to be more skilled in the former serves as an aid to diminishing the latter.

Problem-solving skill seemed to us to be an especially worthy additional component of a comprehensive curriculum. This appeared to be a good training target not only because effective persons seem to be skilled problem solvers but also because delinquent youths, in particular, are frequently lacking or deficient in such problem-solving skills as the ability to diagnose a problem accurately, brainstorm alternatives, consider their consequences, and evaluate the success of a chosen solution. We were especially eager, in the sense of course coordination, to teach youths to effectively problem solve the recurrent diagnostic task of deciding which Structured Learning skills fit which situations and the recurrent evaluative task of monitoring both the quality of one's own skill usage as well as its impact upon others.

Empathy and problem solving, therefore, appear to be worthy additions to the prosocial repertoire of delinquents. Less developed, but clearly a part of our longer term plans, are the development, evaluation, and provision of other psychoeducational courses for such adolescents. Promoting the use of and avoiding the abuse of peer relationships might be the focus of one course. It is a truism in work with adolescents that the peer group is an exceedingly powerful force in shaping and maintaining behavior. A number of earlier interventions designed for delinquent youth, such as Positive Peer Culture (Vorrath & Brendtro, 1974) and Guided Group Interaction (McCorkle, Elias, & Bixby, 1958), sought to capitalize on this peer potency. These interventions were a good beginning and are of more than historical interest. We believe that a psychoeducational training perspective can help take the next steps by teaching youths how to be the most responsive to prosocial peer influences and substantially less responsive to parallel antisocial influences. Advanced Anger Control Training, a sort of postgraduate offering for adolescents who are still chronically angry after completion of the ART program, is another candidate for curricular development. We do not presently know what such a course might consist of. We do know the need for it is real. Other course-length interventions in development or in planning by our research group include Cooperation Training, Building Prosocial Motivation, Understanding Group Processes, Stress Management, and Diagnosing Social Situations.

As such a comprehensive curriculum of prosocial psychoeducational courses becomes available through the development and evaluation efforts of ourselves and others, we indeed hope its use will be prescriptive. In our ideal vision, such courses will both exist and be offered differentially, as needed, for example, courses A, B, and C to one youth, C, D, and E to another, and so forth.

PRESCRIPTIVE REFINEMENT

Most of this book's opening chapter was devoted to the topic of prescriptive intervention: its theoretical value and initial supportive evidence. The research results reported in this book begin to confirm the *initial* prescriptive value of ART for juvenile delinquents. But what *level* of prescriptiveness has been demonstrated? There are what can be called nondifferential, unidifferential, bidifferential, and tridifferential intervention prescriptions (Goldstein & Stein, 1976).

> At the lowest level of prescriptive differentiation, the Nondifferential prescription, an approach to psychotherapy *or* a kind of psychotherapist is specified for a type of patient. Such prescriptions are either declarations or demonstrations that a given set of therapeutic procedures or a given type of psychotherapist is of therapeutic benefit for a given type of patient. . . . Nondifferential prescriptions delimit or differentiate only by implication, but they are more valuable for prescriptive purposes than is the totally nonprescriptive one-true-light position by which psychotherapy "works" not just for a given type of patient, but for all or most types of patients. In an incremental or building-block approach to prescription building, the Nondifferential prescription is the first step.
>   Unlike the Nondifferential . . . the Unidifferential prescription provides an important piece of additional information . . . which psychotherapy or psychotherapies are *not* of apparent effectiveness with the given patient population. . . . Bidifferential prescriptive research systematically varies two of the three essential components of the "proper" outcome question—therapy, therapist, and patient [or training method, type of trainer, and type of trainee]. . . . Tridifferential prescriptive research . . . is the experimental attempt to answer the ultimate prescriptive question: which treatment, for which patient, by which therapist? (pp. 20-24)

The evaluations of the effectiveness of ART presented earlier are examples of nondifferential prescriptive research, and hence should be viewed as but a prescriptive first step. We have demonstrated ART's effectiveness across relevant criteria and, to some extent, settings, but have not begun to identify for which types of youths it is an ineffective technique (unidifferential level), which types of trainers are and are not effective in its utilization (unidifferential level) nor examined type of youth by type of trainer effects (bidifferential level) or youth by trainer by training method interactions (tridifferential level). Our single attempt thus far to move from nondifferential to unidifferential prescriptive levels was a study by Reiner (1985) seeking to identify Interpersonal Maturity Level discriminators of response and nonresponse to ART. Differential results of this analysis did not emerge; ART was equally effective across I-level types. Clearly, therefore, we wish to underscore for others seeking to examine the effectiveness of ART the substantial value at this point of conceptualizing and implementing experimental designs that move beyond the nondifferential prescriptive level.

There is one additional idea we recommend to the prescriptive investigator interested in ART. It concerns the *strategy* that may optimally be employed when conceptualizing such prescriptive research attempts. Strategically, most delinquency intervention research has focused far too exclusively on the delinquent himself. It is fine to formulate, implement, and evaluate multimodal interventions such as ART, which are targeted to the youth alone ("horizontal" interventions), but we believe it is equally important in intervention prescription building and testing to assume and enact a systems perspective. In addition to youth-directed interventions, the systems perspective targets with equal energy the peer, family, and significant-other context in which the youth functions. We have elsewhere developed further the substance of such "vertical interventions" in efforts to reduce school violence by underscoring the need to intervene simultaneously beyond the perpetrators themselves to the teachers, school administration, parents, local community, and elsewhere (Goldstein, Apter, & Harootunian, 1984). Analogously, we believe successful delinquency intervention efforts must also be similarly comprehensive—horizontal and vertical—and thus require prescriptively examined "building blocks" of both types.

PREVENTION

Prevention has become a major force, almost a byword, in human service efforts in the last decade, a perspective clearly also present in the field of juvenile delinquency. Yet, while it is a perspective to be warmly applauded, thus far it has yielded accomplishments more of spirit than of substance. Juvenile delinquency is difficult to predict and difficult to prevent (Loeber & Dishion, 1983; Lundman, 1984; Seidman & Rapkin, 1983). Prediction is relevant, since we must know to whom our preventive efforts ought to be applied. Some valuable progress has been made in recent years in predicting and thus possibly preventing delinquency. Increasingly, early and middle childhood behaviors and circumstances predictive of later juvenile delinquency have been identified (e.g., Dootjés, 1972; S. J. Glick, 1972; Mitchell & Rosa, 1981; Robbins & Ratcliff, 1979). Chief among these predictors are the child's conduct problems, parental discipline and supervision techniques, parental criminality, and the child's poor academic performance (see Loeber & Dishion, 1983, for an excellent review of this predictive literature). The development of effective interventions for such at-risk youngsters has occurred more slowly. Lundman (1984) comments about some of these interventions:

> Prevention of delinquency also remains a stubbornly elusive goal. The Cambridge-Somerville Youth Study's adult counselors were "no more effective than the usual forces in the community in preventing boys from committing delinquent acts." Youth Consultation Service's social workers "failed to prevent delinquency." The Chicago Area Project almost certainly failed to prevent delinquency. . . . Most recently, The National Evaluation of Delinquency Prevention concluded "there is little positive evidence [projects] are effective in preventing delinquency." (p. 224)

Unlike Lundman (1984), we do not conclude from this generally unsuccessful track record that, as he puts it, "it is time to get out of the business of attempting to prevent delinquency" (p. 225). Instead, we would urge, it is time to open a new and different store. We believe that, just as in habilitation interventions, the most favorable results will follow from those delinquency prevention interventions that are both prescriptively designed and implemented, as well as multilevel, in that simultaneous interventions are directed toward both the youth and the significant interpersonal context.

In an effort to operationalize this perspective on prevention, we have simplified the three interventions that constitute ART to approximately 3rd grade level (e.g., McGinnis & Goldstein, 1984) and are examining with youngsters the short- and long-term effectiveness of this potentially preventive intervention. A reciprocal skills-training program is being used with the parents of a subsample of these children. We are too early in the implementation process in this investigation to even get a sense of its probable outcome, so will not speculate upon it save to urge upon the reader serious consideration in the design and conduct of similar preventive intervention evaluations of the prescriptive, multilevel perspective being operationalized here.

SUMMARY

We have with this book sought to introduce the reader, both practitioner and researcher, to Aggression Replacement Training. It is, as we have described at length, a multimodal intervention package designed to simultaneously impact along behavioral, affective, and cognitive channels upon a cluster of delinquency-relevant characteristics. In earlier chapters we examined the empirical base upon which each of the three components of ART rests and, via detailed training manuals, described and illustrated their constituent procedures. The utility and potency of all interventions must in the end be a function not of developer enthusiasm or practitioner acclamation but, instead, of dispassionate experimental scrutiny. We have begun this investigative process and reported in Chapter 8 two investigations whose results provide both initial confirmation of the value of ART for the modification of negative, within-institution behaviors and encouragement for its continued examination as both a within-institution and a within-community intervention. We indeed hope that other investigators, working in different institutional and community settings, will be responsive to these encouraging initial results and add relevant investigative findings of their own.

In this chapter we have sought to chart some promising directions such further research might take. ART, as an intervention oriented toward the reduction of the antisocial and the augmentation of the prosocial in human behavior, may now be profitably examined, we believe, as an in-community training effort, as but part of a larger, more comprehensive psychoeducational curriculum, in a more differentially prescriptive manner, and for its preventive, not only habilitative, potency. We hope others in the research community will join us in this challenging and important pursuit.

Chapter 10

Administrator's Manual for ART

The success of any juvenile justice program, whether it be community based or institutional, lies largely in its administration.* While there is relatively little in the literature that details specific administrative practices that are reliably successful for juvenile justice programming, some recent promising directions have emerged (B. Glick, 1983, 1986). Certainly, there may be key principles of administration that are applicable to all human services systems. However, theory aside, until there are some common tested and established standards to guide administrators of juvenile justice programs, what does exist will remain a potpourri of poorly validated administrative techniques, at best a vague folklore. In addition, progress in juvenile justice administration is hindered by insufficient communication and collaboration among juvenile justice administrators and the near absence of formal professional networking among such administrators in order to share learned skills or successful practices. Therefore, this manual is written for administrators of juvenile justice programs in order to provide initial guidelines for effective juvenile justice program administration, stimulate thoughts about practice of these guidelines, and stir discussion within a class of professionals often rich in implicit skill, yet still in their infancy of formal development. This manual examines the importance of an explicit program philosophy description, the multifaceted role of the administrator, a series of core administrative principles, and a number of implementation problems common in youth programming, along with suggested solutions.

PROGRAM PHILOSOPHY AND DESCRIPTION

The administrator's dream, one might think, is to be able to start from scratch and design and develop a program that does not yet exist, where there are no youths and no staff yet present. Administrators often suffer from what can be called the "if only" syndrome: If only I had more staff, if only there were more money allocated in the budget, if only I did not

---

*The authors wish to thank Daniel V. Gold, youth division counselor at Annsville Youth Center, for his contribution to this chapter.

have to deal with the youth advocates, if only there were no pressure to take more juveniles into the program, if only. . . . Contrary to both the administrator's dream and the "if only" syndrome, it is possible to develop an ambitious program at any point in time, even with limited resources, provided certain key principles are followed and judiciously maintained. Fundamental to any successful administration of a juvenile justice program is a clearly articulated philosophy. (See the Annsville Youth Center statement of philosophy and program description at the end of this chapter.)

Statement of Philosophy

While most administrators do have an implicit, often vague, philosophical framework from which they operate, rarely do administrators take the opportunity to fully think through their operating philosophy or develop a written philosophical statement of youth programming. Even if a philosophy is developed, it is rarely the product of dialogue among the program's policy managers. The administrator's statement of philosophy must be more than just a series of general goals and ethical statements. Optimally, it is a concrete, detailed, written discourse that includes the following topical areas: the nature of youth and the general characteristics of the targeted population served; the nature of staff and expected standards for staff behavior; a detailed description of the nature of the interactions required between youth and staff as well as staff and staff; and an overview of treatment.

More specifically, the nature of youth section in such a statement of philosophy should include perspectives about adolescents and their development. The subject matter should be specific to the population served by the program, and the physiological, psychological, and sociological structures upon which the youth program is developed. This section should, in large part, be based upon developmental theory and knowledge accumulated by researchers in the fields of adolescent development, juvenile justice, and youth aggression. This part of the administrator's statement provides the important context for the framework of program initiatives and operations. It is also within this context that the unique attributes of the adolescent population served by the program are articulated. Thus, the philosophical statement, at the very outset, sets the parameters for program differentiation and individual prescriptiveness.

A second section of the statement of philosophy ideally will deal with the nature of the staff that is to work within the program. The agency's "mission" (e.g., the New York State Division for Youth's Mission

Statement is "Preventing Delinquency through Positive Youth Development") must be translated by the administrator into the standards and expectations required of staff in order to effect positive changes within the adolescents placed in the institution. Such issues as staff roles, the identification of staff attitudes and behaviors, and interpersonal interactions among staff are but a few of the areas that the administrator must address.

Within the context of the nature of staff, there must also be a discussion of optimal youth-staff and staff-staff interactions. Since relationships are an integral part of the delinquent's rehabilitative process, interactions among staff as well as among staff and youth are an important part of the philosophical discussion prior to program development and implementation. For these purposes, the administrator must address ten basic characteristics of staff. These include the following:

- Involvement
- Initiative
- Understanding of self
- Understanding of others
- Openness (in communication and affect)
- Listening ability
- Use of feedback
- Ability to communicate
- Participation in decision-making processes
- Perseverance

Once such orienting statements are clearly articulated about youth and staff, the administrator must begin to address the rather broad area of treatment. Treatment within the context of any juvenile justice program must be defined as the *scientific, planned, organized, structured intervention* in the lives of delinquents in order to facilitate positive and healthy development. Thus, the administrative philosophical statement must address at least three core areas that comprise treatment. These are *evaluation*—assessment, *process*—the intervention used, and *outcome*—the results expected from the treatment interventions. The statement must be particularly specific with regard to assessment: For example, it should describe what areas will be assessed (e.g., vocational development, educational aptitude and achievement, mental abilities, perceptual levels), what instruments will be utilized, and how the assessment will be integrated into the total context of the program. The philosophy statement must detail the treatment strategies and specific interventions to be employed with specific references to relevant theory and techniques, as well as alternative outcomes and the means by which they will be measured.

Program Description

The program's statement of philosophy is one of the most important tasks the administrator must perform in any effort to design, develop, refine, or implement a juvenile justice program. Once developed and published, it is the benchmark from which a myriad of administrative work flows (e.g., program initiatives, staff development, administrative prerogative). The next responsibility of the administrator is to prepare and publish a program description. The program description reflects the facility's philosophy and is a detailed statement that describes who the target population is and how they will be served. Such information as the ages of the youth appropriate for admission, the geographical areas from which they are referred, the ethnic breakdown of the population within the institution, the types of criminal activities best addressed by the program, and the academic and vocational profiles of the residents are all appropriate details to be included in the beginning sections of a program description. It is also important to state those personality attributes that are not likely to be amenable to the program's intervention. This is critical, especially if a statement was included in the program philosophy that espoused the importance of program differentiation and individual prescriptiveness.

After the population is described in relevant detail, the administrator must then articulate the program components and units of service. These areas may include descriptions of the program's counseling, educational, health, and residential services, as well as recreation, religious, and other available resources. Description of these systems may include generic "levels" methodology that systematically moves adolescents from their entry into the program through exit and return to either home, community, or transfer to another facility.

Vital features of the program description, both in spirit and detail, are *safety* and *security*. Without an environment that is safe and secure, there is no rehabilitation, there is no treatment, there is no program. Predictably, there is chaos. It is the administrator's chief responsibility to create an environment that is safe and secure in order for both staff and residents to grow and develop. The primary task, if the administrator is to be successful in achieving the program's mission and goals, is to communicate to the staff and the residents the essence of safety and security. The administrator accomplishes this task in a variety of ways.

First, it is incumbent upon the administrator to verbally state in a variety of forums the importance of safety and security. It must be public knowledge what the administrator demands of residents and staff, what the consequences for infractions are, and how the actions of youth and/ or staff will be met. For example, if the administrator states that no physical aggression will be tolerated within the facility, then the administrator must be willing to follow through with stringent consequences for that violation of safety and security. The administrator must be prepared to press charges against a resident or staff member if the principle of safety and security is violated in this manner. At the very least, the administrator must be willing to implement those administrative processes available to hold staff and youth accountable for violations.

Second, the administrator must articulate the central importance of safety and security through facility policy and directives. And he must be able to implement and manage these policies, procedures, and directives.

Third, the administrator must be able to translate the issues of safety and security into tangible program operations. These include expectations for staff communicated through a system of performance evaluations that specify work expectations and criterion standards for satisfactory performance. Thus, child-care workers, teachers, recreation leaders, administrators, indeed, all staff, will clearly know what is routinely expected of them. Once these standards are identified, the administrator then has the responsibility to ensure via training and supervision that staff are competent in the various safety- and security-relevant tasks required of them.

Fourth, the administrator must also be able to communicate the safety and security issues in concrete fashion to the facility residents. These behavioral expectations, or program norms, must specifically address each aspect of the program and detail the residents' expected behavior required within each program component. The administrator must provide these behavioral expectations in measurable, observable terms for every program area. To develop this list of program "norms," the facility administrator can rely on the program philosophy and program description to systematically define behavioral expectations. Specifically the following program components need to be delineated:

- Youth movement (includes moving between program areas, demeanor, and conversation)
- Language (tone of voice, use of profanity)
- Wake up (personal hygiene, cleanup, breakfast)

- Dining room (receiving food, order of service, tray pickup, delivery)
- Clean up (chores, inspections)
- Classroom (attendance, punctuality, curricula assignments, school decorum)
- Vocational program (use of equipment, stipend jobs)
- Quiet time (leisure time)
- Group and individual counseling
- Recreation (assigned activities, participation)
- Off-campus trips/activities
- Bedtime (personal hygiene, relaxation, lights out)
- Snacks
- Residential and living areas
- Infirmary and sick call

THE ADMINISTRATOR

Once the population description, program definition, and safety/security measures for staff and youth are developed and disseminated throughout the facility, it is the role and responsibility of the facility administrator to translate this philosophy and its consequent program into concrete, functional, operational action. The manner in which the administrator delivers these messages to both staff and residents is critical in setting the tone and climate upon which the programs and services will function and develop. The philosophy and the program description, once articulated, must be restated frequently and consistently by the administrative team if the juvenile justice program is to be successful. Considerable attention needs to be paid to the administrator since the quality of services to residents and standards for program excellence are influenced greatly, for better or worse, by the attributes of the administrator.

What kind of manager is best suited to administer a juvenile justice program? Is there a particular style of management that enhances the juvenile justice program environment so that it operates at maximum efficiency? Certainly the literature is replete with answers to these questions (unlike the program administration practices issues), and some researchers have even critically analyzed the state of the art (Glick, 1986). The experiences of administrators and staff within the New York State Division for Youth and other private child-caring agencies suggest a profile for facility administrators that is amenable to juvenile justice program operations. The following administrator characteristics have been clearly relevant to the successful implementation of the program described in Chapter 8.

Personal Attributes

Staff and residents respond well to administrators who have integrity and a well-established and well-disseminated philosophy for operating youth programs, are proactive rather than reactive when problems arise, and consistently behave with equity and fairness. It may be that the successful juvenile justice administrator is a Boy or Girl Scout graduate in the best sense of the word, in that the administrator is prepared, honest, courteous, and kind. The type of integrity a juvenile justice administrator needs goes beyond the question of choosing "right" and "wrong" to the issue of how high a standard or criterion for right the administrator will choose. The juvenile justice administrator optimally has a well-established credo so that as issues arise there is little doubt as to the administrator's position or that the administrator will be willing to clearly argue that position, yet be willing to listen and change direction if appropriate. The juvenile justice administrator should possess relevant proactive skills and therefore be able to deal effectively with daily problems. The skilled administrator is less likely to have to react to problem situations without due deliberation and is able to take action logically, systematically, and with the benefit of prior anticipation and preparation. Finally, the successful juvenile justice program administrator enjoys a reputation among staff and residents of being consistently fair with issues as well as people. Thus, there is ideally an aura of predictability as the administrator implements the daily operations of the program.

Support of Staff

One of the primary roles of the facility administrator is to establish an environment in which staff can grow and develop, both professionally and personally. It is the role of the administrator and of every supervisor within the facility (including child-care workers, for they are supervisors for the youth) *to be advocates for their subordinates.* Advocating here means to provide the very best situation to foster growth and development by setting high, but achievable, standards; assigning tasks that are challenging; providing rewards that are attainable; and requiring responsible and fair accountability of performance.

Optimism

Yet another important message staff must receive from the facility administrator is the message of hope and optimism. Juvenile justice staff are in a high-pressure often thankless job that frequently leads to feelings of helplessness, if not defeat. It is incumbent upon the administrator to express to staff in very real terms that *for every problem, there is a solution*. Staff need not despair with problems, but should vigorously seek alternatives through a logical, concrete problem-solving model. It is possible in a very practical way for administrators to model hope, optimism, and enthusiasm as they go about their daily work.

Planning and Implementation

Perhaps one of the more important qualities the facility administrator must possess is the ability to balance the day-to-day operations of the program while at the same time providing supervisors and middle managers with future-oriented leadership and direction for continued program development. It is crucial that the administrator constantly remind staff how important they are to the daily operations of the program, because they are the people who can free the administrator to fill the role of long-term "planner." It is desirable, therefore, for the administrator to remind staff that their energies are focused on the here and now, while the administrator concentrates on issues 6 to 9 months in the future. The ability of the facility administrator to manage the tension between immediate needs and long-range plans directly influences the success of program implementation, staff development, new initiatives, and problem resolution.

Delegation of Responsibility

Yet one final attribute the program administrator must possess is the ability to delegate responsibilities with authority and accountability. It is important that administrators relieve themselves of tasks that can be accomplished by other staff, so that attention can be focused on planning, monitoring, managing, and directing. However, the administrator must be willing to delegate responsibility with commensurate authority so as not to undermine the chain of command or other organizational structure that is functional within the institution. Accountability is maintained as the administrator monitors, provides feedback to staff, trains, and appropriately interacts with supervisors and middle managers. Now that a number of the desirable qualities and attributes of the facility administrator have been identified, the administrative principles that are the underpinnings of a successful juvenile justice program will be examined.

ADMINISTRATIVE PRINCIPLES

Principles of effective administration must be responsive to relevant features of the system in which they will be utilized. Thus the development of such principles must begin by a careful examination of the system. How is the system structured? Who is responsible for what? What are the lines of communication? How are problems identified and resolved? All of these questions are fundamental to the development of an effective juvenile justice program. The administrator must answer each of these questions decisively and deliberately. All of the answers must be a logical extension of the statement of philosophy that has been developed and published.

There are certain systems principles that are central to the administration of quality programs and services. The following principles have evolved from the participatory management system adopted at Annsville Youth Center.

Principle 1: No Pain, No Gain

Simply stated, this principle asserts that there can be no staff growth and development without some pain, discomfort, or distress experienced by the staff through the process of growth. While this may seem contradictory to all that has been said before, it really is not. Pain does not imply punishment, nor does it imply malice. In this context, it is an admission that if the administrator truly wishes to provide an environment for staff to grow and develop and is interested in staff professional advancement, then it is incumbent upon that administrator to take whatever action is necessary to meet those objectives. For example, many administrators agonize over progressive disciplinary action taken toward staff in the hope of extinguishing inappropriate behavior. Many administrators conduct supervisory meetings or investigatory proceedings to begin to develop the necessary staff attitude or work ethic. And many staff express frustration with either the system or themselves as they gain new skills and knowledge.

Principle 2: Give Respect to Get Respect

There is a New Testament teaching that states: "Do unto others as you would have them do unto you." It is a basic administrative principle that mandates that one must treat others with respect. Respect should be shown by the administrator for the staff members' job knowledge, skill level, and position. Respect also implies esteem for oneself and one's position, accomplishments, and productivity. The interaction between the administrator's perception of the staff and the staff members' self-perception creates a mutual respect for position and job function. When staff members are able to fully understand their own position and function, no matter what position they have within the organization, then they may freely give and receive feedback with dignity, without fear, and without the feeling of being threatened. Thus, respect includes one's reputation with others as well as one's feelings of pride about oneself. When respect is given freely, very often it is reciprocated.

Principle 3: Acknowledge Effort, Reward Results

One of the most difficult responsibilities of a juvenile justice administrator is to evaluate the performance of staff. Objectivity is obviously critical as staff receive feedback relative to what they do and how well they do it. Administrators often give confusing or unnecessarily negative messages to employees relative to their work performance, including skill development levels, ability, and productivity. A closer look at communication between the administrator and staff often reflects that administrators do not adequately differentiate between effort and achievement. How often do employees receive "outstanding" ratings on job evaluations even though they do only what is expected of them? In addition, it is often the case that the supervisor has rated the employee's motivation or willingness rather than actual performance. That case is reflected in such comments as these: "This employee is always willing to try to complete the tasks in an outstanding manner" or "This employee always tries to do the very best job all of the time." These statements reflect effort, and ought not to be considered evaluation for work productivity. The administrator must be able to separate the employee's willingness from the employee's ability. In the same vein, the supervisor needs to be clear about those issues that reflect the employees' attitude and affect, as well as those that are objective work outcomes. The guideword then for the facility administrator is to reinforce among all supervisory personnel the need to recognize and acknowledge effort and motivation among staff and positively reinforce and reward employees as they achieve goals and objectives.

Principle 4: Bureaucracies Complicate
What Staff Make Simple

Every system, every organization, no matter how large or small, creates its own bureaucratic structure within which it operates. Juvenile justice administrators often have a tendency to complicate things. As one climbs the administrative ladder within an organization, the tendency to complicate often simple matters seems to increase. Add to that the frequently found division of roles and responsibilities, and it is no surprise that many administrations accomplish little or no problem solving.

What is crucial is the degree to which the facility administrator is able to concretely, simply, and with crisp and concise communication, take action. At Annsville, the administrator often reminds managers that one of the administrator's roles is to be 6 months ahead of where first line and middle managers are. Thus it makes it easier for the managers to put the administrator's comments into longer term perspective and keep operational, day-to-day goals clear and targeted. Another similar technique is for administrators to restate and clarify the differences between system-wide (e.g., agency) issues, agendas, and problems, as opposed to organization-wide (facility or institution) concerns.

Principle 5: Administrative Tolerance for Organized Ambiguity Is Necessary to Maximize Organizational Flexibility and Program Tolerance

This principle begins with the premise that one of the primary responsibilities of the facility administrator is planning. It is the facility administrator who is responsible for formulating goals, directing energy toward the completion of objectives, and ensuring that all staff efforts are on target. In order to do this successfully, the facility administrator must be able to keep in balance a variety of goals and program initiatives, while at the same time directing staff activity toward specific day-to-day outcomes. Many times the balance between the two needs seems contradictory. It is this tension that often creates a sense of ambiguity for managers within the organization. Often staff want immediate answers to questions they ask or solutions to problems they pose. The administrator may know the long-term answer or general direction to point staff for problem resolution, but often must refrain from giving information and purposefully causes ambiguity within the organization. If problem resolution information and direction are given too soon, the administrator may stifle staff members' creativity, and the participatory management style may be sacrificed. This is but an example of what the administrator must deal with on a daily basis. Withholding information or direction does create tension and perpetuate dissonance, but, when done carefully, creates an environment that maximizes staff's ability to generate program alternatives and enhance organizational flexibility.

Principle 6: The More, the Merrier When It Comes to Problem Solving, Policy Development, and Program Initiatives

The Annsville bias is that the administrator build an administrative model that values broad participation of staff. Further, the administrative system needs to communicate explicitly to staff that there is an open, accessible, responsible team of managers able and willing to listen. The participatory model of administration solicits input from all staff at all levels within the institution and cuts across supervisory lines as well as organizational units. The result, when properly managed, is an environment in which morale of staff is high, there is ownership of task and accomplishment, productivity and performance level of staff is above standard, and there is an abundance of new ideas and creativity. The administrator who adopts a participatory model of administration must have a tolerance for dialogue and debate of issues, not be threatened by challenges from subordinates, and be nonthreatening to subordinates who desire to participate. Further, the administrator must be willing and able to change positions, alter opinions, consider alternatives, and reverse decisions (based upon input from staff) without compromising policy or authority.

Systems responsive to the philosophy presented need not be meek or unaccountable. In fact, such systems allow greater flexibility for administrators by incorporating such features as standards for successful achievement, criteria for optimal performance, tolerance for error, and value of learning, as well as expectations for continued program growth and personnel development. It is incumbent upon the administrator to integrate appropriate management style, supervisory protocol, personnel resources, and administrative principles so as to guarantee the best of quality service to the residents and an attractive learning environment for staff.

While there are basic models of administration that have been traditionally used within human services systems, the administrator of the juvenile justice program must take great care to develop a model specific to the program or service that must be managed. One must be vigilant to avoid adopting an administrative model out of convenience because of supervisory pressure or because of tradition. On the contrary, the administrator needs to design, develop, or adapt an administrative model/system based upon the mission, people, and environment of the particular institution. We have shared these principles of sound administration in order to represent but one perspective. We leave to individual readers the task of selecting and modifying these principles to fit their own context and needs.

IMPLEMENTATION PROBLEMS

Organizing the Idea

One of the first problems that the Annsville facility administration faced vis à vis the Aggression Replacement Training concept was how to organize the idea into an operational program: how to take the ideal and translate it into what was practical, given the parameters of the existing program, budget, personnel resources, and political realities. The strategy used for solving this problem follows.

Strategy

The Annsville administration began by stating the issue as clearly and concisely as possible. Special attention was paid to the philosophy statement and program description developed earlier in order to state Annsville's needs and how the new program would respond to the facility's mission and objective. In general, the administrative team attempted to specify what was required to provide a quality service to the residents. They also articulated their next steps clearly and targeted actions.

Research developments at Syracuse University paralleled program interests of the Annsville administration and thus the beginning of a collaborative, working relationship was initiated. This collaborative effort provided the foundation upon which the ART program eventually was formulated and implemented.

After contact with Syracuse University was made and a collaborative effort begun, the next step was to organize a functioning planning group. The facility's administrative team served as the planning group, along with the university researchers. The planning group's task was to take the basic program and develop a practical implementation plan. In other words, once the basic nature of ART was developed, the purpose of the group was to answer such questions as how to present the program to staff and residents, how to involve staff and then residents in the program, and how to initiate and maintain enthusiasm. The planning group needed to deal with a spectrum of issues that included program development, tactical implementation, integration of research needs of the university and program services to residents, as well as unplanned problems that evolved.

As the planning group convened, both on a frequent regular schedule and an ad hoc basis, all members became increasingly aware of group dynamics. Such issues as task versus relationship, productivity, cohesion, and role conflict all needed attention. As the group met together, it became evident that a series of roles developed that in retrospect were critical dynamics of a planning effort of this type. Once the group was cognizant of these roles, members contributed significantly from their own skill and technical knowledge, but, more importantly, provided a consistent function to the group that was predictable. These role functions, whose descriptions follow, also proved useful when the group needed to make assignments and divide task responsibilities.

The dreamer is an individual who possesses the ability to be abstract and conceptualize ideas. He is not blocked by obstacles, perceived or real (such as staff resource issues or budget constraints), organizational or functional, but motivates the planning group members through expressions of what should be and potentially can be. He frequently encourages and supports creative, individual expression of thoughts and ideas. As the identified leader of the group, the dreamer exhibits an administrative tolerance for dissent in order to maximize flexibility and broaden program alternatives. In effect, the dreamer is able to implement administrative Principles 2 (Give Respect to Get Respect) and 5 (Administrative Tolerance for Organized Ambiguity is Necessary to Maximize Organizational Flexibility and Program Tolerance).

The strategizer is a creative individual who is able to identify several alternatives and define these choices in a concrete fashion. Her contribution is to translate the dreamer's concepts into less abstract terms. She assists in forming a healthy socioemotional climate by maintaining the balance between the task-oriented individuals and the more abstract conceptualizers. The strategizer often uses administrative Principle 3 (Acknowledge Effort, Reward Results) most effectively.

The pragmatist assists in the maintenance of the process through the ability to identify problems, obstacles, and resources. He, like the strategizer, is adept at maintaining a balance within the group between the ideal and the real. In addition, the pragmatist provides a critical analysis of the suggestions presented by the strategizer and the concepts provided by the dreamer. The pragmatist relies upon administrative Principles 1 (No Pain, No Gain) and 3 (Acknowledge Effort, Reward Results) in order to accomplish his role.

The implementer possesses the special skills and abilities necessary to translate the chosen strategy into reality. This individual is a logistics person who reasons logically, objectively, and concretely and can balance the parameters of program budget as well as personnel resources. The implementer relies on administrative Principle 4 (Bureaucracies Complicate What Staff Make Simple) to get things done.

After the planning group was selected, one of the most important things the administrative team did was to agree upon a planning process. The planning process dictated a structured, organized approach to problem identification and resolution that facilitated the group's ability to remain task-oriented and productive. The system adopted for use is the "Problem Identification Model." A worksheet (Figure 6) was developed to structure energy and to allow enlightened, informed decisions that capitalized on maximum input from the greatest number of participants to be made.

By definition, a problem is a situation or condition that is undesirable and should be improved. It is the gap that exists between what is and

Figure 6. Problem Identification Worksheet

1 RE: _____

DECISION
CENTER: _____

CONTACT
PERSON: _____

PHONE: _____

NEW YORK STATE
DIVISION FOR YOUTH
ANNSVILLE YOUTH CENTER

ATTN: _____

2 PROBLEM STATEMENT (Brief summary of what is wrong. Include supporting data, if available.)

☐ Continued on back)

5 POLICY GOAL (Ideal state of problem correction.)

3 POSSIBLE CAUSES (What or who is the source of the problem?)

4 EFFECTS (What are the consequences of the problem?)

DIRECT (Primary):

INDIRECT (Secondary):

6 CURRENT EFFORTS (What is being done about the problem now?)

7 POSSIBLE STRATEGIES (What can be done to address the cause(s) or effect(s) of the problem?)

261

what should be. The problem statement (see section 2 of Figure 6) should focus on the nature and magnitude of the problem (using appropriate data where possible), the status and progress of the problem (is it getting larger or smaller, better or worse), how long the problem has existed, why it is a problem, and who is affected by the problem.

In section 3 (see Figure 6) who and what caused the problem are described. It is important to answer such questions as "What are the major factors contributing to the problem?"; "Why have these factors caused or created the problem?"; "Who or what is involved in the cause of the problem?"; and "Are the causes internal or external to the facility?"

The effects section (section 4) of the Problem Identification Worksheet should indicate the negative or undesired impact or consequences of the problem. The direct, or primary, effects of the problem indicate who or what is directly affected by the problem, how they are affected, and to what degree they are affected. The indirect, or secondary, effects indicate those consequences that result from the direct effect of the problem. Impact on other groups or units within the facility, as well as how this problem relates to other problems, should also be identified in this section.

The policy goal (section 5) states the general or overall result that should be achieved and identifies what *should be* done in order to eliminate the problem; it is the long-range accomplishment that is to be achieved over time. It is important that the goal statement include an action verb (e.g., to improve, to increase, to decrease, to eliminate) and a clear result to be achieved.

The current efforts section (section 6) describes what is presently being done about the problem. This statement should include what the facility is doing about the problem, what other groups are doing about the problem, and a brief description of results. The possible strategies section (section 7) is a complete list of the different ways in which the problem may be resolved. Any reasonable strategy that will change the undesirable situation, either partially or entirely, should be identified. The strategy list should be a logical result of the causes and/or results described in the problem statement. Strategies need to be reasonable, feasible, defensible, and implementable. As many strategies as possible should be listed, in order of priority.

The planning process we have just described is important to learn and must be used, practiced, and monitored in order for it to become a useful tool. The use of this planning model facilitated the planning group's effort to design and implement ART in a relatively short time period.

Getting Administrative Approval

Even when an innovative, creative idea exists, one that appears to be useful to the facility program and likely to increase the quality of service to residents, getting administrative approval for the idea is often a problem. The central office administration has different focuses than a facility, and if the system is decentralized, the regional administration may have yet a third viewpoint. How the facility administration gets the necessary permission to implement the program is critical to the program's initiation and use.

Strategy

The Annsville facility administration was eager to implement ART without unnecessary delay. There was substantial fear that administrative Principle 4 (Bureaucracies Complicate What Staff Make Simple) could cause the loss of the opportunity to implement ART. Indeed, there was time pressure in the form of the beginning of the academic year at the university as well as the school year in the facility. The planning group designed a 10-week ART intervention in a time frame that, with few exceptions, precluded holidays and included an uninterrupted block of time. Once the internal capabilities of the facility as well as the external realities of the Division for Youth and the State were assessed, the group proceeded as follows.

The group prepared and communicated a clear statement to administrative superiors regarding the nature of the program and its desirability. The statement included a series of Problem Identification Worksheets that defined what agency and regional objectives were being addressed, as well as the results expected in terms of services to residents.

Next, the group prepared an implementation plan. This included a timetable for accomplishing the details of the program. Information about activities, implementers, and time needed, as well as desired outcomes, was necessary. The ART Implementation Plan (see Figure 7) also included a statement of additional resources being sought in order to accomplish the tasks of the project.

The facility administration also gave the regional managers and agency administrators two specific assurances. First, the facility director guaranteed that the introduction of the ART program would not compromise the safety and security of the residents in the facility or the staff. Second, the regional and central office managers were told that no additional or new monies would be requested in order to implement the program.

Figure 7.

Task/Activity	3/84	4/84	5/84	6/84	7/84	8/84	9/84	10/84	11/84	12/84	1/85
Develop Concept, Gain Approvals	▓	▓									
Develop Facility Objectives		▓									
Develop Grant Proposal			▓								
Convene Planning Group				▓							
Train Staff							▓				
Pretest Youth							▓				
ART Program—Two Treatment Groups								▓	▓	▓	
Posttest Youth										▓	▓
Train Remainder of Staff											▓
ART Program—Entire Facility											
Posttest First and Second Groups of Youth											
Transition Planning											
Ongoing ART Programming											

The ART Implementation Plan

2/85	3/85	4/85	5/85	6/85	7/85	8/85	9/85	10/85	11/85	12/85	Individual Responsible/Comments
											Facility Director, University Collaborator
											Facility Director
											University Collaborator
											Facility Administration
											Facility Director, University Collaborator
											University Collaborators, Facility Staff, Volunteers
											Counselors, Youth Division Aides
											University Collaborators, Volunteers, Facility Staff
											University Collaborator
▓	▓	▓									Counselors, Youth Division Aides, Teachers
		▓									Volunteers, Facility Staff
				▓	▓	▓	▓				Planning Group
								▓	▓	▓	Facility Staff

265

Setting the Climate

The planning group faced the same challenge as most juvenile justice administrators when implementing a new program: how to establish an appropriate environment in order to promote and nurture the development of the program. It is Annsville's stated philosophy (see end of chapter) that administrators have the task of creating a physical and psychological environment in which new ideas and initiatives may prosper and in which staff can grow and develop. An appropriate analogy, since Annsville is located in rural farm land of upstate New York and many of the staff hail from farms, is the climate needed for newly sown seeds to grow, develop, and prosper. A poor climate will yield a crop failure in farming; a poor climate in a facility will yield failure to meet program mission, goals, and objectives. Thus, the planning group took a number of steps to create an optimal climate for the new program to prosper, an effort directed toward both staff and residents.

Strategy

A series of general staff meetings were held. Involved in these staff meetings were counselors, teachers, youth division aides, secretaries, maintenance persons, cooks, and medical staff, that is, essentially all facility staff as well as the university researchers (see administrative Principle 6—The More, the Merrier When It Comes to Problem Solving, Policy Development, and Program Initiatives). At the meetings, philosophy and mission were reviewed with staff and how ART would contribute to the achievement of these stated program goals was discussed. Staff concerns regarding how the program would affect the residents, as well as their own roles and responsibilities were explored. These meetings provided staff with a forum to discuss issues so that they would not view the implementation of a new program as an additional burden that would extend their obligation to the facility or their working hours or offer them only abstract, impractical tools. It was important to demonstrate the participatory model of administration and have staff perceive that their input was desired, necessary, and useful. Further, it was the administration's desire to have staff view the ART program as an opportunity to acquire new skills that would contribute to their developing into more effective professionals within the juvenile justice system.

It was just as important to establish an appropriate climate for residents. To generate enthusiasm, excitement, and acceptance among residents for the ART program, a sense of anticipation was created among them. An ambitious publicity campaign that included fliers, posters, and news announcements suggested something new and unprecedented was coming to Annsville. Posters were designed by residents and placed in conspicuous places (e.g., dining hall, educational wing, dormitory areas). Counselors were instructed to use their group counseling sessions to begin discussing with residents a special program beginning just at Annsville, just for Annsville youth. The program was described to residents as one that would help them to deal more effectively with anger. Anticipation was further heightened by the fact that residents were informed that at least initially not all units were going to be selected for the ART program. As the beginning of ART grew closer, new posters and fliers replaced those that merely promised something new was coming to Annsville. The something new was given a name; residents were informed that "Angerbusters" was coming. In making a concerted effort to establish a climate that increased participation, alleviated concerns, and heightened anticipation, the planning group received a bountiful harvest of enthusiasm, willingness, and commitment—certainly from staff and, more ambivalently, from residents too.

Identifying and Selecting Staff

Another element that was vital to the success of ART was the ability of the planning group to identify and select motivated staff members capable of leading effective Structured Learning, Anger Control Training, or Moral Education groups. Such questions as how to select staff and how to assign staff to the program who were *willing* and *able* to make a contribution to the research and program goals of the project needed to be resolved.

Strategy

The planning group at Annsville first sought to identify those skills that staff needed to possess in order to implement ART effectively. This assessment was completed separately for each program component.

Structured Learning was formally designated by the education supervisor to be acceptable as part of the affective education curriculum required by the New York State Education Department. Thus, teachers and youth division aides, who are regularly scheduled to assist teachers during school hours, were chosen as the groups from which to select the Structured Learning trainers.

The trainer competencies required for Anger Control Training are closely related to those relevant for behavior management. Since Division for Youth counselors and youth division aides (child-care workers) are assigned the job responsibility of resident behavior management, and indeed are usually technical experts in this domain, the planning group decided to select Anger Control trainers from this core of individuals.

In order to conduct Moral Education sessions, an individual must possess the ability to conceptualize and comprehend abstract concepts and categorize such concepts with aptitude and fluency. The planning group wanted to identify staff who had such abstract reasoning abilities, could synthesize information and ideas, interpret discussions within a group quickly, and be verbally proficient.

Once potentially effective staff for each ART component had been identified, they were provided with an interest survey form which they were requested to complete. The planning group reemphasized that this first round of the ART program was voluntary and that those staff who were interested in participating should select the component that had the most appeal for them. One goal in doing so was to maintain the positive climate that was established in the facility among staff and residents. It was imperative that the enthusiasm, energy, and optimism already created be sustained.

After collecting the surveys, the planning group reviewed the survey forms and matched individual interests with earlier estimates of which staff members would likely be proficient in which ART components. Thus, a combination of self-selection as well as administration's knowledge of individual staff member's strengths and skills was employed in selecting trainers from the counselor, teacher, and youth division aide staff.

Identifying and Selecting Residents

The identification and selection of residents posed a greater challenge for the planning group. The group had to determine how to maintain the safety and security of the residents and the staff within the facility and still implement an effective program, which of the residents were to be involved, how to integrate program needs with research requirements, and how to ethically offer the program to some residents and not other residents.

Strategy

Annsville Youth Center has a resident population of 60 youths who range in age from 14 to 17 years. Annsville endorses a team, or unit, concept with 5 units of 12 youth each. A youth division counselor is designated "unit manager" and is responsible for providing direct services to youth assigned to that unit. Counselors also provide supervision to the youth division aides assigned to their unit.

As the selection process for residents began, counselors collected data relative to residents' length of stay and projected release dates. Thus the group could plan for the research requirement that youths in the treatment units (those involved with ART) remain in the program for at least the 12 weeks necessary to complete pretesting, intervention, and posttesting. Based upon this information, the planning group reassigned three youths to other units (not selected for ART) who were scheduled for release during the first phase of the program. New admissions were randomly assigned to the two treatment units. In selecting the treatment units, the planning group consciously set a goal to retain the integrity of the existing program and thus integrated the three types of ART classes into the facility's ongoing academic and vocational class schedule, as well as group counseling sessions.

Motivating Residents

It was not enough to pique the interest of residents who were selected to participate in ART without addressing the issue of how to keep the residents involved until they developed their own intrinsic value for and interest in the program. The planning group's concern was how to motivate residents already interested as well as increase the involvement of those who apparently had little or no desire to participate.

Strategy

Since the goal was to enhance the motivation of those residents already participating in ART, as well as to increase the desire to participate of residents who were not part of the original research project but who were to become involved as the project was integrated throughout the entire facility, the planning group carefully designed and selected several reinforcement strategies. Reinforcers were introduced gradually, according to a schedule that was sensitive to program issues, safety and security standards, and resident needs.

The first reinforcer, one that was predictably potent, was to provide each group with an off-grounds pizza party for every two homework assignments completed when at least five youths in a unit had done so. A second action taken to motivate residents was to post the Structured Learning Skill of the Week in the facility log room (a place where all staff must be sometime during their shift) as well as the team counseling offices (a place where residents convened during the day). Staff, whether they were directly involved in teaching ART or not, were encouraged to verbally commend residents when they saw them using the skill appropriately. Staff were also encouraged to remind residents of the skill knowledge that they possessed and to help them practice their newly learned skills in appropriate situations.

In order to more systematically teach staff how to reward skilled resident behaviors, The Transfer Coach (see Appendix B) was developed and distributed. Team meetings, general staff meetings, and one-on-one supervision were used to involve all staff in this effort. Building on the spirit of The Transfer Coach, controlled situations were planned in which residents would experience success in using their newly acquired skills outside of the training context. In one instance, a youth counselor was aware that a youth assigned to his team had a complaint regarding a broken drawer on his bed. The counselor reviewed the skill "Expressing a Complaint" with the youth and then helped him identify the most appropriate person to whom the complaint should be expressed, in this case the maintenance person. Prior to the youth's approaching the maintenance person, the counselor contacted the latter and made him aware that the youth would be seeking him out in order to express his complaint. By setting up the situation, the counselor ensured an appropriate response to the skill trial. The appropriate staff response and a repaired drawer were thus reinforcers for the youth, ensuring that he would continue using this skill.

The natural propensity for youth to form groups was also used as a reinforcer. In this case the planning group encouraged a prosocial gang, the "Angerbusters" and gave an Angerbuster T-shirt to every resident who completed the 10-week program. The black T-shirt with the red emblem was awarded to each trainee in a special ceremony by the facility director (Dr. Glick) and the university collaborator (Dr. Goldstein). Finally, each trainee was presented with a Certificate of Achievement (see Figure 8), again in a special ceremony, as they completed the basic 10-week curriculum. The facility director also took time at special events, such as the facility Christmas party, the summer picnic, or the fall Olympics, to recognize those residents who had completed the program during the preceding time period.

Scheduling

Proper scheduling is an essential part of any successful program. The logistics of staff training, resident testing, and implementation of a new program must be well planned. How to transform program goals into operational realities, what implementation was possible given the resources available, how to keep overtime costs at a minimum, and how to complement existing programs without depleting personnel are some of the questions that needed to be addressed. Described next are

Figure 8. Certificate of Achievement

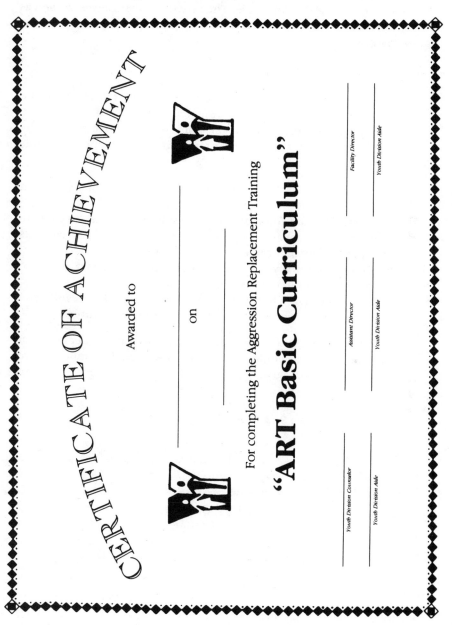

271

the staff training, resident testing, and program implementation schedules utilized for ART at Annsville. The schedules themselves, as well as the concerns and problems encountered in their development, are also provided.

Strategy

Staff training schedule. Once the staff had been selected for the program, a training schedule was designed to provide them with the background knowledge and hands-on skills necessary to implement the program (Figure 9). Of prime importance in the development of this schedule were the following:

1. How many staff should be trained in each program component at one time?
2. How many staff could be removed from the regular work schedule without jeopardizing the safety and security of the residents and still maintain regular programming?
3. Could temporary services staff be used to avoid overtime expenditures to cover required shifts?
4. Could the staff who were trained be scheduled for training on their regular work days to avoid overtime expenditures?

In view of Annsville's limited staffing capability, it was decided that small training groups would be optimal. Eight staff members were trained as Structured Learning group leaders. A total of four staff were

Figure 9. ART Staff Training Schedule

Training	Monday	Tuesday	Wednesday	Thursday	Friday
Structured Learning	Group A 9 A.M.–5 P.M.	Group A 9 A.M.–5 P.M.			
Anger Control Training		Group B 9 A.M.–5 P.M.	Group B 9 A.M.–5 P.M.		
Moral Education				Group C 9 A.M.–5 P.M.	Group C 9 A.M.–5 P.M.

Key
Group A—Four teachers and four youth division aides
Group B—Two youth division counselors and four youth division aides
Group C—Two youth division counselors and four youth division aides

actually needed for the two classes, but double the required number were scheduled for training to ensure that a reserve of trainers was available. For the Anger Control Training and Moral Education components, groups of six staff members each were used with two staff members identified as reserve trainers. Each training session was planned as a 2-day session, 8 hours each day. This allowed sufficient time for the trainers to become familiar with their component of the ART program procedures, materials, and format. The training schedule also allowed ample time for staff to practice and lead mock groups. The training for the three components was scheduled during a 1-week time frame and was offered the week before the program began with the residents.

Where possible, staff were trained on regular work days to avoid overtime expenditures. Temporary services staff were reassigned to cover gaps created in scheduling. By making these adjustments, the use of overtime was unnecessary. Alternative class activities were planned and two substitute teachers were called in to allow four of the regular teachers to be trained. Overall during the training, regular program activities were maintained, minimum staffing requirements were realized, and the training sessions were successfully implemented without major costs or program disruption.

Resident testing schedule. In order to evaluate the effectiveness of ART at Annsville, all 60 of the residents were pre- and posttested on measures relevant to the three components of the program (see Figure 10). This testing effort posed special problems of consistency and staff-

Figure 10. ART Youth Testing Schedule

Time	Monday	Tuesday	Wednesday	Thursday	Friday
9–10 A.M.	I_a SL	III_a SL	V_a SL	II_a ME	IV_a ME
10:30–11:30 A.M.	I_b SL	III_b SL	V_b SL	II_b ME	IV_b ME
2–3 P.M.	II_a SL	IV_a SL	I_a ME	III_a ME	V_a ME
3:30–4:30 P.M.	II_b SL	IV_b SL	I_b ME	III_b ME	V_b ME

Key

Team I, II, III, IV, V—Each number represents one team of 12 residents. Each subscript (e.g., I_a, I_b) represents a team subgroup of 6 residents.

SL—Structured Learning test.

ME—Moral Education test.

ing. However, a testing schedule was developed and the necessary staffing organized for implementation.

The greatest challenge was presented by the requirements of the tests designed to measure the direct effects of Structured Learning and Moral Education. An adult recorder was needed to write down the verbatim responses of each resident to the tape recording of situational questions for each component that was played to him. Finding people to do the recording and scheduling residents for testing were concerns. Funding the available manpower to accomplish this task was prohibitive, and so the planning group sought outside assistance. Volunteers, university students, advisory board members, and support staff were all used to accomplish the one-on-one recording task. The facility chaplain solicited volunteers during community church services. University students were recruited by university colleagues. The facility director announced the need for resources at the monthly advisory board meetings. Support staff included personnel from the administrative/business office, maintenance, food services, and health services. All were identified as possible resources to accomplish the testing tasks. Once a group of recorders was identified and available the testing schedule was finalized. Residents were tested in groups of six at a time. The testing period lasted 1 hour, and made it possible to test two groups each morning and afternoon, Monday through Friday. The 60 residents were divided into 10 groups of 6 residents each to be individually tested. It took 5 days to test the total facility population. Designing the schedule in this way allowed the volunteers to sign up for time slots for which they were available at their convenience.

The testing completed by persons other than the residents themselves was less difficult to implement. The youth division counselors assigned to each of the five residential teams completed the Kendall-Wilcox Behavior Rating Scale, the study's measure of impulsiveness, for each of the residents on their unit. Each week, a youth division aide on each unit completed a Behavior Incident Report—Form A, for each resident, as the study's ongoing measure of acting-out behavior. All the required testing was completed the week preceding and the week following the ART intervention. It was done efficiently and inexpensively. Scheduling residents for testing in small groups did not cause any major interruptions to the regular program. Matching available resources with scheduling needs proved to be the most effective implementation plan to accomplish the testing.

Program schedule. Once the residents had been selected and pretested for the program, the planning group developed a schedule in order to establish when the residents' classes would be conducted. The program intervention was designed for 10 weeks, exclusive of the pre- and posttesting. In designing the program schedule, the following conditions were required:

1. Each resident was to receive one class in Structured Learning Training, Anger Control Training, and Moral Education each week.
2. Structured Learning Training and Anger Control Training class size was set at 6 residents each. Moral Education was to involve the entire unit of 12 residents.
3. All classes were to be 1 hour in duration.
4. The research design required that classes be distributed throughout the week in order to provide opportunities for spaced learning and completion of homework. Thus, ART classes could not be offered three consecutive days to one group but rather on Monday, Wednesday, Friday or Tuesday, Thursday, Saturday schedules.
5. The schedule of classes had to be coordinated with the work schedules of the staff who were selected to conduct the training.
6. Substitute staff needed to be identified who could be available to maintain "regular" program coverage during the time training staff taught their classes.
7. Time periods needed to be identified during the "regular" program day so residents would not resent attending ART sessions because they felt they were being denied an activity they enjoyed (e.g., gym, recreation).

Figure 11 describes the ART program implementation that was developed as a result of the aforementioned considerations.

After carefully evaluating these conditions, the planning group decided the following: The Structured Learning classes were to be scheduled from 3-4 P.M. on Monday and Wednesday. Thus, the evening youth division aides who were scheduled 4 P.M. to midnight were readjusted to 2:30-10:30 P.M. on those days. This did not seriously affect the evening supervision of residents and did not involve changing the days these staff were to work. Having the Structured Learning training class at these times was also optimal for the teacher-trainers who co-trained with the youth division aides. Classes were at the end of the school day and overlapped into a noninstructional period. This helped to minimize any disruptions to the regular school program and avoided substitute coverage problems.

Figure 11. ART Program Implementation Schedule

Monday	Wednesday	Friday
I_a ACT	I_b ACT	
9:20–10:20 A.M.	9:20–10:20 A.M.	
I_b SL	I_a SL	I ME
3–4 P.M.	3–4 P.M.	3:45–4:45 P.M.
IV_b SL	IV_a SL	IV ME
3–4 P.M.	3–4 P.M.	3:45–4:45 P.M.
IV_a ACT	IV_a ACT	
7:30–8:30 P.M.	7:30–8:30 P.M.	

Key

Team I, IV—Each number represents one team of 12 residents. Each subscript
  (e.g., 1_a, 1_b) represents a team subgroup of 6 residents.

SL—Structured Learning class.

ACT—Anger Control Training class.

ME—Moral Education class.

The Anger Control Training classes were to be taught Monday and Wednesday both in the morning and evening. This arrangement was to coincide with the "regular" work schedule of the staff trainers. No staffing adjustments were necessary and no substitute coverage problems were created. The residents who were trained were simply excused from their classes (Individualized Education Plans allowed for residents' continued learning independent of class attendance) or activities at the specified times in order to attend Anger Control Training classes. One cautionary note should be emphasized at this point relative to this scheduling pattern. Since the groups of residents had these classes the *same time* each week, they either missed an academic class (in the morning) or a recreational activity (in the evening). Thus it was important for staff to be aware of the motivational levels of individuals in these groups and intervene appropriately with either encouragement, increased attention, or whatever reinforcer was acceptable in the program for that particular youth.

The Moral Education classes were scheduled for Friday during the regularly scheduled counseling period. Since 12 residents on each unit met together in the Moral Education classes, the regular counseling format and time period was convenient to utilize. The youth division counselor and youth division aide trainers were already scheduled to work at these times, except for one of the youth division aides whose pass days were Thursday and Friday. This staff member voluntarily agreed to work for the hour in order to cover the class each Friday. Thus, no work schedule changes had to be made and no substitute program activities were necessary.

From the very outset, the planning group determined that all program initiatives would be integrated into the routine program activities and schedules, whenever practical. Also the group ensured that whatever schedule was developed would not duplicate or supplant existing schedules. Thus, every effort was made to fit the ART class schedule, as was done with the training and testing schedules, into the existing resident program schedules and staff work schedules. This program development policy helped to eliminate disruptions to the "regular" program and avoided the use of overtime expenditures.

Maintaining the Program

Starting a program is generally easier than maintaining it. When something new is introduced sensitively and systematically, staff are motivated to learn and eager to try, and they desire to be successful. Once the program is established, the sense of innovativeness wanes, and the problem of maintaining staff energy levels, perseverance to task, and ongoing program activity becomes predominant. Dealing with the daily operations given limited staff resources, maintaining energy levels when staff are tired, dealing with personnel shortages to maintain the new program given other priorities, and defusing staff frustration are all issues that must be addressed in order to sustain the new initiative. The primary question that administrators constantly struggle with is not whether a program is useful, but whether the program should be continued given specific priorities and resources. There is a critical juncture point when most new, innovative programs are dropped. It is at this point, when the program is still vulnerable because not all the administrative logistical problems have been resolved, that often neither staff nor administrators are strong enough to persevere with their innovation. The tenacity of the planning group needs to prevail at this time over the assertion that the program is not do-able or continue-able, and something new should be tried.

Strategy

The administrative team was aware that there would be a point in time when the program would have to be expanded from a research effort into a facility-wide program. Thus, as the research period drew to completion, the group began to look at those activities that required closure or transition.

Training. The planning group determined that additional training was required. A phase of training "master trainers," individuals within the facility who could continue the training and supervision function first offered through the university researchers, was begun. The university researchers designed training and then co-trained with those facility staff designated as "master trainers." Again, the purpose was to develop a cadre of trainers within the facility to provide this function after the research phase of the project had ended. A practicum was provided to these individuals during which time they practiced the training and supervision skills. These "master trainers" were selected across staff role, function, and position.

Data collection. The instruments used to collect the research data were institutionalized within Annsville wherever practical. Those standardized tests, as well as staff-designed instruments, were defined in terms of purpose of information-gathering, such as behavioral indices, classification and placement, and case review. The Behavior Incident Report, for example, was used to indicate reduction in a resident's aggressive behavior such as cursing, fighting, mushing (pushing one's hand into the face of another in an intimidating manner without causing physical harm or contact), and restraint.

Schedules. The schedule that was developed for the original research design was maintained. The same principles used to design the schedules for two teams during the research phase were used for five teams as we shifted into the facility-wide program.

The planning group reevaluated the ART curricula utilized during the research phase of the project and decided that Structured Learning would continue as part of the affective education program taught by teachers during school. Each youth division aide and counselor was asked to complete a skills checklist (Goldstein et al., 1980) to assess residents' skills. Residents were grouped by skill-deficiency cluster within established academic groups. New admissions were assigned to Structured Learning classes based upon academic group designation and skill-deficiency assessment. Upon completion of 10 Structured Learning skills, new residents were certified as having completed the Structured Learning component of the basic curriculum.

We discontinued the advanced (post-10 weeks) Anger Control Training classes as we determined them to be redundant. Instead, we scheduled the 10-week basic Anger Control Training curriculum during the evening hours for all new admissions. Additionally, we modified the procedures for the Anger Control Training classes by standardizing the Structured Learning skills taught during the last 3 weeks of the program.

The skills we decided were important to teach all residents in a basic curriculum included Keeping Out of Fights, Responding to Anger, and Dealing with an Accusation. Booster Anger Control Training sessions were designed, also to be provided during evening hours for designated residents who required additional practice. Moral Education was continued during regular group counseling sessions for groups of 12 residents, no matter when they were admitted to the facility or what their progress through ART.

CONCLUSION

This chapter was included to provide the reader with an administrative perspective on the implementation of the ART program. Often, with program development initiatives the mistaken assumption is made that the administrators of the program are aware of and have the necessary supporting knowledge for successful implementation. This chapter presented those philosophical positions that must be explicit to everyone involved in a program, followed by a series of administrative principles that are generic for any successful juvenile program. Finally those critical core techniques that must be addressed for a successful ART program to occur were provided. A copy of the Annsville program description and philosophy follows in full as a model for administrators.

Readers are encouraged to incorporate these suggestions into their own styles of leadership and administrative organization. While the state of the art for juvenile justice administrators is yet emerging, what is included in this chapter will, it is hoped, stimulate others to think more fully about the nature and substance of effective juvenile justice administration.

The Annsville Youth Center:
A Program Description and Philosophy

PHILOSOPHICAL STATEMENT

Nature of Youth—General Characteristics

In Western culture the period between the ages of 12 and 19 has generally been referred to as the period of adolescence.* This period of

---

*This program description was written by: Barry Glick, Ph.D., Facility Director; Thomas Coultry, Program Decision Center Manager; Paul Fiore, Education Decision Center Manager; Dan Gold, Support Services Decision Center Manager; Suzanne Walker, Fiscal Decision Center Manager; and Royal Savoy, Physical Plant Decision Center Manager of the Annsville Youth Center. Elizabeth Brown, Stenographer; Tina Noble, Typist.

time, characterized by emotional turmoil and stress, comprises a developmental process in which youth move from the dependency and immaturity of childhood toward the physical, psychological, and social maturity of adulthood.

Physiologically, this maturational process includes changes in size (e.g., height, weight); changes in physiological structure (e.g., development of sexual glands and organs; growth of pubic hair, coarser skin, oily secretions); and changes in hormones and other chemical secretions that affect physiological growth, emotions, and behavior.

Psychologically, there is a desire for independence and development of one's identity. Adolescents exhibit an inflated sense of responsibility. They desire the privilege of decision-making like adults, but have not acquired the skills nor discipline necessary for effective and appropriate decision-making. Adolescents frequently question the authority and values of parents, teachers, and significant others (e.g., youth division aides, teachers, counselors), yet continue to have a strong need for adult approval. They tend to be idealistic and establish goals for themselves that are often unrealistic.

Socially, adolescents begin moving away from the family group and exhibit a strong need for peer recognition. The peer group becomes a powerful influence and affects adolescents' behavior and attitudes.

Annsville Youth

The adolescents admitted to Annsville Youth Center share all of the characteristics attributed to the typical adolescent. However, unlike the typical adolescent, Annsville youth have been unsuccessful in their transition between childhood and adulthood. They have often been the victims of a "deprivation syndrome" in which they have not received the appropriate direction, nurturing, encouragement, or guidance from significant adults. Thus, they have been unable to develop the prosocial attitudes and values to be successful adults. Many of them have been exposed to extremely poor role models and have been the victims of severe emotional deprivation during their early childhood years. Annsville youth typically are deficient in both academic skills and interpersonal relationship skills. Essentially, they are impulsive, lacking planning skills, decision-making skills, problem-solving skills, negotiating skills, and the ability to appropriately control and deal with their anger. The result of these deficiencies has frequently been involvement in delinquent activities, verbal and physical aggression, and the acceptance of an antisocial value system.

Despite early deprivation and the development of a negative value system, it is the belief at the Annsville Youth Center that youth admitted to Annsville can, with the proper interventions from staff, become productive citizens of the Annsville community as well as society. Annsville Youth Center staff provide youth a habilitation program that is structured, with controlled program standards and behavioral expectations. In addition to programs within the institution, there are opportunities in the community planned for youth that allow them to practice what they have learned within the institution as well as problem solve typical adolescent predicaments within the community.

Nature of Staff

Annsville's mission is to assist youth to become productive, functional, and fully integrated citizens of society. Thus, the needs of the youth dictate the type and nature of staff required to effect their positive change. (Remember, youth at Annsville have suffered long with poor and inappropriate role models. Annsville youth have been socially and emotionally deprived. Their negative self-concept and antisocial values are well developed.) It is imperative that Annsville staff be impeccable role models while working with youth in the center. Adolescents need staff whom they can emulate, who convey a genuine concern and caring, with unconditional positive regard and empathic understanding. As positive role models, staff must be ever cognizant of their interpersonal interactions with both youth and colleagues and exhibit an ability to appropriately handle conflict, decision-making, problem solving, and planning. In order to demonstrate a genuine concern for youth, staff must be warm and friendly, yet firm in holding youth accountable to expectations for their growth and development. Annsville will need a staff capable of achieving a delicate balance between establishing close, personal relationships with youth and yet performing roles as adult authority figures.

Youth-Staff—Staff-Staff Interactions

Critical to the treatment process are the interactions between staff and youth. Maslow's hierarchy of needs (Maslow, 1970) is a theory in which the foundation for youth and development begins with the creation of a physically and psychologically safe and secure environment. Consequently, staff must initially develop and continually sustain a physically safe (e.g., appropriate shelter, adequate clothing, wholesome food, clean environment) and psychologically safe (e.g., clearly established norms for behavior, structured activity and routines, predictability in relationships) environment.

Once a safe, secure environment is established, it is equally crucial that staff are both capable and willing to differentiate their interactions and interventions with youth. While youth who enter Annsville are skill deficient (academically and interpersonally) and have failed to act responsibly, they are at different levels in terms of skill development. Staff must individualize their interactions with Annsville youth if a youth's potential is to be maximally effected.

The youth at Annsville are placed in the facility because they made poor decisions and have acted irresponsibly in the community. Staff, if they are to be effective in their interactions, must be able to modify or change their own behavior depending on the situation and the youth involved. Staff will continually be involved in both *directive behavior* (i.e., telling the youth what to do, where to do it, when to do it, and how to do it) as well as *supportive behavior* (i.e., listening to the youth and providing support, encouragement, and reinforcement). The professional staff person is adept at knowing when it is appropriate to be directive and when it is appropriate to be supportive, based on the situation and the maturity level of the youth involved. Initially, staff will interact in a highly directive and in a low supportive manner (especially with a new admission) with a youth who is unwilling or unable to act in a responsible manner. As the youth matures and demonstrates his ability and willingness to accept and fulfill his responsibilities, staff will gradually move toward providing the youth with low directive and low supportive behavior. Thus youth are provided with an opportunity to demonstrate learned skills independently and responsibly.

As staff engage in the serious profession of being change agents, it must be recognized that their interactions and interventions with one another are as crucial to the habilitative process as their interventions and interactions with youth. To be successful in their mission, staff must work cooperatively and supportively with one another as members of the treatment team as well as the Annsville Center at large. Inherent in this team spirit are characteristics that all staff need to possess:

1. *Involvement:* ability to develop and demonstrate a commitment to the group with which one works as well as a commitment to the Annsville program
2. *Initiative:* willingness to accept responsibility and to contribute more than may be required even when it may seem risky or beyond one's role or function
3. *Understanding of Self:* ability to possess a knowledge of one's own feelings, values, beliefs, abilities, limitations, and needs
4. *Understanding of Others:* willingness to explore and listen to what others (co-workers) feel, believe, think, and need

5. *Openness:* ability to say what is on one's mind; the ability and willingness to confront peers constructively to enhance job performance; a realistic appraisal of where one stands
6. *Listening Ability:* willingness and ability to listen carefully to what others say and mean and to listen for necessary information and instructions; willingness to ask questions to assist in better understanding of what one has heard
7. *Use of Feedback:* ability to accept constructive criticism from others, learn from one's experiences, and make changes that will improve job performance
8. *Communication:* ability to share and receive information/data with co-workers
9. *Participation in Decision Making:* willingness to take the time and energy to share in the decision-making process
10. *Perseverance:* commitment to (does not abandon) youth or staff with whom one is working; ability to work under stress without giving up

Treatment

While involvement, initiative, understanding of self, understanding of others, openness, listening ability, use of feedback, communication, decision making, and perseverance are characteristics crucial to team work, they are also characteristics essential to effective treatment. For the staff at Annsville, treatment is a *scientific, planned, organized, structured intervention* into the lives of youth to facilitate positive and healthy development. In the application of treatment, what differentiates professionals from nonprofessionals is the ability of professionals to make conscious use of self. This means that they are aware of the intervention they are using in a specific situation and have consciously selected it. This scientific, planned, organized, structured intervention is diametrically opposed to an unconscious, commonsense approach often referred to as "flying by the seat of one's pants." Treatment as we have defined it is comprised of three primary components: evaluation (assessment), process (interventions), and outcome (results).

Assessment

The first of these components, evaluation, provides us with the essential data critical to the planning of our treatment process. Consequently, as youth are admitted to Annsville we will in the first 2 weeks conduct a series of assessments to evaluate the youth's perception of his world and his interactions with others (Jesness I-Level System), academic skills (Woodcock-Johnson), vocational skills (test battery), and physical health (physical examination).

Interpersonal Maturity Level Classification System (I-Level)

The I-Level system focuses on ways in which the delinquent perceives himself and his world, especially in terms of emotions and motivations, as well as his ability to understand what is happening between himself and others. There are seven successive stages of interpersonal maturity that characterize psychological development. They range from the least mature, which resembles the interpersonal interactions of a newborn infant, to an ideal of social maturity that is seldom or never reached in our present culture. Each of the seven stages, or levels, is defined by a crucial interpersonal problem that must be solved before further progress toward maturity can occur. All persons do not necessarily work their way through each stage, but rather may become fixed at a particular level and therefore perceive their world at that level of maturity. The range of maturity levels typically found in adolescent populations is from maturity level 2 (I_2) to maturity level 5 (I_5). Within each maturity level there is a subtype categorization that represents the individual's response to his view of the world. The instrument used to identify a youth's interpersonal maturity level is the Jesness Inventory (Jesness, 1962). The Jesness Inventory is comprised of 155 true-false statements which are designed to measure the reactions of adolescents to a wide range of content.

Woodcock-Johnson Psychoeducational Battery

The Woodcock-Johnson test, developed by Richard Woodcock and M. Bonner Johnson (Woodcock, 1978), is a valuable tool for the education program at Annsville Youth Center.

This test was selected for use because it is a widely accepted and valid standardized test of psychological development and educational skills. For purposes of our education program each student is pretested in four main "clusters." The four clusters and their subdivisions are as follows:

Reading	*Mathematics*
Letter-Word Identification	Calculation
Word Attack	Applied Problems
Passage Comprehension	

Written Language	*Knowledge*
Dictation	Science
Proofing	Social Studies
	Humanities

After the student is tested, results are sent to Albany and to each teacher. Teachers study the results of the pretest and use the results in conjunction with the student's other background information to develop his Individualized Education Plan (IEP). The posttest scores help the education staff to determine students' growth and give vital information to the facility or school district in which the discharged student is placed. The Woodcock-Johnson test is just one tool, but a vital one in the Annsville Youth Center's commitment to quality education.

Vocational Assessment

Within 30 days after arrival at Annsville each resident is given a battery of tests. Each test focuses on a factor that relates to the resident's ability to find or keep a job. A similar battery of tests is given again just prior to the resident's departure. A determination can be made regarding his progress toward job readiness. The following is a description of each test administered and how it relates to job readiness:

Work Relevant Attitudes Inventory (WRAI). The Work Relevant Attitudes Inventory was developed by Regis Walther (1975) over the course of 7 years of testing and development with disadvantaged youth and evaluation of Manpower programs for disadvantaged youth. Three primary factors were found to be predictive of the employee status of disadvantaged youth.

1. *Optimism:* This is a 4-item scale that reflects the degree of optimism a person feels. Clients are provided with statements such as "You feel lazy" and are asked the degree to which they agree with them. Scores on this scale are positively correlated with employment outcomes. That is, youth with more optimistic outlooks on life are more likely to have successful employment experiences than those who are pessimistic.

2. *Self-Confidence:* This 4-item scale is very similar in nature to the optimism scale. Including items such as "You feel like a failure," this scale reflects the degree of self-confidence a person may possess. Persons who are low in self-confidence are often not as successful in employment as those who possess a high degree of self-confidence.

3. *Unsocialized Attitudes:* This construct appears to be very similar to that which other theorists have labeled attitudes toward authority. This is an 8-item scale that reflects the degree to which respondents evince attitudes that would be disruptive in a workplace. Items such as "Most people cannot be trusted" measure this variable.

Rotter Scale. The Internal-External Attitudes Scale (Rotter, 1966) is an instrument developed to describe the extent to which a person believes that he can influence and control events by his own efforts or that external factors are controlling him. This instrument attempts to determine where a person considers his "locus of control" to be located. It can be within himself or outside himself. If the locus of control is within an individual, he will view success as a function of his characteristics and efforts; the opposite would be true for a person who perceives his locus of control to be manipulated externally. This test is a 7-item instrument; each respondent is asked to rate (1-4 points) whether he agrees a lot, agrees a little, disagrees a little, or disagrees a lot with statements descriptive of where he perceives his locus of control to be.

Office of Youth Development Scales (OYD). These scales were developed by the Behavioral Research and Evaluation Corporation for the Office of Youth Development (1975) within HEW as part of a national assessment of youth needs and youth program impact. The scales have been extensively tested with scores on perceived access to occupational and education roles showing a strong relationship to self-reported delinquency and subsequent changes in employment status.

Further evidence of the importance of these dimensions is provided by the National Longitudinal Surveys of Youth (Andrisani, 1977). Both occupational aspirations and expectancy of reaching aspirations (measured with a different scale) were found to effect changes over time in the employment status of a national sample of youth. In this research, youth with similar backgrounds, experience, location, skills, and initial jobs were compared and followed over time to control for other relevant employment-related factors. Thus, there is strong empirical evidence of a link between these dimensions and both delinquency and employment status over time.

These dimensions have strong theoretical appeal in terms of both delinquent behavior and employment status over time. In terms of delinquent behavior, youth with little expectation of school or occupational success may have no stake in conformity and may feel that they place little in jeopardy if they engage in illegal behaviors. Additionally, illegal behavior may be perceived as the only way to financial reward. Concerning employment outcomes, expectancy of success will probably motivate the youth to (1) seek employment; (2) confidently approach work tasks; (3) overcome minor initial failures; and (4) persevere during the inevitable long transition period before receiving stable, meaningful, and well-paid employment.

Youth and family job history schedule. This demographic schedule is designed to measure the job history of the youth and his family. Depending on age, past work efforts are a valid indicator of likely efforts to be made after the program and may reveal problems likely to recur. The family composition and socioeconomic status of the family are also initial indicators of possible barriers.

Work Behavior Rating Scale. This scale (Piccola, French, & Leve, 1982) was adapted from instruments designed by Ralph Piccola (Tryon) and Mark French (Brookwood), field tested and revised, and finally revised in layout by Peter Leve (Cass). There are three primary purposes in collecting this data: (1) to describe the range of behavioral strengths and problems youth have with respect to work, along dimensions considered important to work behavior; (2) to see how well the factors correlate with future employment problems revealed in a follow-up study; and (3) to validate other scales being used through intercorrelation of this data with other scales. The scale consists of 15 items measuring behavior of primary concern to employers. Item 16 measures pure *ability* in the work area apart from work behaviors of concern.

Program for Assessing Youth Employment Skills (PAYES). Designed for use as a counseling tool with youth enrolled in work-training programs, the Program for Assessing Youth Employment Skills (Educational Testing Service, 1967) is a battery of paper-and-pencil measures. Developmental level, content, verbal level, format, and method of administration were tailored to overcome a number of deficiencies often attributed to conventional tests when used with youth from poverty-level backgrounds who are also minority group members with low verbal skills. The chosen measures were meant to reflect trainee behaviors considered relevant to work training program purposes and goals and to meet some of the informational needs of program professionals (e.g., counselors, planners, administrators, or evaluators). The measurement constructs are embodied in a variety of factors reflective of attitudinal, practical reasoning and vocational interest. Originally, 13 separate test booklets combined pictorial and verbal information to sample responses in the three major areas of measurements. The most current edition of PAYES consists of 8 guidance measures contained in 3 separate booklets; however, we have chosen those we consider most valid—Job Knowledge, Job Seeking Skills, and Vocational Interests. They provide valuable baseline data that meet the training needs of the average member of the Division for Youth Service population.

Medical Examination/Health Assessment

Annsville Youth Center conducts a medical examination/assessment for each youth so that health problems/needs are promptly identified and then appropriately treated. Upon admission, each resident is given a screening interview to determine if the youth has any health problems that require immediate medical attention. A complete medical examination includes but is not limited to the following elements: (1) health history; (2) physical examination (within 1 week), dental check (within 2 weeks), and mental health check (within 3 weeks); (3) audiological and ophthalmological examination; (4) laboratory testing; (5) chest X-ray; and (6) radiological or medical specialty consultive services. In addition, each youth's immunization status is determined, health problems and plans are recorded, and records are checked to be sure a signed Authorization and Consent Form for Medical, Psychiatric, Surgical, and Dental Treatment is present.

Youth admitted to Annsville are also evaluated by our professional child-care staff (youth division aides and youth division counselors) through interviews and behavioral observations. In appropriate instances youth are referred to the Mobile Mental Health Team Psychologist for a psychological evaluation utilizing both projective and non-projective tests. At the conclusion of 45 days, the youth's assigned counselor will prepare an initial Problem Oriented Service Plan that clearly outlines the treatment strategies for the next 45 days.

Interventions

The foundation for our treatment strategies/interventions at Annsville is a psychosocial education model. Reality Therapy (Glasser, 1965) is one intervention especially appropriate for youth at Annsville for the following reasons:

1. Typically, Annsville youth are skill deficient in their interpersonal interactions and have both failed and acted irresponsibly in attempting to meet their basic needs for safety, security, love, acceptance, and self-worth.

2. The basic principles of Reality Therapy can be implemented by all staff and utilized in all areas of the program (education, counseling, recreation).
3. Reality Therapy lends itself to individualization in order to meet the needs of youth at their particular level of development.
4. Since Reality Therapy is behaviorally based, goals may be established to improve a youth's self-esteem.
5. Reality Therapy is a fairly simple process to understand and teach to both youth as well as adults.

The primary goal of Reality Therapy is to assist an irresponsible individual to become more responsible in order that he may fulfill his own needs without violating or infringing upon the needs of others.

Reality Therapy, unlike more conventional or traditional forms of therapy, places emphasis on the present ("here and now") rather than attempting to provide insight into past behavior and/or motivations. Reality Therapy is concerned with assisting the individual to function better now. Initially, this requires that staff become involved with youth in a caring and personally warm manner. (Cautionary Note: This does not mean that staff are buddies or friends but are caring adults who are both positive role models and willing to hold youth accountable for their actions.)

Beyond an involvement with youth, staff will provide youth with an opportunity to learn behaviors that will assist them to meet their needs for acceptance, love, and self-worth. At Annsville, we believe this will be best accomplished through the integration of Reality Therapy with Aggression Replacement Training, a multitherapeutic modality comprised of three primary components.

1. *Structured Learning* (SL) is a systematic, organized psychoeducational intervention to teach prosocial behaviors in interpersonal life skills. It provides youth with alternative behavior to aggression and irresponsible behavior.
2. *Anger Control Training* (ACT) is a systematic approach to teaching awareness of the activators of anger. It teaches the inhibition of anger, aggression, and antisocial behavior.
3. *Moral Reasoning* is designed to assist youth in placing a high value on the prosocial skills they have acquired through SL and ACT. Thus, upon leaving Annsville, youth will be motivated to transfer their newly acquired skills to the community. Through the effective transfer and maintenance of these skills, Annsville's youth will become fully productive citizens of society.

PROGRAM DESCRIPTION

Population

Adolescent youth ages 14 to 17 are referred to Annsville Youth Center from all regions of the state. At this time approximately 50 percent of the facility's population are from the New York City region, the other 50 percent are from upstate areas of New York, including the cities of Syracuse, Rochester, and Albany. Generally speaking, the ethnicity of the population has been 40 percent Caucasian, 50 percent black, 9 percent Hispanic, and 1 percent Native American. Ninety-four percent of the admitted youth are adjudicated Juvenile Delinquents (JD's): 29 percent Title II and 65 percent Title III. Approximately 5 percent of the youth are admitted as Conditions of Probation (COP) and 1 percent as Persons In Need of Supervision (PINS). The majority of youth admitted to Annsville Youth Center are persons who lack the skills to interact successfully with most adults and peers in a community setting. These youth have committed criminal offenses such as auto theft, assaults, and burglaries. In addition, the statutory crimes of truancy and ungovernable behavior have been an integral part of the residents' characteristics before they were admitted to the Center.

The median age of the youth is 15. The average reading and math levels are grades 6.9 and 5.2, respectively. Youth generally have very limited vocational experiences due to truancy and/or behavior problems; most have never been employed. Residents exhibit a lack of motivation coupled with a sense of failure and limited ego strengths. They are often unable to conceptualize any information. This problem is exacerbated by lengthy absences from a formal school setting. Approximately one-third of the population has been classified as handicapped or is suspected of being handicapped. The predominant classifications of the resident youth are emotionally disturbed and learning disabled. A small percentage have mild mental retardation problems as well as visual and speech handicaps.

The referral process begins with the division's youth service team worker who compiles assessment reports, probation reports, recent psychological and medical reports, educational material, and problem-oriented service plans. A referral package is sent to the intake officer at the center and reviewed to determine if the youth is appropriate for the program. Parameters for acceptance include ability to function in a large peer group setting and some socialization skill and physical functionability. Youth with serious physical handicaps, severe mental retardation, or psychotic or severe mental illness are not considered appropriate candidates. Youth with a history of homosexuality, arson, suicidal tendencies, or extreme violent behavior are also inappropriate referrals. Once a youth is determined to be appropriate for the program, an admission date is set or the youth is put on the active waiting list until an opening is available.

Counseling

At Annsville there are five teams of 12 residents, with each team having an assigned counselor. The primary objective of the counseling program is to assist youth to develop prosocial methods of interacting with others so that they will become productive, functional citizens of both the Annsville community and their home communities.

Group counseling sessions are held on a daily basis, Monday through Friday. Emphasis is placed on behavior management and the resident's use of his Structured Learning and Anger Control Training skills. Formal individual sessions are held with each resident, at least once a week, with emphasis on developing future plans and also dealing with more personal issues not appropriate for the group process.

Education

The education program at the Annsville Youth Center is a unique and quality program that allows all youth the opportunity to excel in both academics and vocational study. Both areas are staffed by highly competent and caring professionals and paraprofessionals who are skilled in instructing delinquent youth.

Academically, the program is designed to include math, English, science, and social studies for *all* students. It provides remedial or special education services for those students identified as having learning deficiencies. In addition, each student's needs are analyzed and a detailed Individualized Education Plan (IEP) is developed.

Students also explore a wide variety of vocational skills and take such courses as Job Readiness, Building Maintenance, Ceramics, Auto Body, Auto Mechanics, and Wood Shop. "Hands on" experience is stressed in all classes. For students who show exceptional ability in a vocational area, a stipend program allows the resident to earn wages and learn more advanced job related skills.

In addition, the academic and vocational programs are coordinated to complement each other. The small teacher-pupil ratio (1:10 maximum) allows each resident the opportunity to receive individual help that cannot be offered in many other school settings.

Religion

The aim of all religious education is to help people discern, respond to, and be transformed by the presence of God in their lives, as well as to work for the continuing transformation of the world in the light of this perception of God. The Annsville program recognizes that in adolescent development, spiritual growth is as important to maturity and the development of the fully integrated personality as is intellectual, emotional, and physical growth.

Youth come to Annsville spiritually deprived, with little previous religious education, and have had poor faith models in their home and previous environment. The inadequate development of their relationship to God is a strong contributing factor to their poor self-image and their lack of self-confidence. They generally lack the inner spiritual strength and self-discipline to cope with their emotions and problems and they lack the religious perspective that provides meaning and direction to life.

The Annsville religious program attempts to expose the adolescent to the notion of a loving God and to help him respond freely to that God according to his own conscience. Chaplains work closely together to give the youth the experience of God's love and to help the youth understand what moral response God expects of them in this life. The chaplains have an initial interview with each youth soon after he is admitted to the facility. At this interview they seek to establish a good rapport with the youth and to demonstrate their approachability and future availability for personal and confidential counseling. The youth attend weekly religious education classes at which they are exposed to the beliefs of various religious traditions such as Christianity, Judaism, Buddhism, Hinduism, and Islam. The classes are also used to try to inculcate in the youth sound spiritual and moral values. Youth also have the opportunity to attend religious services at various local churches of their own choice.

The Annsville religious program aims at giving the youth a knowledge and experience of a loving God, so that when they leave Annsville they will possess the spiritual and moral capacity to lead productive and happy lives. It is a goal of the program to enable youth to cope with life's problems as well as give them the spiritual vision necessary to bring about a better life for themselves and for others.

Recreation

The recreation activities comprise another major component of the program. These activities are conducted during the evenings and on weekends. The on-grounds activities are structured and scheduled by living units. Each unit is rotated between the recreation room, gymnasium, handball court, and team offices on a daily basis. The team youth development aide supervises and conducts the scheduled activities in each area to ensure proper participation and adherence to program rules and expectations. Pool, basketball, foose ball, weight lifting, TV, and quiet games are some of the activities provided. Inter-unit competitions are also often scheduled to help build team cohesiveness and pride.

Off-grounds activities are provided for select residents from each unit on the weekends. Opportunities to attend movies, dances, sports events, rollerskating, and so forth are given to those residents who participate in a positive manner in the overall program. Groups of ten residents and two staff are scheduled to attend the various off-campus activities.

A great deal of attention is paid to the ways in which residents spend their leisure time. A daily evaluation is made to determine whether a youth uses his recreation time in positive or negative ways. Of concern is each resident's ability to organize his time well, his ability to deal with peer pressure to join a clique, to interact fairly and effectively with others, and to conduct himself in a respectful and socially acceptable manner in the community.

CONCLUSION

The Annsville Program is an integrated, planned habilitation effort to assist youth to become productive, functional citizens of society. The staff at Annsville, caring yet firm adult role models, complement treatment initiatives that facilitate youth to learn prosocial skills, control aggression, and develop abilities to evaluate their values and morals. Our brief interactions with youth are not completely realized unless youth return to their communities without repeating delinquent activities or making poor decisions. While we know our program works for youth when they are in our environment, their real success depends upon either their ability to use what they learn at Annsville when they return to their homes or the availability in their home communities of a similar environment in which to continue the habilitation process.

Appendix A
Assessment and
Research Instruments

1. Direct Situations Test (DT)
2. Minimal Generalization Situations Test (MGT)
3. Extended Generalization Situations Test (EGT)
4. Kendall-Wilcox Self-Control Scale
5. Sociomoral Reflections Measure
6. Behavior Incident Report—Form A
7. Behavior Incident Report—Form B
8. Community Adjustment Rating Scale

A1: Direct Situations Test (DT)

(This test should be prerecorded for presentation. Do
not record the skill names in parentheses.)

On the tape you are about to hear, there are brief descriptions of situations people often get into. As you listen, you will hear situations described one at a time, and then you will be asked after each one what you would do if you were in that situation. So, for each situation you hear, please try to pretend to yourself that it is really happening to you, and then tell what you believe you would *actually* do in that situation. Tell your answer to the person at your table, and he or she will write it down. Your answer will be kept in the strictest confidence.

Thank you for your cooperation.

(*Skill 1. Expressing a Complaint*)

1   The Parole Board has just held you another 6 months. You think you should be able to go home because you haven't broken any of the rules. What would you do?

2   You are always doing the hardest work in the kitchen. None of the other workers are helping you out. What would you do?

3   You just bought a pair of sneakers and left the store, and now you realize that they didn't give you the correct change. They shortchanged you. What would you do?

4   You share a room at home with your brother, who is always using your things without asking you. What would you do?

(*Skill 2. Responding to the Feelings of Others*)

5   One of the residents assigned to your unit is very upset. He has just been held at the Parole Board. What would you do?

6   A resident who is a friend of yours tells you that he has just received a letter from his girlfriend, and she has broken up with him. What would you do?

7   A friend has just told you that his brand new sneakers have been stolen. What would you do?

8   A resident that you know in another unit is upset because his parents, who promised to visit him for the last 3 weeks, have not shown up. What would you do?

(*Skill 3. Preparing for a Stressful Conversation*)

9   You are scheduled to appear before the commissioners at the Parole Board, who will decide whether you will stay longer in this facility. You will have to speak to the commissioners about this. What would you do?

10   You have been caught smoking a joint and you know that you will have to speak about it to your counselor, who is coming in on the next shift. What would you do?

11   You have to go talk to a staff person, your teacher, to discuss an earlier incident in which you have been disrespectful and have cursed at her. What would you do?

12   You have to go to the facility nurse and tell her you think that you may have VD. What would you do?

(*Skill 4. Responding to Anger*)

13   A resident in your unit is angry with you because he feels that you have cut in front of him in the dinner line. What would you do?

14   A staff member is angry with you because you have not followed his directions for cleaning up your unit office. What would you do?

15   It is 2:00 A.M. and you have just arrived home. Your mother is very angry because you were supposed to be home not later than 10:30 P.M. What would you do?

16   Your counselor is angry because your unit has continued to be in last place on Unit of the Week for the last 5 weeks. What would you do?

(*Skill 5. Keeping Out of Fights*)

17   Another resident has just come up to you and demanded that you give him cigarettes. What would you do?

18   You just found out who stole your sneakers. What would you do?

19   Another resident has just bumped into you and made you spill your drink and drop your tray of food on the floor. What would you do?

20   Another resident has just told you that you are a stupid ass because of the color of your skin. What would you do?

(*Skill 6. Helping Others*)

21 A resident has just been told that his parents are here for their visit, but he has been assigned to work in the kitchen. What would you do?

22 A new resident has just been admitted to the program. It is the first time he has ever been away from home. What would you do?

23 The resident who is sitting next to you in math class is having trouble understanding the assignment. What would you do?

24 You are walking down the street and you notice a woman standing beside her car, which has a flat tire. What would you do?

(*Skill 7. Dealing with an Accusation*)

25 You are accused by a store owner of taking a new pair of pants from his store. What would you do?

26 Your teacher accuses you of being lazy and always refusing to do your work. What would you do?

27 You are accused by your counselor of having set off a fire alarm. What would you do?

28 Your friends accuse you of always thinking of yourself first. What would you do?

(*Skill 8. Dealing with Group Pressure*)

29 Three residents have just asked you to go AWOL with them. You really don't like it in the facility, but you want to do well in the program. What would you do?

30 Several members of your unit tell you that they're going to steal cigarettes from a resident who is a member of another unit, and they want you to be the lookout. What would you do?

31 You've just been released home and it's your first week in school. Some of your old friends have decided that they are going to skip the day and not go to school. They have just asked you to come with them. What would you do?

32 Three friends pull over in a car you think they may have stolen. They ask you to get in and go for a ride. What would you do?

(*Skill 9. Expressing Affection*)

33 You have been in the program for about 45 days. Your parents have just arrived for their first visit. You are really excited about seeing them. What would you do?

34   Your counselor has just helped you to work out a very serious problem. What would you do?

35   You have really made a lot of progress in your reading, and it's time for you to be released from the program. You must say good-bye to your reading teacher. What would you do?

36   Your girlfriend has just told you on the telephone that she loves you. What would you do?

(*Skill 10. Responding to Failure*)

37   You have just received the results of your GED exam and have found out that you did not pass. What would you do?

38   You spent 3 weeks trying to help your little brother learn how to ride a bicycle, and he still has not learned. What would you do?

39   In woodshop, you have been working on building a bookcase, but it just does not come out right. What would you do?

40   You have just found out that your unit failed inspection after you have worked hard all week to clean. What would you do?

This completes the situations tape. Thank you for your cooperation!

A2: Minimal Generalization Situations Test (MGT)

(This test should be prerecorded for presentation. Do
not record the skill names in parentheses.)

On the tape you are about to hear, there are brief descriptions of situations people often get into. As you listen, you will hear situations
described one at a time, and then you will be asked after each one what
you would do if you were in that situation. So, for each situation you
hear, please try to pretend to yourself that it is really happening to you,
and then tell what you believe you would *actually* do in that situation.
Tell your answer to the person at your table, and he or she will write it
down. Your answer will be kept in the strictest confidence.

Thank you for your cooperation.

(Skill 1. Expressing a Complaint)

1   You are having lunch at the facility and you just took the first
bite of your sandwich. Something tastes really spoiled. What
would you do?

2   You are restricted for being disrespectful. You feel the staff provoked you and that it is unfair. What would you do?

3   Your teacher keeps giving you work that is too easy. It's the same
work over and over again, and you are really bored. What would
you do?

4   You are not getting along with the other residents in your unit,
and you want to be transferred to another unit. What would you
do?

(Skill 2. Responding to the Feelings of Others)

5   A new resident in your unit really looks sad. He tells you he is
very homesick. What would you do?

6   A resident who is a good friend of yours tells you that he has just
learned that his girlfriend is pregnant. What would you do?

7   A resident in your unit has just told the unit that his mother died
of cancer last night. What would you do?

8   Today there was a new admission to your unit, and he doesn't
know anyone. What would you do?

(*Skill 3. Preparing for a Stressful Conversation*)

9   Your counselor has just told you that you will have to talk with the resident who accused you of stealing his sneakers. What would you do?

10   You have to telephone your mother this afternoon and tell her that you got into a fight, so the Parole Board may hold you for several months. What would you do?

11   You and another resident had a physical confrontation, and staff members tell you that you must sit down with him after lunch and work it out. What would you do?

12   You have an appointment tomorrow to talk to your school's football coach about trying out for the team. He is known to be a very tough guy. What would you do?

(*Skill 4. Responding to Anger*)

13   A resident in your unit has just gotten heavily sanctioned. He says that you started the fight with him last week that made this happen, and he's very angry with you. What would you do?

14   Some of the members of your unit are angry because you fouled an opposing player, he scored, and your unit lost the basketball game. What would you do?

15   The cook who is serving the food is angry with you because he just heard you tell another resident how bad it tastes. What would you do?

16   A resident threatens you and the rest of your unit about getting even with whoever took his commissary. What would you do?

(*Skill 5. Keeping Out of Fights*)

17   Another resident tells you that he has rights to the chair you are sitting in at the unit office. What would you do?

18   You lost your privileges because someone told your counselor that you were smoking cigarettes in the bathroom, and you just found out who told. What would you do?

19   A resident to whom you lent a pack of cigarettes is now refusing to pay you back. What would you do?

20   Your mother's boyfriend is drunk and getting a little nasty. It looks like he's getting up to come over and hit you. What would you do?

(*Skill 6. Helping Others*)

21 Two unit members got into a dumb argument, and now it looks like they are about to get into a fight neither of them wants. What would you do?

22 Your teacher has asked if there is anyone in your class who would help her move some boxes. What would you do?

23 Your mother has to go to work, your older sister is still sleeping, and there is no one else to watch your little brother. What would you do?

24 A friend of yours wants to go to the movies, but doesn't have enough money. What would you do?

(*Skill 7. Dealing with an Accusation*)

25 You are accused by your counselor of always getting other residents to do your dirty work for you. What would you do?

26 A resident in your unit accused you of being a homosexual. What would you do?

27 Your mother accuses you of taking $10 from her wallet. What would you do?

28 A neighbor at home accuses you of being just like your father, a no-good bum. What would you do?

(*Skill 8. Dealing with Group Pressure*)

29 You are at a party in a friend's house and some of the other guys ask you to help search for any liquor in the house. What would you do?

30 The members of your unit want to win the decorating contest for the holidays, and they are all on your case because you really have not been doing your job very well. What would you do?

31 Three residents are pressuring you to become a 5 percenter, but you don't want to. What would you do?

32 You know that four members of your unit were smoking marijuana last night. During group counseling your counselor asks you what you know about the incident. What would you do?

(*Skill 9. Expressing Affection*)

33 The cooks at the facility have just made you a cake for your birthday. What would you do?

34   You are on an emergency home leave because your grand-mother, who has spent the most time raising you, is very sick. You are visiting her in the hospital. What would you do?

35   Your little brother, who is 10 years old, is getting high every day. You really care for him a lot. What would you do?

36   You are leaving the facility after a year and have to say good-bye to another resident, who has become the best friend you ever had. What would you do?

(*Skill 10. Responding to Failure*)

37   You wanted to do at least 30 pushups in a row, but could only do 23. What would you do?

38   Your basketball team just lost the championship game. What would you do?

39   You have just been told that your grades are not good enough for you to be advanced to the next grade level. What would you do?

40   You were hoping to get your ceramics project completed by the time you left for your release, but now you realize that you are not going to finish it on time. What would you do?

This completes the situations tape. Thank you for your cooperation!

A3: Extended Generalization Situations Test (EGT)

(This test should be presented live by the tester. Do
not present the skill names in parentheses.)

You are about to hear brief descriptions of situations people often get
into. As you listen, you will hear situations described one at a time, and
then you will be asked after each one what you would do if you were in
that situation. So, for each situation you hear, please try to pretend to
yourself that it is really happening to you, and then tell what you believe
you would actually do in that situation. Tell me your answer, and I will
write it down. Your answer will be kept in the strictest confidence.

(*Skill 1. Expressing a Complaint*)

1   Pretend I am your counselor. I always seem to have time to talk
to the other residents in your unit, but I never seem to have time
to talk with you. What would you do?

2   Pretend I am your mother. On your home visits I always want
you in by 10:30, but you don't want to come home that early.
What would you do?

(*Skill 2. Responding to the Feelings of Others*)

3   Pretend I am your brother. On your home visit you learn that I
have just failed my GED exam. What would you do?

4   Pretend I am your closest friend. I have just told you I found out
today that my parents are getting separated. What would you
do?

(*Skill 3. Preparing for a Stressful Conversation*)

5   Pretend I am the Facility Vocational Specialist. You have a job
interview with me today at 2:00. What would you do?

6   Pretend I am the Facility Director. You are sitting outside my
office, waiting to see me about your escape attempt last night.
What would you do?

(*Skill 4. Responding to Anger*)

7   Pretend I am your teacher. I am angry with you because you
were disruptive during class. What would you do?

8   Pretend I am another resident in your unit. I am angry with you
because I lent you my leather coat for your home visit and you
have come back from the visit without it. What would you do?

(*Skill 5. Keeping Out of Fights*)

9   Pretend I am a new resident, just admitted to the facility. I came up to you and called you a punk and a sucker. What would you do?

10   Pretend I am the other team's pitcher in a baseball game. You have just come to bat and I call you a chickenshit. What would you do?

(*Skill 6. Helping Others*)

11   Pretend I am a staff member. We are on a field trip. I am pretty busy doing different things, and I complain to you that now I have to do the cooking. What would you do?

12   Pretend I am another resident in your unit. I am sitting alone, on my bed, looking very sad. What would you do?

(*Skill 7. Dealing with an Accusation*)

13   Pretend I am the facility cook. I have just accused you of taking food from the kitchen. What would you do?

14   Pretend I am a police officer. You are walking down the street. I stop you and accuse you of burglarizing a house. What would you do?

(*Skill 8. Dealing with Group Pressure*)

15   Pretend I am an old friend of yours. You are on a home visit and I have just asked you to join me and another old friend in snatching a purse from an old lady who is walking down the street. What would you do?

16   Pretend I am a member of your unit. Two other unit members and I have just come to you and asked you to join us tonight in beating up a new resident whom no one seems to like. What would you do?

(*Skill 9. Expressing Affection*)

17   Pretend I am your best and oldest friend. It is your first week home after being released from the facility. You have not seen me for a year, and now you spot me walking toward you on the street. What would you do?

18   Pretend I am your mother. I have just given you a new coat you like very much for your birthday. What would you do?

(Skill 10. Responding to Failure)

19 Pretend you are alone. You applied for a job at a factory downtown, and you really wanted it a lot, but you just found out someone else got it. What would you do?

20 Pretend I am your friend. You spent a lot of time helping me to solve a problem I am having, but I have just told you that it didn't work, and that the problem is as bad as ever. What would you do?

This completes the situations. Thank you for your cooperation!

A4: Kendall-Wilcox Self-Control Scale

Name of Youth _____

Rater _____ Date _____

Please rate this youth according to the descriptions below by circling the appropriate number. The underlined 4 in the center of each row represents where the average youth would fall on this item. Please do not hesitate to use the entire range of possible ratings.

1. When the youth promises to do something, can you count on him or her to do it?

        1   2   3   4   5   6   7
     always   never

2. Does the youth butt into games or activities even when he or she hasn't been invited?

        1   2   3   4   5   6   7
     never   often

3. Can the youth deliberately calm down when he or she is excited or all wound up?

        1   2   3   4   5   6   7
     yes   no

4. Is the quality of the youth's work all about the same or does it vary a lot?

        1   2   3   4   5   6   7
     same   varies

5. Does the youth work for long-range goals?

        1   2   3   4   5   6   7
     yes   no

6. When the youth asks a question, does he or she wait for an answer, or jump to something else (e.g., a new question) before waiting for an answer?

        1   2   3   4   5   6   7
     waits   jumps

Note. From Kendall, P. C., & Wilcox, L. E. (1979). Self-control in children: Development of a rating scale. *Journal of Consulting and Clinical Psychology, 47,* 1020–1030. Copyright 1979 American Psychological Association. Reprinted by permission of publisher and author.

7. Does the youth interrupt inappropriately in conversation with peers or wait his or her turn to speak?

1   2   3   <u>4</u>   5   6   7

waits   interrupts

8. Does the youth stick to what he or she is doing until he or she is finished with it?

1   2   3   <u>4</u>   5   6   7

yes   no

9. Does the youth follow the instructions of responsible adults?

1   2   3   <u>4</u>   5   6   7

always   never

10. Does the youth have to have everything right away?

1   2   3   <u>4</u>   5   6   7

no   yes

11. When the youth has to wait in line, does he or she do so patiently?

1   2   3   <u>4</u>   5   6   7

yes   no

12. Does the youth sit still?

1   2   3   <u>4</u>   5   6   7

yes   no

13. Can the youth follow suggestions of others in group projects, or does he or she insists on imposing his or her own ideas?

1   2   3   <u>4</u>   5   6   7

able to follow   imposes

14. Does the youth have to be reminded several times to do something before he or she does it?

1   2   3   <u>4</u>   5   6   7

never   always

15. When reprimanded, does the youth answer back inappropriately?

1   2   3   <u>4</u>   5   6   7

never   always

16. Is the youth accident prone?

1   2   3   <u>4</u>   5   6   7

no   yes

17. Does the youth neglect or forget regular chores or tasks?

    1   2   3   <u>4</u>   5   6   7

    never   always

18. Are there days when the youth seems incapable of settling down to work?

    1   2   3   <u>4</u>   5   6   7

    never   often

19. Would the youth more likely grab a smaller toy today or wait for a larger toy tomorrow, if given the choice?

    1   2   3   <u>4</u>   5   6   7

    wait   grab

20. Does the youth grab for the belongings of others?

    1   2   3   <u>4</u>   5   6   7

    never   often

21. Does the youth bother others when they are trying to do something?

    1   2   3   <u>4</u>   5   6   7

    no   yes

22. Does the youth break basic rules?

    1   2   3   <u>4</u>   5   6   7

    never   always

23. Does the youth watch where he or she is going?

    1   2   3   <u>4</u>   5   6   7

    always   never

24. In answering questions does the youth give one thoughtful answer or blurt out several answers all at once?

    1   2   3   <u>4</u>   5   6   7

    one answer   several

25. Is the youth easily distracted from his or her work or chores?

    1   2   3   <u>4</u>   5   6   7

    no   yes

26. Would you describe this youth more as careful or careless?

    1   2   3   <u>4</u>   5   6   7

    careful   careless

27. Does the youth play well with peers (follows rules, waits turn, cooperates)?

          1   2   3   <u>4</u>   5   6   7

          yes   no

28. Does the youth jump or switch from activity to activity rather than sticking to one thing at a time?

          1   2   3   <u>4</u>   5   6   7

          sticks to one   switches

29. If a task is at first too difficult for the youth, will he or she get frustrated and quit or first seek help with the problem?

          1   2   3   <u>4</u>   5   6   7

          seek help   quit

30. Does the youth disrupt games?

          1   2   3   <u>4</u>   5   6   7

          never   often

31. Does the youth think before he or she acts?

          1   2   3   <u>4</u>   5   6   7

          always   never

32. If the youth paid more attention to his or her work, do you think he or she would do much better than at present?

          1   2   3   <u>4</u>   5   6   7

          no   yes

33. Does the youth do too many things at once, or does he or she concentrate on one thing at a time?

          1   2   3   <u>4</u>   5   6   7

          one thing   too many

A5: Sociomoral Reflections Measure

Name _____

Age _____ Date _____

(This exercise should be presented live by the tester.)

Listen to the following problems and tell me your answers to the questions after them.

Problem One

In Europe, a woman was near death from a special kind of cancer. There was one drug that the doctors thought might save her. It was a form of radium that a druggist in the same town had recently discovered. The drug was expensive to make, but the druggist wanted people to pay ten times what the drug cost him to make.

The sick woman's husband, Heinz, went to everyone he knew to borrow the money, but he could only get together about half of what the druggist wanted. Heinz told the druggist that his wife was dying and asked him to sell it cheaper or to let him pay later. But the druggist said, "No. I discovered the drug and I'm going to make money from it." So the only way Heinz could get the drug would be to break into the druggist's store and steal it.

Heinz has a problem. He should help his wife and save her life. But, on the other hand, the only way he could get the drug she needs would be to break the law by stealing the drug.

What should Heinz do?

should steal/should not steal/can't decide (choose one)

Why?

Let's change things about the problem and see if you still have the opinion you chose (should steal, should not steal, or can't decide). Also, we want to find out about the things you think are important in this and other problems, especially *why* you think those things are important.

Note. John Gibbs/Keith Widaman, *SOCIAL INTELLIGENCE: Measuring the Development of Sociomoral Reflection,* © 1982, pp. 193–200. Adapted with permission of Prentice-Hall, Inc. Englewood Cliffs, NJ.

Please try to help us understand your thinking by SAYING AS MUCH AS YOU CAN TO EXPLAIN YOUR OPINIONS—EVEN IF YOU HAVE TO STATE YOUR EXPLANATIONS MORE THAN ONCE. Don't just say "same as before." If you can explain better or use different words to show what you mean, that helps us even more.

1. What if Heinz's wife asks him to steal the drug for her? Should Heinz:

      steal/not steal/can't decide (choose one)?

a. How important is it for a husband to do what his wife asks, to save her by stealing, even when he isn't sure whether that's the best thing to do?

      very important/important/not important (choose one)

b. WHY IS THAT VERY IMPORTANT/IMPORTANT/NOT IMPORTANT (whichever one you chose)?

2. What if Heinz doesn't love his wife? Should Heinz:

      steal/not steal/can't decide (choose one)?

a. How important is it for a husband to steal to save his wife, even if he doesn't love her?

      very important/important/not important (choose one)

b. WHY IS THAT VERY IMPORTANT/IMPORTANT/NOT IMPORTANT (whichever one you chose)?

3. What if the person dying isn't Heinz's wife but instead a friend (and the friend can get no one else to help)? Should Heinz:

      steal/not steal/can't decide (choose one)?

a. How important is it to do everything you can, even break the law, to save the life of a friend?

      very important/important/not important (choose one)

b. WHY IS THAT VERY IMPORTANT/IMPORTANT/NOT IMPORTANT (whichever one you chose)?

4. What about for a stranger? How important is it to do everything you can, even break the law, to save the life of a stranger?

      very important/important/not important (choose one)

a. WHY IS THAT VERY IMPORTANT/IMPORTANT/NOT IMPORTANT (whichever one you chose)?

5. What if the druggist just wants Heinz to pay what the drug cost to make, and Heinz can't even pay that? Should Heinz:

> steal/not steal/can't decide (choose one)?

a. How important is it for people not to take things that belong to other people?

> very important/important/not important (choose one)

b. WHY IS THAT VERY IMPORTANT/IMPORTANT/NOT IMPORTANT (whichever one you chose)?

6. How important is it for people to obey the law?

> very important/important/not important (choose one)

a. WHY IS THAT VERY IMPORTANT/IMPORTANT/NOT IMPORTANT (whichever one you chose)?

7. What if Heinz does steal the drug? His wife does get better, but in the meantime, the police take Heinz and bring him to court. Should the judge:

> jail Heinz/let Heinz go free/can't decide (choose one)?

a. How important is it for judges to go easy on people like Heinz?

> very important/important/not important (choose one)

b. WHY IS THAT VERY IMPORTANT/IMPORTANT/NOT IMPORTANT (whichever one you chose)?

8. What if Heinz tells the judge that he only did what his conscience told him to do? Should the judge:

> jail Heinz/let Heinz go free/can't decide (choose one)?

a. How important is it for judges to go easy on people who have acted out of conscience?

> very important/important/not important (choose one)

b. WHY IS THAT VERY IMPORTANT/IMPORTANT/NOT IMPORTANT (whichever one you chose)?

9. What if Heinz's wife never had cancer? What if she was only a little sick, and Heinz stole the drug to help her get well a little sooner? Should the judge:

> jail Heinz/let Heinz go free/can't decide (choose one)?

a. How important is it for judges to send people who break the law to jail?

very important/important/not important (choose one)

b. WHY IS THAT VERY IMPORTANT/IMPORTANT/NOT IMPOR-TANT (whichever one you chose)?

Problem Two

Joe is a 14-year-old boy who wants to go to camp very much. His father promised him he could go if he saved up the money for it himself. So Joe worked hard at his paper route and saved up the $40 it cost to go to camp and a little more besides. But just before camp was going to start, his father changed his mind. Some of the father's friends decided to go on a special fishing trip, and Joe's father was short of the money it would cost. So he told Joe to give him the money Joe had saved from the paper route. Joe doesn't want to give up going to camp, so he thinks of refusing to give his father the money.

Joe has a problem. Joe's father promised Joe he could go to camp if he earned and saved up the money. But, on the other hand, the only way Joe could go would be by disobeying and not helping his father.

What should Joe do?

should refuse/should not refuse/can't decide (choose one)

Why?

Let's change things about the problem and see if you still have the opinion you chose (should refuse, should not refuse, or can't decide). Also, we want to find out about the things you think are important in this and other problems, and especially *why* you think those things are important. Please try to help us understand your thinking by SAYING AS MUCH AS YOU CAN TO EXPLAIN YOUR OPINIONS—EVEN IF YOU HAVE TO STATE YOUR EXPLANATIONS MORE THAN ONCE. Don't just say "same as before." If you can explain better or use different words to show what you mean, that's even better.

1. What if Joe hadn't earned the money? What if the father had simply given the money to Joe and promised Joe could use it to go to camp—but now the father wants the money back for the fishing trip? Should Joe:

refuse/not refuse/can't decide (choose one)?

a. How important is it for parents to keep their promises about let-ting their children keep money—even when their children never earned the money?

very important/important/not important (choose one)

b. WHY IS THAT VERY IMPORTANT/IMPORTANT/NOT IMPOR-TANT (whichever one you chose)?

2. What about keeping a promise to a friend? How important is it to keep a promise, if you can, to a friend?

very important/important/not important (choose one)

a. WHY IS THAT VERY IMPORTANT/IMPORTANT/NOT IMPOR-TANT (whichever one you chose)?

3. What about to anyone? How important is it to keep a promise, if you can, even to someone you hardly know?

very important/important/not important (choose one)

a. WHY IS THAT VERY IMPORTANT/IMPORTANT/NOT IMPOR-TANT (whichever one you chose)?

4. What if Joe's father hadn't *told* Joe to *give* him the money, but had just *asked* Joe if he would *lend* the money? Should Joe:

refuse/not refuse/can't decide (choose one)?

a. How important is it for children to help their parents, even when their parents have broken a promise?

very important/important/not important (choose one)

b. WHY IS THAT VERY IMPORTANT/IMPORTANT/NOT IMPOR-TANT (whichever one you chose)?

5. What if Joe did earn the money, but Joe's father did not promise that Joe could keep the money? Should Joe:

refuse/not refuse/can't decide (choose one)?

a. How important is it for parents to let their children keep earned money—even when the parents did not promise their children that they could keep the money?

very important/important/not important (choose one)

b. WHY IS THAT VERY IMPORTANT/IMPORTANT/NOT IMPOR-TANT (whichever one you chose)?

6. What if the father needs the money not to go on a fishing trip, but instead to pay for food for the family? Should Joe:

refuse/not refuse/can't decide (choose one)?

a. How important is it for children to help their parents—even when it means that the children won't get to do something they want to do?

very important/important/not important (choose one)

b. WHY IS THAT VERY IMPORTANT/IMPORTANT/NOT IMPOR-TANT (whichever one you chose)?

A6: Behavior Incident Report—Form A

INSTRUCTIONS: Check which behavior the resident exhibited during the past week. Be sure to check only the one(s) that represent the youth's cumulative behavior. For example, checking "restrained" may include "involved in bickering" or "involved in physical fights."

Yes	No	
		Instigated arguments/fights.
		Threatened, harassed, intimidated (sold wolf-tickets).
		Verbally abusive (cursed).
		Failed to calm down when requested.
		Upset when he could not do something immediately.
		Became antagonistic when registering complaint.
		Involved in bickering, squabbling.
		Argued when told what to do.
		Used profanity/vulgar language.
		Was short tempered and quick to show anger.
		Was aggravated or abusive when frustrated.
		Involved in physical fights.
		Threw articles, e.g., chair, plate, tray, pool balls, etc.
		Damaged state/personal property.
		Slammed doors, punched walls, kicked locker.
		Restrained.
		Pushed, mushed.
		Displayed offensive gestures.
		OTHER: Specify _____

Resident's Name: _____

Date: _____

Completed by: _____

Team #: _____

A7: Behavior Incident Report—Form B

INSTRUCTIONS: Check which behavior the resident exhibited during the past week.

Yes	No	
		Instigated an argument or fight.
		Provided advice or in other ways helped others when they were upset or needed help.
		Threatened, harrassed, intimidated.
		Expressed a criticism or complaint appropriately.
		Failed to calm down when requested.
		Expressed himself in an appropriate manner when frustrated or upset.
		Became antagonistic when registering complaint.
		Accepted criticism without flaring up.
		Was involved in bickering or squabbling.
		Expressed feelings appropriately when he failed at something.
		Argued when told what to do.
		Controlled his temper.
		Used profanity or vulgar language.
		When he failed was able to try again.
		Was short tempered and quick to show anger.
		Identified future negative consequences for poor behavior.
		Was involved in a physical fight.
		Expressed or answered an accusation appropriately when accused by another resident.
		Threw articles e.g., chair, plate, tray, pool balls, etc.
		Calmed down in a reasonable amount of time when angry or aggravated.
		Damaged state/personal property.
		Was able to wait when he couldn't have his way right away.
		Slammed doors, punched walls, kicked locker.
		Expressed an opinion different from the group's.
		Was restrained.

Form B *(cont.)*

Showed understanding of someone else's feelings.

Pushed, mushed.

Responded to someone else's anger without getting angry.

Displayed offensive gestures.

Expressed warm feelings, liking, or affection to someone else.

Resident's Name: _____

Date: _____

Completed by: _____

Unit #: _____

A8: Community Adjustment Rating Scale

Name of ex-resident: _____

Rater: _____

Please rate the exresident's adjustment since discharge from his youth facility. For each item listed below, in addition to your rating, please provide a brief comment explaining the reason for your rating.

		3 Excellent	2 Good	1 Fair	0 Poor
A.	Home and family adjustment				
	Comment:				

		3 Excellent	2 Good	1 Fair	0 Poor
B.	School adjustment				
	Comment:				

		3 Excellent	2 Good	1 Fair	0 Poor
C.	Work adjustment				
	Comment:				

		3 Excellent	2 Good	1 Fair	0 Poor
D.	Peer adjustment				
	Comment:				

		3 Excellent	2 Good	1 Fair	0 Poor
E.	Legal adjustment				
	Comment:				

Appendix B
The Transfer Coach

Programs that try to change the behavior of aggressive adolescents often succeed only at a certain time and in a certain place. That is, the program works, but only at or shortly after the time it occurred and only in the same place where it occurred. Thus, a program may make a youth behave better during and immediately after the weeks it is going on and in the facility where it took place. But a few weeks later, or when out on a field trip, home visit, or elsewhere outside the facility, the youth may be as aggressive as ever. This temporary success followed by a relapse to old, negative ways of behaving is what we would call a *failure of transfer*. Transfer failures are much more the rule than the exception with delinquent or aggressive youth. During Aggression Replacement Training (ART) in addition to instruction in skills, adolescents receive a great deal of support, enthusiasm, encouragement, and reward for their efforts. After ART, many of them may receive very little support, reward, or other positive response. So the common failure of transfer should not surprise us.

Yet, this outcome can be prevented. Newly learned and thus fragile constructive skills need not fade away after ART. If attempts by adolescents to use such skills in the real world are met with success—support, enthusiasm, encouragement, reward—the skill use will continue, aggression will decrease, and other positive benefits will result. Research has shown that it is people like yourself—facility staff, community workers, parents, friends, peers, teachers, employers—who are in the ideal position to provide this exceedingly valuable skill-promoting support and reward. *You* can be a powerful transfer coach, helping make sure that the curriculum of skills practiced in ART turns into long-term or even permanent learning. What is this skills curriculum, and exactly how can you help?

THE SKILLS CURRICULUM

Adolescents in ART go to three classes each week. One is Moral Reasoning, designed to promote higher levels of ethical understanding. A second class each week is Anger Control Training, teaching techniques for reducing and managing feelings of anger in provoking situations. The third class is Structured Learning, in which a series of constructive skills is taught each one of which is a positive alternative to the destructive or aggressive responses usually shown by the adolescents in certain situations.

Transfer coaches should respond with praise and encouragement when a youth, finding himself in a provoking situation (one in which he usually would respond with anger) responds instead by using one or more of the anger-reducing techniques he learned in Anger Control Training. These techniques are ignoring the provocation or turning away, counting to ten, pausing and taking deep breaths, or imagining himself to be at a calm or peaceful place. If the transfer coach can reward such behavior, the likelihood that it will continue increases a great deal.

An equal or greater impact can be made by the transfer coach when it comes to the Structured Learning skills. When each skill is taught, it is broken down into the small number of behaviors or steps that actually make up the skill. The behavioral steps *are* the skill. The transfer coach should look for, encourage, and reward the following behaviors when they occur.

STRUCTURED LEARNING SKILLS

Skill 1. Expressing a Complaint

1. Define what the problem is and who is responsible for it.
2. Decide how the problem might be solved.
3. Tell that person what the problem is and how it might be solved.
4. Ask for a response.
5. Show that you understand his/her feelings.
6. Come to agreement on the steps to be taken by each of you.

Skill 2. Responding to the Feelings of Others (Empathy)

1. Observe the other person's words and actions.
2. Decide what the other person might be feeling and how strong the feelings are.
3. Decide whether it would be helpful to let the other person know you understand his/her feelings.
4. Tell the other person, in a warm and sincere manner, how you think he/she is feeling.

Skill 3. Preparing for a Stressful Conversation

1. Imagine yourself in the stressful situation.
2. Think about how you will feel and why you will feel that way.
3. Imagine the other person in the stressful situation. Think about how that person will feel and why.
4. Imagine yourself telling the other person what you want to say.
5. Imagine what he/she will say.
6. Repeat the above steps using as many approaches as you can think of.
7. Choose the best approach.

Skill 4. Responding to Anger

1. Listen openly to what the other person has to say.
2. Show that you understand what the other person is feeling.
3. Ask the other person to explain anything you don't understand.
4. Show that you understand *why* the other person feels angry.
5. If it is appropriate, express your thoughts and feelings about the situation.

Skill 5. Keeping Out of Fights

1. Stop and think about why you want to fight.
2. Decide what you want to happen in the long run.
3. Think about other ways to handle the situation besides fighting.
4. Decide on the best way to handle the situation and do it.

Skill 6. Helping Others

1. Decide if the other person might need and want your help.
2. Think of the ways you could be helpful.
3. Ask the other person if he/she needs and wants your help.
4. Help the other person.

Skill 7. Dealing with an Accusation

1. Think about what the other person has accused you of.
2. Think about why the person might have accused you.
3. Think about ways to answer the person's accusations.
4. Choose the best way and do it.

Skill 8. Dealing with Group Pressure

1. Think about what the other people want you to do and why.
2. Decide what you want to do.
3. Decide how to tell the other people what you want to do.
4. Tell the group what you have decided.

Skill 9. Expressing Affection

1. Decide if you have good feelings about the other person.
2. Decide whether the other person would like to know about your feelings.
3. Decide how you might best express your feelings.
4. Choose the right time and place to express your feelings.
5. Express affection in a warm and caring manner.

Skill 10. Responding to Failure

1. Decide if you have failed.
2. Think about both the personal reasons and the circumstances that have caused you to fail.
3. Decide how you might do things differently if you tried again.
4. Decide if you want to try again.
5. If it is appropriate, try again, using your revised approach.

SPECIFIC COACHING TECHNIQUES

Specific statements, procedures, and techniques that you may find valuable in your attempts to be an effective transfer coach follow.

Prompting

Under the pressure of real-life situations both in and out of the facility, adolescents may forget all or part of the Structured Learning skills (or anger-reducing techniques) they were taught, and learned, earlier. If their anxiety isn't too great or their forgetting too complete, all that may be needed in order to perform the skill correctly is some prompting. Prompting is reminding the person *what* to do (the skill), *how* to do it (the steps), *when* to do it (now, or the next time the situation occurs), *where* to do it (and where not to), and/or *why* to use the skill here and now (describing the positive outcomes expected).

Encouraging

Offering encouragement to adolescents to use a given skill assumes they know it well enough (thus, they do not need prompting), but are reluctant to use it. Encouragement may be necessary, therefore, when the problem is lack of motivation rather than lack of knowledge. Encouragement can often best be done by gently urging them to try using what they know, by showing *your* enthusiasm for the skill being used, and by communicating optimism about the likely positive outcome of use of the skill.

Reassuring

For particularly anxious youths, skill transfer attempts will be more likely to occur if you are able to reduce the threat of failure. Reassurance is often an effective threat-reduction technique. "You can do it," "I'll be there to help if you need it," and "You've used the other skills well, I think you'll do fine with this one too" are examples of the kinds of reassuring statements the transfer coach can fruitfully provide.

Rewarding

The most important contribution by far that the transfer coach can make for skill transfer is to provide (or help someone else provide) rewards for using a skill correctly. Rewards may take the form of approval, praise, or compliments or may consist of special privileges, points, tokens, recognition, or other reinforcers built into a facility's management system. All of these rewards will, in very substantial ways, increase the likelihood of continued skill uses in new settings and at later times. The most powerful reward that can be offered, however, is the success of the skill itself. If a youth prepares well for a stressful conversation and the conversation then goes very well, that reward (the successful conversation itself) will help the skill transfer more than any other reward. The same conclusion, that success increases transfer, applies to all of the Structured Learning skills (and all of the Anger Control Training anger reducers). Thus, whenever you have or can create the opportunity, reward a youth's skill use by helping it work. Respond positively to a complaint if it is reasonable and try to have others also respond positively. Reciprocate or at least show appreciation for affection when it is expressed appropriately (i.e., by following the steps for Expressing Affection). Try to react with whatever behaviors on your part signal your awareness of effective and appropriate skill use. If you do so, and encourage other important people in the adolescents' environment to do so also, fragile skills will become lasting skills, and ART will have been successful.

References

Adair, J. G., & Schachter, B. S. (1972). To cooperate or to look good? The subject's and experimenter's perceptions of each other's intentions. *Journal of Experimental Social Psychology, 8,* 74–85.

Adams, S. (1961). *Assessment of the psychiatric treatment program, phase I* (Research Report No. 21). Sacramento, CA: California Department of the Youth Authority.

Adams, S. (1962). The PICO project. In N. Johnston, L. Savitz, & M. E. Wolfgang (Eds.), *The sociology of punishment and correction.* New York: Wiley.

Adkins, W. R. (1970). Life skills: Structured counseling for the disadvantaged. *Personnel and Guidance Journal, 49,* 108–116.

Adkins, W. R. (1974). Life coping skills: A fifth curriculum. *Teachers College Record, 75,* 507–526.

Agee, V. L. (1979). *Treatment of the violent incorrigible adolescent.* Lexington, MA: Lexington Books.

Agee, V. L. (1986). Institutional treatment programs for the violent juvenile. In S. J. Apter & A. P. Goldstein (Eds.), *Youth violence: Programs and prospects.* Elmsford, NY: Pergamon.

Agras, W. S. (1967). Transfer during systematic desensitization therapy. *Behavior Research and Therapy, 5,* 193–199.

Allport, F. H. (1924). *Social psychology.* New York: Houghton-Mifflin.

Andrisani, P. (1977). *Work attitudes and labor market experience: Evidence from the National Longitudinal Surveys.* Washington, DC: Employment and Training Administration.

Arbuthnot, J. (1973). Relationships between maturity of moral judgment and measures of cognitive abilities. *Psychological Reports, 33,* 945–946.

Arbuthnot, J. (1975). Modification of moral judgment through role-playing. *Developmental Psychology, 11,* 319–324.

Arbuthnot, J., & Faust, A. (1981). *Teaching moral reasoning: Theory and practice.* New York: Harper & Row.

Arbuthnot, J., & Gordon, D. A. (1983). Moral reasoning development in correctional intervention. *Journal of Correctional Education, 34,* 133–138.

Argyle, M., Trower, P., & Bryant, B. (1974). Explorations in the treatment of personality disorders and neuroses by social skill training. *British Journal of Medical Psychology, 47,* 63–72.

Atrops, M. (1978). *Behavioral plus cognitive skills for coping with provocation in male offenders.* Unpublished doctoral dissertation, Fuller Theological Seminary, Pasadena, CA.

Bailey, W. (1966). *Correctional outcome: An evaluation of 100 reports.* Unpublished manuscript, University of California at Los Angeles, School of Social Welfare.

Bandura, A. (1969). *Principles of behavior modification.* New York: Holt, Rinehart & Winston.

Bandura, A. (1973). *Aggression: A social learning analysis.* Englewood Cliffs, NJ: Prentice-Hall.

Beck, C., Sullivan, E. V., & Taylor, P. (1972). Stimulating transition to post-convention morality: The Pickering High School study. *Interchange, 17,* 28–37.

Bem, S. L. (1967). Verbal self-control: The establishment of effective self-instruction. *Journal of Experimental Psychology, 74,* 485–491.

Bender, N. N. (1976). Self-verbalization versus tutor verbalization in modifying impulsivity. *Journal of Educational Psychology, 68,* 347–354.

Bergin, A. E., & Strupp, H. H. (1972). *Changing frontiers in the science of psychotherapy.* Chicago: Aldine.

Berlin, R. (1976). *Teaching acting-out adolescents prosocial conflict resolution through structured learning training of empathy.* Unpublished doctoral dissertation, Syracuse University, NY.

Bernstein, K., & Christiansen, K. (1965). A resocialization experiment with short-term offenders. *Scandinavian Studies in Criminology, 1,* 35–54.

Blasi, A. (1980). Bridging moral cognition and moral action: A critical review of the literature. *Psychological Bulletin, 88,* 1–45.

Blatt, M., Colby, A., & Speicher, B. (1974). *Hypothetical dilemmas for use in moral discussions.* Cambridge, MA: Moral Education and Research Foundation, Harvard University.

Blatt, M., & Kohlberg, L. (1975). The effects of classroom moral discussion upon children's level of moral judgment. *Journal of Moral Education, 4,* 129–161.

Bornstein, M., Bellack, A. S., & Hersen, M. (1980). Social skills training for highly aggressive children: Treatment in an inpatient psychiatric setting. *Behavior Modification, 4,* 173–186.

Bornstein, P. H., & Quevillon, R. P. (1976). The effects of a self-instructional package on overactive preschool boys. *Journal of Applied Behavior Analysis, 9,* 179–188.

Braswell, L., Kendall, P. C., & Urbain, E. S. (1982). A multistudy analysis of the role of socioeconomic status (SES) in cognitive-behavioral treatments with children. *Journal of Abnormal Child Psychology, 10,* 443–449.

Braukmann, C. J., & Fixsen, D. L. (1975). Behavior modification with delinquents. In M. Hersen, R. M. Eisler, & P. M. Miller (Eds.), *Progress in behavior modification* (Vol. 1). New York: Academic.

Braukmann, C. J., Fixsen, D. L., Phillips, E. L., Wolf, M. M., & Maloney, D. M. (1974). An analysis of a selection interview training package for predelinquents at Achievement Place. *Criminal Justice and Behavior, 1,* 30–42.

Braukmann, C. J., Maloney, D. M., Phillips, E, L., & Wolf, M. M. (1973). *The measurement and modification of heterosexual interaction skills of predelinquents at Achievement Place.* Unpublished manuscript, University of Kansas, Lawrence.

Brody, S. R. (1978). The effectiveness of sentencing—A review of the literature (Home Office Research Study #35). London: H.M.S.O.

California Department of the Youth Authority. (1967). *James Marshall treatment program* [Mimeo].

Callantine. M. F., & Warren, J. M. (1955). Learning sets in human concept formation. *Psychological Reports, 1,* 363–367.

Camp, B. W. (1977). Verbal mediation in young aggressive boys. *Journal of Abnormal Psychology, 86,* 145–153.

Camp, B. W., Blom, G., Hebert, F., & VanDoorninck, W. (1977). "Think aloud": A program for developing self-control in young aggressive boys. *Journal of Abnormal Child Psychology, 5,* 157–169.

Campagna, A. F., & Harter, S. (1975). Moral judgment in sociopathic and normal children. *Journal of Personality and Social Psychology, 31,* 199–205.

Carney, F. J. (1966). *Summary of studies on the derivation of base expectancy categories for predicting recidivism of subjects released from institutions for the Massachusetts Department of Corrections.* Boston: Massachusetts Department of Corrections.

Carroll, J. L., & Nelson, E. A. (1979). *Explorations in the evaluation of the moral development of pre-adolescents.* Unpublished manuscript.

Carroll, J. L., & Rest, J. R. (1981). Development in moral judgment as indicated by rejection of lower-stage statements. *Journal of Research in Personality, 15,* 538–544.

Coats, K. I. (1979). Cognitive self-instructional training approach for reducing disruptive behavior of young children. *Psychological Reports, 44,* 127–134.

Colby, A., Kohlberg, L., Fenton, E., Speicher-Dubin, B., & Lieberman, M. (1977). Secondary school moral discussion programmes led by social studies teachers. *Journal of Moral Education, 6,* 90–111.

Colby, A., Kohlberg, L., & Gibbs, J. (1979). *The longitudinal study of moral judgment.* Paper presented at the meeting of the Society for Research in Child Development, San Francisco.

Conger, J. J., Miller, W. C., & Walsmith, C. R. (1965). Antecedents of delinquency: Personality, social class, and intelligence. In P. H. Mussen, J. J. Conger, & J. Kagen (Eds.), *Readings in child development and personality*. New York: Harper & Row.

Copeland, A. P. (1981). The relevance of subject variables in cognitive self-instructional programs for impulsive children. *Behavior Therapy, 12,* 520–529.

Copeland, A. P. (1982). Individual difference factors in children's self-management: Toward individualized treatments. In P. Karoly & F. H. Kanfer (Eds.), *Self-management and behavior change: From theory to practice*. New York: Pergamon.

Craft, M., Stephenson, G., & Granger, C. (1964). A controlled trial of authoritarian and self-governing regimes with adolescent psychopaths. *American Journal of Orthopsychiatry, 34,* 543–554.

Crain, D. (1977). *Awareness and the modification of anger problems*. Unpublished doctoral dissertation, University of California at Los Angeles.

Cronbach, L. J., & Snow, R. E. (1977). *Aptitudes and instructional methods*. New York: Irvington.

Curry, J. F., Wiencrot, S. I., & Koehler, F. (1984). Family therapy with aggressive and delinquent adolescents. In C. R. Keith (Ed.), *The aggressive adolescent*. New York: Free Press.

Damon, W. (1980). Structural-developmental theory and the study of moral development. In M. Windmiller, H. Lambert, & E. Turiel (Eds.), *Moral development and socialization*. Boston: Allyn & Bacon.

Davidson, W. S., II, & Seidman, E. (1974). Studies of behavior modification and juvenile delinquency: A review, methodological critique, and social perspective. *Psychological Bulletin, 81,* 998–1011.

De Lange, J. M., Lanham, S. L., & Barton, J. A. (1981). Social skills training for juvenile delinquents: Behavioral skill training and cognitive techniques. In D. Upper & S. M. Ross (Eds.), *Behavioral group therapy, 1981: An annual review*. Champaign, IL: Research Press.

Dickie, J. (1973). *Private speech: The effect of presence of others, task and intrapersonal variables*. Unpublished doctoral dissertation, Michigan State University, East Lansing.

Dootjés, I. (1972). Predicting juvenile delinquency. *New Zealand Journal of Criminology, 5,* 157–171.

Douglas, V. I., Parry, P., Marton, P., & Garson, C. (1976). Assessment of a cognitive training program for hyperactive children. *Journal of Abnormal Child Psychology, 4,* 389–410.

Dreikurs, R., Grunwald, B. B., & Pepper, F. C. (1971). *Maintaining sanity in the classroom*. New York: Harper & Row.

Duncan, C. P. (1958). Transfer after training with single versus multiple tasks. *Journal of Experimental Psychology, 55,* 63–73.

Edelman, E. M., & Goldstein, A. P. (1981). Moral education. In A. P. Goldstein, E. G. Carr, W. S. Davidson, & P. Wehr (Eds.), *In response to aggression.* Elmsford, NY: Pergamon.

Edelman, E. M., & Goldstein, A. P. (1984). Prescriptive relationship levels for juvenile delinquents in a psychotherapy analog. *Aggressive Behavior, 10,* 269–278.

Educational Testing Service. (1967). *PAYES: Program for Assessing Youth Employment Skills.* New York: Cambridge Book.

Elardo, P., & Cooper, M. (1977). *AWARE: Activities for social development.* Reading, MA: Addison-Wesley.

Elder, J. P., Edelstein, B. A., & Narick, M. M. (1979). Adolescent psychiatric patients: Modifying aggressive behavior with social skills training. *Behavior Modification, 3,* 161–178.

Ellis, H. (1965). *The transfer of learning.* New York: Macmillan.

Empey, L. T. (1969). Contemporary programs for convicted juvenile offenders: Problems of theory, practice and research. In D. J. Mulvihill & M. M. Tumin (Eds.), *Crimes of violence* (Vol. 13). Washington, DC: U. S. Government Printing Office.

Enright, R. D. (1980). An integration of social cognitive development and cognitive processing: Educational applications. *American Educational Research Journal, 17,* 21–41.

Epps, S., Thompson, B. J., & Lane, M. P. (1985). *Procedures for incorporating generalization programming into interventions for behaviorally disordered students.* Unpublished manuscript, Iowa State University, Ames, IA.

Fagan, J. A., & Hartstone, E. (1984). Strategic planning in juvenile justice—Defining the toughest kids. In R. A. Mathias, P. DeMuro, & R. S. Albinson (Eds.), *Violent juvenile offenders.* San Francisco: National Council on Crime and Delinquency.

Faust, D., & Arbuthnot, J. (1978). Relationship between moral and Piagetian reasoning and the effectiveness of moral education. *Developmental Psychology, 14,* 435–436.

Federal Bureau of Investigation. (1975). *Uniform crime report.* Washington, DC: U. S. Government Printing Office.

Federal Bureau of Investigation. (1978). *Uniform crime report.* Washington, DC: U. S. Government Printing Office.

Feindler, E. L. (1979). *Cognitive and behavioral approaches to anger control training in explosive adolescents.* Unpublished doctoral dissertation, West Virginia University, Morgantown.

Feindler, E. L. (1981). *The art of self-control.* Unpublished manuscript, Adelphi University, Garden City, NY.

Feindler, E. L., & Fremouw, W. J. (1983). Stress inoculation training for adolescent anger problems. In D. Meichenbaum & M. E. Jaremko (Eds.), *Stress reduction and prevention.* New York: Plenum.

Feindler, E. L., Latini, J., Nape, K., Romano, J., & Doyle, J. (1980). *Anger reduction methods for child-care workers at a residential delinquent facility.* Presented at the meeting of the Association for the Advancement of Behavior Therapy, New York.

Feindler, E. L., Marriott, S. A., & Iwata, M. (1984). Group anger control training for junior high school delinquents. *Cognitive Therapy and Research, 8,* 299–311.

Feldman, R. A., Caplinger, T. E., & Woodarski, J. S. (1983). *The St. Louis conundrum: The effective treatment of antisocial youths.* Englewood Cliffs, NJ: Prentice-Hall.

Feshbach, N. D. (1982). Empathy training and the regulation of aggression in elementary school children. In R. M. Kaplan, V. J. Konecni, & R. Novaco (Eds.), *Aggression in children and youth.* Alphen den Rijn, The Netherlands: Sijthoff/Noordhoff.

Feshbach, N. D., & Feshbach, S. (1969). The relationship between empathy and aggression in two age groups. *Developmental Psychology, 1,* 102–107.

Fischman, A. (1984). *Evaluation of the effectiveness of structured learning with abusive parents.* Unpublished master's thesis, Syracuse University, NY.

Fischman, A. (1985). *Skill transfer enhancement in structured learning of abusive parents.* Unpublished doctoral dissertation, Syracuse University, NY.

Fleetwood, R. S., & Parish, T. S. (1976). Relation between moral development test scores of juvenile delinquents and their inclusion in a moral dilemma discussion group. *Psychological Reports, 39,* 1075–1080.

Fleming, D. (1976). *Teaching negotiation skills to pre-adolescents.* Unpublished doctoral dissertation, Syracuse University, NY.

Fodor, E. M. (1972). Delinquency and susceptibility to social influence among adolescents as a function of level of moral development. *Journal of Social Psychology, 86,* 257–260.

Fraenkel, J. R. (1976). The Kohlberg bandwagon: Some reservations. *Social Education, 40,* 216–222.

Freedman, B. J., Rosenthal, L., Donahoe, C. P., Schlundt, D. G., & McFall, R. M. (1978). A social behavioral analysis of skill deficits in delinquent and nondelinquent adolescent boys. *Journal of Consulting and Clinical Psychology, 46,* 1448–1462.

Garrity, D. (1956). *The effects of length of incarceration upon parole adjustment and estimation of optimum sentence.* Unpublished doctoral dissertation, University of Washington, Seattle.

Gensheimer, L. K., Mayer, J. P., Gottschalk, R., & Davidson, W. S. (1986). Diverting youth from the juvenile justice system: A meta-analysis of intervention efficacy. In S. J. Apter & A. P. Goldstein (Eds.), *Youth violence: Programs and prospects.* Elmsford, NY: Pergamon.

Gerson, R., & Damon, W. (1975). *Relations between moral behavior in a hypothetical-verbal context and in a practical, "real-life" setting.* Paper presented at the meeting of the Eastern Psychological Association, New York.

Gibbs, J. C., Arnold, K. D., Ahlborn, H. H., & Cheesman, F. L. (1984). Facilitation of sociomoral reasoning in delinquents. *Journal of Consulting and Clinical Psychology, 52,* 37–45.

Gibbs, J. C., Widaman, K. F., & Colby, A. (1982). *Social intelligence: Measuring the development of sociomoral reflection.* Englewood Cliffs, NJ: Prentice-Hall.

Glaser, D. (1973, November). *The state of the art of criminal justice evaluation.* Paper presented at the meeting of the Association for Criminal Justice Research, Los Angeles.

Glasser, W. (1965). *Reality therapy.* New York: Harper & Row.

Glick, B. (1983). Juvenile delinquency. In A. P. Goldstein (Ed.), *Prevention and control of aggression.* Elmsford, NY: Pergamon.

Glick, B. (1986). Programming for juvenile delinquents: An administrative perspective. In S. J. Apter & A. P. Goldstein (Eds.), *Youth violence: Programs and prospects.* Elmsford, NY: Pergamon.

Glick, S. J. (1972). Identification of predelinquents among children with school behavior problems as basis for multiservice treatment program. In S. Glueck & E. Glueck (Eds.), *Identification of predelinquents: Validation studies and some suggested uses of Glueck table.* New York: Intercontinental Medical Books.

Golden, R. (1975). *Teaching resistance-reducing behavior to high school students.* Unpublished doctoral dissertation, Syracuse University, NY.

Goldstein, A. P. (1973). *Structured learning therapy: Toward a psychotherapy for the poor.* New York: Academic.

Goldstein, A. P. (Ed.). (1978). *Prescriptions for child mental health and education.* Elmsford, NY: Pergamon.

Goldstein, A. P. (1981). *Psychological skill training.* Elmsford, NY: Pergamon.

Goldstein, A. P., Apter, S. J., & Harootunian, B. (1984). *School violence.* Englewood Cliffs, NJ: Prentice-Hall.

Goldstein, A. P., Glick, B., Reiner, S., Zimmerman, D., Coultry, T., & Gold, D. (in press). Aggression Replacement Training: A comprehensive intervention for juvenile delinquents. *Journal of Correctional Education.*

Goldstein, A. P., & Goedhart, A. (1973). The use of structured learning for empathy enhancement in paraprofessional psychotherapist training. *Journal of Community Psychology, 1,* 168–173.

Goldstein, A. P., & Kanfer, F. H. (1979). *Maximizing treatment gains: Transfer enhancement in psychotherapy.* New York: Academic.

Goldstein, A. P., Keller, H., & Erné, D. (1985). *Changing the abusive parent.* Champaign, IL: Research Press.

Goldstein, A. P., & Michaels, G. Y. (1985). *Empathy: Development, training and consequences.* Hillsdale, NJ: Erlbaum.

Goldstein, A. P., Monti, P. J., Sardino, T. J., & Green, D. J. (1977). *Police crisis intervention.* Elmsford, NY: Pergamon.

Goldstein, A. P., & Rosenbaum, A. (1982). *Aggress-Less.* Englewood Cliffs, NJ: Prentice-Hall.

Goldstein, A. P., Sherman, M., Gershaw, N. J., Sprafkin, R. P., & Glick, B. (1978). Training aggressive adolescents in prosocial behavior. *Journal of Youth and Adolescence, 7,* 73–92.

Goldstein, A. P., & Sorcher, M. (1973a, March). Changing managerial behavior by applied learning techniques. *Training and Development Journal,* 36–39.

Goldstein, A. P., & Sorcher, M. (1973b). *Changing supervisor behavior.* Elmsford, NY: Pergamon.

Goldstein, A. P., Sprafkin, R. P., & Gershaw, N. J. (1976). *Skill training for community living: Applying structured learning therapy.* Elmsford, NY: Pergamon.

Goldstein, A. P., Sprafkin, R. P., Gershaw, N. J., & Klein, P. (1980). *Skillstreaming the adolescent: A structured learning approach to teaching prosocial skills.* Champaign, IL: Research Press.

Goldstein, A. P., & Stein, N. (1976). *Prescriptive psychotherapies.* Elmsford, NY: Pergamon.

Grant, J. (1986). *Problem solving training for delinquent youth.* Unpublished doctoral dissertation, Syracuse University, NY.

Grant, J., & Grant, M. Q. (1959). A group dynamics approach to the treatment of nonconformists in the navy. *Annual of the American Academy of Political and Social Sciences, 322,* 126–135.

Gray, A. L., & Dermody, H. E. (1972). Reports of casework failure. *Social Casework, 16,* 207–212.

Green, R. A., & Murray, E. J. (1973). Instigation to aggression as a function of self-disclosure and threat to self-esteem. *Journal of Consulting and Clinical Psychology, 40,* 440–443.

Greenleaf, D. (1977). *Peer reinforcement as transfer enhancement in structured learning therapy.* Unpublished master's thesis, Syracuse University, NY.

Grim, P. F., Kohlberg, L., & White, S. H. (1968). Some relationships between conscience and attentional processes. *Journal of Personality and Social Psychology, 8,* 239–252.

Grimes, P. (1974). *Teaching moral reasoning to eleven-year-olds and their mothers: A means of promoting moral growth.* Unpublished doctoral dissertation, Boston University.

Grinder, R. E. (1964). Relations between cognitive dimensions of conscience in middle childhood. *Child Development, 35,* 881–891.

Gross, A. M., Brigham, T. A., Hopper, C., & Bologna, N. C. (1980). Self-management and social skills training: A study with predelinquent youths. *Criminal Justice and Behavior, 7,* 161–184.

Gruber, R. P. (1971). Behavior therapy: Problems in generalization. *Behavior Therapy, 2,* 361–368.

Guerney, B. G., Jr. (1977). *Relationship enhancement.* San Francisco: Jossey-Bass.

Gurr, T. R. (1979). On the history of violent crime in Europe and America. In H. D. Graham & T. R. Gurr (Eds.), *Violence in America: Historical and comparative perspectives.* Beverly Hills, CA: Sage.

Guttman, E. S. (1970). Effects of short-term psychiatric treatment for boys in two California Youth Authority institutions. In D. C. Gibbons (Ed.), *Delinquent behavior.* Englewood Cliffs, NJ: Prentice-Hall.

Guzzetta, R. A. (1974). *Acquisition and transfer of empathy by the parents of early adolescents through structured learning training.* Unpublished doctoral dissertation, Syracuse University, NY.

Haan, N. (1975). Hypothetical and actual moral reasoning in a situation of civil disobedience. *Journal of Personality and Social Psychology, 32,* 255–270.

Haan, N., Smith, M. B., & Block, T. (1968). The moral reasoning of young adults: Political-social behavior, family background, and personality correlates. *Journal of Personality and Social Psychology, 10,* 183–201.

Hare, M. A. (1976). *Teaching conflict resolution situations.* Paper presented at the meeting of the Eastern Community Association, Philadelphia.

Harris, S., Mussen, P., & Rutherford, E. (1976). Some cognitive, behavioral and personality correlates of maturity of moral judgment. *Journal of Genetic Psychology, 128,* 123–135.

Harrison, R. M., & Mueller, P. (1964). *Clue hunting about group counseling and parole outcome.* Sacramento, CA: California Department of Corrections.

Hartig, M., & Kanfer, F. H. (1973). The role of verbal self-instructions in children's resistance to temptation. *Journal of Personality and Social Psychology, 25,* 259–267.

Hartshorne, J., & May, M. A. (1928). *Studies in the nature of character: Vol. 1. Studies in deceit.* New York: Macmillan.

Hawley, R. C., & Hawley, I. L. (1975). *Developing human potential: A handbook of activities for personal and social growth.* Amherst, MA: Education Research Associates.

Hazel, J. S., Schumaker, J. B., Sherman, J. A., & Sheldon-Wildgen, J. (1981). *ASSET: A social skills program for adolescents.* Champaign, IL: Research Press.

Heath, B. L. (1978). *Application of verbal self-instructional training procedures to classroom behavior management.* Unpublished doctoral dissertation, University of Minnesota, Minneapolis.

Heiman, H. (1973). Teaching interpersonal communications. *North Dakota Speech and Theatre Association Bulletin, 2,* 7–29.

Higa, W. R. (1973). *Self-instructional versus direct training in modifying children's impulsive behavior.* Unpublished doctoral dissertation, University of Hawaii, Honolulu.

Hoffman, M. (1970). Moral development. In P. Mussen (Ed.), *Carmichael's manual of child psychology.* New York: Wiley.

Hollin, C. R., & Courtney, S. A. (1983). A skill training approach to the reduction of institutional offending. *Personality and Individual Differences, 4,* 257–264.

Hollin, C. R., & Henderson, M. (1981). The effects of social skills training on incarcerated delinquent adolescents. *International Journal of Behavioral Social Work, 1,* 145–155.

Holstein, C. B. (1976). Irreversible, stepwise sequence in the development of moral judgment: A longitudinal study of males and females. *Child Development, 47,* 51–61.

Hudgins, W., & Prentice, N. M. (1973). Moral judgment in delinquent and nondelinquent adolescents and their mothers. *Journal of Abnormal Psychology, 82,* 145–152.

Hummel, J. (1980). *Session variability and skill content as transfer enhancers in structured learning training.* Unpublished doctoral dissertation, Syracuse University, NY.

Hunt, D. E. (1972). Matching models for teacher training. In B. R. Joyce & M. Weil (Eds.), *Perspectives for reform in teacher education.* Englewood Cliffs, NJ: Prentice-Hall.

Jennings, R. L. (1975). *The use of structured learning techniques to teach attraction enhancing skills to residentially hospitalized lower socioeconomic emotionally disturbed children and adolescents: A psychotherapy analogue investigation.* Unpublished doctoral dissertation, University of Iowa, Iowa City.

Jesness, C. F. (1962). *Jesness Inventory, Form G.* Palo Alto, CA: Consulting Psychologists Press.

Jesness, C. F. (1965). *The Fricot Ranch study.* Sacramento: California Department of the Youth Authority.

Jones, M. (1953). *The therapeutic community.* New York: Basic Books.

Kagan, J. (1966). Reflection-impulsivity: The generality and dynamics of conceptual tempo. *Journal of Abnormal Psychology, 71,* 17–24.

Kahn, A. J. (1965). A case of premature claims. *Crime and Delinquency, 20,* 233–240.

Karoly, P., & Steffen, J. J. (Eds.). (1980). *Improving the long-term effects of psychotherapy.* New York: Gardner.

Kassenbaum, G., Ward, D., & Wilner, D. (1979). *Prison treatment and its outcome.* New York: Wiley.

Kaufmann, H., & Feshbach, S. (1963). The influence of anti-aggressive communications upon the response to provocation. *Journal of Personality, 31,* 428–444.

Kazdin, A. (1980). *Research design in clinical psychology.* New York: Harper & Row.

Keasey, C. B. (1977). Young children's attribution of intentionality to themselves and others. *Child Development, 48,* 261–264.

Keith, C. R. (1984). Individual psychotherapy and psychoanalysis with the aggressive adolescent: A historical review. In C. R. Keith (Ed.), *The aggressive adolescent.* New York: Free Press, 191–208.

Keller, F. S. (1966). A personal course in psychology. In R. Ulrich, T. Stachnik, & J. Mabry (Eds.), *Control of human behavior.* Glenview, IL: Scott Foresman.

Kendall, P. C. (1977). On the efficacious use of verbal self-instructional procedures with children. *Cognitive Therapy and Research, 1,* 331–341.

Kendall, P. C., & Braswell, L. (1985). *Cognitive-behavioral therapy for impulsive children.* New York: Guilford.

Kendall, P. C., & Wilcox, L. E. (1979). Self-control in children: Development of a rating scale. *Journal of Consulting and Clinical Psychology, 47,* 1020–1030.

Kiesler, D. J. (1969). A grid model for theory and research. In L. D. Eron & R. Callahan (Eds.), *The relation of theory to practice in psychotherapy.* Chicago: Aldine.

Kifer, R. E., Lewis, M. A., Green, D. R., & Phillips, E. L. (1974). Training predelinquent youths and their parents to negotiate conflict situations. *Journal of Applied Behavior Analysis, 7,* 357–364.

Kirschenbaum, H. (1975). Recent research in values education. In J. R., Meyer, B. Burnham, & J. Chotvat (Eds.), *Values education: Theory, practice, problems, prospects.* Waterloo, Ontario: Wilfrid Laurier University Press.

Klausmeier, H. J., Rossmiller, R. A., & Sailey, M. (1977). *Individually guided elementary education.* New York: Academic.

Kleiman, A. (1974). *The use of private speech in young children and its relation to social speech.* Unpublished doctoral dissertation, University of Chicago.

Klett, C. J., & Moseley, E. C. (1963, November). *The right drug for the right patient* (Report No. 54). Washington, DC: Cooperative Studies in Psychiatry, Veterans Administration, U.S. Government Printing Office.

Knight, D. (1969). *The Marshall Program: Assessment of a short-term institutional treatment program* (Research Report No. 56). Sacramento, CA: California Department of the Youth Authority.

Kohlberg, L. (1969). Stage and sequence: The cognitive-developmental approach to socialization. In D. A. Goslin (Ed.), *Handbook of socialization theory and research.* Chicago: Rand McNally.

Kohlberg, L. (1971a). From is to ought: How to commit the naturalistic fallacy and get away with it in the study of moral development. In T. Meschel (Ed.), *Cognitive development and epistemology.* New York: Academic.

Kohlberg, L. (1971b). Stages of moral development as a basis for moral education. In C. M. Beck, B. S. Crittendon, & E. V. Sullivan (Eds.), *Moral education: Interdisciplinary approaches.* Toronto: University of Toronto Press.

Kohlberg, L. (Ed.). (1973). *Collected papers on moral development and moral education.* Cambridge, MA: Center for Moral Education, Harvard University.

Kohlberg, L. (1976). Moral stages and moralization: The cognitive-developmental approach. In T. Lickona (Ed.), *Moral development and behavior: Theory, research, and social issues.* New York: Holt, Rinehart, & Winston.

Kohlberg, L., Kauffman, K., Scharf, P., & Hickey, J. (1975). The just community approach to corrections: A theory. *Journal of Moral Education, 4,* 243–260.

Kohlberg, L., & Kramer, R. G. (1969). Continuities and discontinuities in childhood and adult moral development. *Human Development, 12,* 93–120.

Kohlberg, L., & Turiel, E. (1971). Moral development and moral education. In G. S. Lesser (Ed.), *Psychology and educational practice.* Chicago: Scott Foresman.

Kohlberg, L., Yaeger, J., & Hjertholm, E. (1968). Private speech: Four studies and a review of theories. *Child Development, 39,* 691–736.

Kopel, S., & Arkowitz, H. (1975). The role of attribution and self-perception in behavior change: Implications for behavior therapy. *Genetic Psychology Monographs, 92,* 175–212.

Kramer, R. (1968). *Changes in moral judgment response pattern during late adolescence and young adulthood: Retrogression in a developmental sequence.* Unpublished doctoral dissertation, University of Chicago.

Krebs, R. L. (1967). *Some relationships between attention and resistance to temptation.* Unpublished doctoral dissertation, University of Chicago.

Kuhn, D. (1976). Short-term longitudinal evidence for the sequentiality of Kohlberg's early stages of moral judgment. *Developmental Psychology, 12,* 162–166.

Kurtines, W., & Grief, E. B. (1974). The development of moral thought: Review and evaluation of Kohlberg's approach. *Psychological Bulletin, 81,* 453–470.

Lack, D. Z. (1975). *Problem-solving training, structured learning training, and didactic instruction in the preparation of paraprofessional mental health personnel for the utilization of contingency management techniques.* Unpublished doctoral dissertation, Syracuse University, NY.

Lavin, G. K., Trabka, S., & Kahn, E. M. (1984). Group therapy with aggressive and delinquent adolescents. In C. R. Keith (Ed.), *The aggressive adolescent.* New York: Free Press.

Lee, D. Y., Hallberg, E. T., & Hassard, H. (1979). Effects of assertion training on aggressive behavior in adolescents. *Journal of Counseling Psychology, 26,* 459–461.

Lee, L. C. (1971). The concomitant development of cognitive and moral modes of thought: A test of selected deductions from Piaget's theory. *Genetic Psychology Monographs, 83,* 93–146.

Liberman, B. (1970). *The effect of modeling procedures on attraction and disclosure in a psychotherapy analogue.* Unpublished doctoral dissertation, Syracuse University, NY.

Lickona, T. (1976). Critical issues in the study of moral development and behavior. In T. Lickona (Ed.), *Moral development and behavior: Theory, research, and social issues.* New York: Holt, Rinehart, & Winston.

Lipton, D., Martinson, R., & Wilks, J. (1975). *The effectiveness of correctional treatment: A survey of treatment evaluation studies.* New York: Praeger.

Little, V. L., & Kendall, P. C. (1979). Cognitive-behavioral interventions with delinquents: Problem solving, role-taking, and self-control. In P. C. Kendall & S. D. Hollon (Eds.), *Cognitive-behavioral interventions.* Orlando, FL: Academic.

Litwack, S. E. (1976). *The use of the helper therapy principle to increase therapeutic effectiveness and reduce therapeutic resistance: Structured learning therapy with resistant adolescents.* Unpublished doctoral dissertation, Syracuse University, NY.

Loeber, R., & Dishion, T. (1983). Early predictors of male delinquency: A review. *Psychological Bulletin, 94,* 68–99.

Long, S. J., & Sherer, M. (1984). Social skills training with juvenile offenders. *Child & Family Behavior Therapy, 6,* 1–12.

Lopez, M. (1977). *The effects of overlearning and prestructuring in structured learning therapy with geriatric patients.* Unpublished doctoral dissertation, Syracuse University, NY.

Lopez, M., Hoyer, W. J., Goldstein, A. P., Gershaw, N. J., & Sprafkin, R. P. (1982). Predicting social skill acquisition and transfer by psychogeriatric inpatients. *International Journal of Behavioral Geriatrics, 1,* 43–46.

Lundman, R. J. (1984). *Prevention and control of delinquency.* New York: Oxford University Press.

Luria, A. R. (1961). *The role of speech in the regulation of normal and abnormal behavior.* New York: Liveright.

Magaro, P. A. (1969). A prescriptive treatment model based upon social class and premorbid adjustment. *Psychotherapy: Theory, Research and Practice, 6,* 57–70.

Mallick, S. K., & McCandless, B. R. (1966). A study of catharsis of aggression. *Journal of Personality and Social Psychology, 4,* 591–596.

Maloney, D. M., Harper, T. M., Braukmann, C. J., Fixsen, D. L., Phillips, E. L., & Wolf, M. M. (1976). Teaching conversation-related skills to predelinquent girls. *Journal of Applied Behavior Analysis, 9,* 371.

Martinson, R. (1974, Spring). What works? Questions and answers about prison reform. *The Public Interest,* 22–54.

Maslow, A. H. (1970). *Motivation and personality.* New York: Harper & Row.

Matefy, R. E., & Acksen, B. A. (1976). The effect of role-playing discrepant positions on change in moral judgments and attitudes. *The Journal of Genetic Psychology, 128,* 189–200.

Matson, J. L., Esveldt-Dawson, K., Andrasik, F., Ollendick, T. H., Petti, T., & Hersen, M. (1980). Direct, observational, and generalization effects of social skills training with emotionally disturbed children. *Behavior Therapy, 11,* 522–531.

May, J. R., & Johnson, H. J. (1973). Physiological activity to internally elicited arousal and inhibitory thoughts. *Journal of Abnormal Psychology, 82,* 239–245.

Mayer, J. P., Gensheimer, L. K., Davidson, W. S., & Gottschalk, R. (1986). Social learning treatment within juvenile justice: A meta-analysis of impact in the natural environment. In S. J. Apter & A. P. Goldstein (Eds.), *Youth violence: Programs and prospects.* Elmsford, NY: Pergamon.

McCorkle, L., Elias, A., & Bixby, F. (1958). *The Highfields story: A unique experiment in the treatment of juvenile delinquency.* New York: Holt.

McCullough, J. P., Huntsinger, G. M., & Nay, W. R. (1977). Self-control treatment of aggression in a 16-year-old male. *Journal of Consulting and Clinical Psychology, 45,* 322–331.

McGinnis, E., & Goldstein, A. P. (1984). *Skillstreaming the elementary school child: A guide for teaching prosocial skills.* Champaign, IL: Research Press.

McNamee, S. (1977). Moral behaviour, moral development and motivation. *Journal of Moral Education, 7,* 27–31.

Meichenbaum, D. H. (1977). *Cognitive-behavior modification: An integrative approach.* New York: Plenum.

Meichenbaum, D. H., Gilmore, J. B., & Fedoravicius, A. (1971). Group insight versus group desensitization in treating speech anxiety. *Journal of Consulting and Clinical Psychology, 36,* 410–421.

Meichenbaum, D. H., & Goodman, J. (1969). The developmental control of operant motor responding by verbal operants. *Journal of Experimental Child Psychology, 7,* 553–565.

Meichenbaum, D. H., & Goodman, J. (1971). Training impulsive children to talk to themselves: A means of developing self-control. *Journal of Abnormal Psychology, 77,* 115–126.

Minkin, N., Braukmann, C. J., Minkin, B. L., Timbers, G. D., Timbers, B. J., Fixsen, D. L., Phillips, E. L., & Wolf, M. M. (1976). The social validation and training of conversation skills. *Journal of Applied Behavior Analysis, 9,* 127–139.

Mitchell, S. & Rosa, P. (1981). Boyhood behaviour problems as precursors of criminality: A fifteen-year follow-up study. *Journal of Child Psychology and Psychiatry, 22,* 19–33.

Monahan, J., & O'Leary, K. D. (1971). Effects of self-instruction and rule-breaking behavior. *Psychological Reports, 29,* 1059–1066.

Moon, J. R., & Eisler, R. M. (1983). Anger control: An experimental comparison of three behavioral treatments. *Behavior Therapy, 14,* 493–505.

Mussen, P. H. (1963). *The psychological development of the child.* Englewood Cliffs, NJ: Prentice-Hall.

Mussen, P. H., Conger, J. J., Kagan, J., & Gerwitz, J. (1979). *Psychological development: A life-span approach.* New York: Harper & Row.

Nisan, M., & Kohlberg, L. (1978). *University and cross-cultural variance in moral development: A longitudinal and cross-sectional study in Turkey.* Unpublished manuscript, Center for Moral Education, Harvard University, Cambridge, MA.

Novaco, R. W. (1975). *Anger control: The development and evaluation of an experimental treatment.* Lexington, MA: D. C. Heath.

Novaco, R. W. (1977). A stress inoculation approach to anger management in the training of law enforcement officers. *American Journal of Community Psychology, 5,* 327–346.

Novaco, R. W. (1978). Anger and coping with stress. In J. Foreyt & D. Rathjen (Eds.), *Cognitive behavior therapy: Therapy, research and practice.* New York: Plenum.

Novaco, R. W. (1979). The cognitive regulation of anger and stress. In P. C. Kendall & S. D. Hollon (Eds.), *Cognitive-behavioral interventions.* Orlando, FL: Academic.

Office of Youth Development. (1975). *Theory validation and aggregate national data.* Boulder, CO: Behavioral Research and Evaluation Corporation.

O'Leary, K. D., O'Leary, S., & Becker, W. C. (1967). Modification of a deviant sibling interaction pattern in the home. *Behavior Research and Therapy, 5,* 113–120.

Ollendick, T. H., & Hersen, M. (1979). Social skills training for juvenile delinquents. *Behavior Research and Therapy, 17,* 547–555.

Orenstein, R. (1973). *Effect of teaching patients to focus on their feelings on level of experiencing in a subsequent interview.* Unpublished doctoral dissertation, Syracuse University, NY.

Orne, M. T. (1962). On the social psychology of the psychological experiment: With particular reference to demand characteristics and their implications. *American Psychologist, 17,* 776–783.

Osgood, C. E. (1953). *Method and theory in experimental psychology.* New York: Oxford University Press.

Palkes, H., Stewart, M., & Kahana, B. (1968). Porteus Maze performance of hyperactive boys after training in self-directed verbal commands. *Child Development, 39,* 817–826.

Palmer, T. (1973). Matching worker and client in corrections. *Social Work, 18,* 95–103.

Palmer, T. (1975). Martinson revisited. *Journal of Research in Crime and Delinquency, 12,* 133–152.

Patterson, G. R., & Anderson, D. (1964). Peers as social reinforcers. *Child Development, 35,* 951–960.

Patterson, G. R., Cobb, J. A., & Ray, R. S. (1973). A social engineering technology for retraining the families of aggressive boys. In H. E. Adams & I. P. Unikel (Eds.), *Issues and trends in behavior therapy.* Springfield, IL: Charles C. Thomas.

Patterson, G. R., Reid, J. G., Jones, R. R., & Conger, R. E. (1975). *A social learning approach to family intervention* (Vol. 1). Eugene, OR: Castalia.

Pentz, M. A. (1980). Assertion training and trainer effects on unassertive and aggressive adolescents. *Journal of Counseling Psychology, 27,* 76–83.

Peters, R. S. (1978). The place of Kohlberg's theory in moral education. *Journal of Moral Education, 7,* 147–157.

Piaget, J. (1932). *The moral judgment of the child.* London: Routledge & Kegan Paul.

Piccola, R., French, M., & Leve, P. (1982). *The Work Behavior Rating Scale.* Unpublished manuscript, Albany, NY.

Pressley, M. (1979). Increasing children's self-control through cognitive interventions. *Review of Educational Research, 49,* 319–370.

Pulkkinen, L., & Saastomoinen, M. (1986). Cross-cultural perspectives on youth violence. In S. J. Apter & A. P. Goldstein (Eds.), *Youth violence: Programs and prospects.* Elmsford, NY: Pergamon.

Raleigh, R. (1977). *Individual versus group structured learning therapy for assertiveness training with senior and junior high school students.* Unpublished doctoral dissertation, Syracuse University, NY.

Raths, L. E., Harmin, M., & Simon, S. B. (1966). *Values and teaching: Working with values in the classroom.* Columbus, OH: Charles Merrill.

Redl, F., & Wineman, D. (1957). *The aggressive child.* New York: Free Press.

Redner, R., Snellman, L., & Davidson, W. S. (1983). Juvenile delinquency. In R. J. Morris & T. R. Kratochwill (Eds.), *The practice of child therapy.* Elmsford, NY: Pergamon.

Reiner, S. (1985). *Interpersonal maturity level as a measure of differential responsiveness to aggression replacement training.* Unpublished master's thesis, Syracuse University, NY.

Rest, J. R. (1979). *Development in judging moral issues.* Minneapolis: University of Minnesota Press.

Rest, J. R., Turiel, E., & Kohlberg, L. (1969). Level of moral development as a determinant of preference and comprehension of moral judgments made by others. *Journal of Personality, 37,* 225–252.

Riessman, F. (1965). The "helper" therapy principle. *Social Work, 10*(2), 27–32.

Rimm, D. C., & Litvak, S. B. (1969). Self-verbalization and emotional arousal. *Journal of Abnormal Psychology, 74,* 181–187.

Robbins, L. N., & Ratcliff, K. S. (1979). Risk factors in the continuation of childhood antisocial behavior into adulthood. *International Journal of Mental Health, 7,* 96–116.

Robin, A. L. (1981). A controlled evaluation of problem-solving communication training with parent-adolescent conflict. *Behavior Therapy, 12,* 593–609.

Robin, A. L., Kent, R., O'Leary, K. D., Foster, S., & Prinz, R. (1977). An approach to teaching parents and adolescents problem-solving communication skills: A preliminary report. *Behavior Therapy, 8,* 639–643.

Robinson, J., & Smith, G. (1971). The effectiveness of correctional programs. *Crime and Delinquency, 17,* 67–80.

Robinson, R. (1973). *Evaluation of a structured learning empathy training program for lower socioeconomic status home-aide trainees.* Unpublished master's thesis, Syracuse University, NY.

Rogers, C. R. (1957). The necessary and sufficient conditions of therapeutic personality change. *Journal of Consulting Psychology, 21,* 95–103.

Romig, D. A. (1978). *Justice for our children: An examination of juvenile delinquency rehabilitation programs.* Lexington, MA: Lexington Books.

Rosenkoetter, L. I., Landman, S., & Mazak, S. G. (1980). Use of moral discussion as an intervention with delinquents. *Psychological Reports, 46,* 91–94.

Rothman, J. R. (1980). The relationship between moral judgment and moral behavior. In M. Wendmiller, N. Lambert, & E. Turiels (Eds.), *Moral development and socialization.* Boston: Allyn & Bacon.

Rotter, J. B. (1966). Generalized expectancies for internal versus external control of reinforcement. *Psychological Monographs, 80* (Whole No. 609).

Ruma, E. H., & Mosher, D. L. (1967). Relationship between moral judgment and guilt in delinquent boys. *Journal of Abnormal Psychology, 72,* 122–127.

Rundle, L. (1977). *The stimulation of moral development in the elementary school and the cognitive examination of social experience: A fifth grade study.* Unpublished doctoral dissertation, Boston University.

Russell, P. L., & Brandsma, J. M. (1974). A theoretical and empirical integration of the rational-emotive and classical conditioning theories. *Journal of Consulting and Clinical Psychology, 42,* 389–397.

Rutter, M., & Giller, H. (1983). *Juvenile delinquency: Trends and perspectives.* New York: Guilford.

Saltzstein, H. D., Diamond, R. M., & Belenky, M. (1972). Moral judgment level and conformity behavior. *Developmental Psychology, 7,* 327–336.

Sarason, I. G., & Ganzer, V. J. (1973). Modeling and group discussion in the rehabilitation of juvenile delinquents. *Journal of Counseling Psychology, 20,* 442–449.

Sarason, I. G., & Sarason, B. R. (1981). Teaching cognitive and social skills to high school students. *Journal of Consulting and Clinical Psychology, 49,* 908–918.

Schlichter, K. J., & Horan, J. J. (1981). Effects of stress inoculation on the anger and aggression management skills of institutionalized juvenile delinquents. *Cognitive Therapy and Research, 5,* 359–365.

Schmidlin, S. S. (1977). *Moral judgment and delinquency: The effect of institutionalization and peer pressure.* Unpublished doctoral dissertation, University of Florida, Gainesville.

Schneiman, R. (1972). *An evaluation of structured learning and didactic learning as methods of training behavior modification skills to lower and middle socioeconomic level teacher-aides.* Unpublished doctoral dissertation, Syracuse University, NY.

Schrader, C., Long, J., Panzer, C., Gillet, D., & Kornbath, R. (1977). *An anger control package for adolescent drug abusers.* Paper presented at the meeting of the Association for the Advancement of Behavior Therapy, Atlanta.

Schwartz, G. E. (1971). Cardiac responses to self-induced thoughts. *Psychophysiology, 8,* 462–467.

Schwartz, S. H., Feldman, K. A., Brown, M. E., & Heingartner, A. (1969). Some personality correlates of conduct in two situations of moral conflict. *Journal of Personality, 37,* 41–57.

Sealy, A., & Banks, C. (1971). Social maturity, training, experience, and recidivism amongst British borstal boys. *British Journal of Criminology, 11,* 245–264.

Sechrest, L., White, S. O., & Brown, E. D. (1979). *The rehabilitation of criminal offenders: Problems and prospects.* Washington, DC: National Academy of Sciences.

Seidman, E., & Rapkin, B. (1983). Economics and psychosocial dysfunction: Toward a conceptual framework and prevention strategies. In R. D. Felner, L. A. Jasson, J. N. Moritsugu, & S. S. Farber (Eds.), *Preventive psychology.* Elmsford, NY: Pergamon.

Serna, L. A., Schumaker, J. B., Hazel, J. S., & Sheldon, J. B. (in press). Teaching reciprocal social skills to parents and their delinquent adolescents. *Journal of Clinical Child Psychology.*

Shoemaker, M. E. (1979). Group assertion training for institutionalized male delinquents. In J. S. Stumphauzer (Ed.), *Progress in behavior therapy with delinquents.* Springfield, IL: Charles C. Thomas.

Shore, E., & Sechrest, L. (1961). Concept attainment as a function of number of positive instances presented. *Journal of Educational Psychology, 52,* 303–307.

Simon, S. B., Howe, L. W., & Kirschenbaum, H. (1972). *Values clarification: A handbook of practical strategies for teachers and students.* New York: Hart.

Simon, S. B., & Olds, S. W. (1976). *Helping your child learn right from wrong: A guide to values clarification.* New York: McGraw-Hill.

Simpson, E. L. (1974). Moral development research: A case of scientific cultural bias. *Human Development, 17,* 81–106.

Slavson, S. R. (1964). *A textbook in analytic group psychotherapy.* New York: International Universities Press.

Snyder, J. J., & White, M. J. (1979). The use of cognitive self-instructions in treatment of behaviorally disturbed adolescents. *Behavior Therapy, 10,* 227–235.

Solomon, E. (1977). *Structured learning therapy with abusive parents: Training in self-control.* Unpublished doctoral dissertation, Syracuse University, NY.

Spatz-Norton, C. (1985). *An evaluation of prosocial skill training plus aggression-control training with chronically aggressive children.* Unpublished doctoral dissertation, Syracuse University, NY.

Spence, A. J., & Spence, S. H. (1980). Cognitive changes associated with social skills training. *Behavioral Research and Therapy, 18,* 265–272.

Spence, S. H. (1981). Differences in social skills performance between institutionalized juvenile male offenders and a comparable group of boys without offence records. *British Journal of Clinical Psychology, 20,* 163–171.

Spence, S. H. (1982). Social skills with young offenders. In P. Feldman (Ed.), *Developments in the study of criminal behaviour* (Vol. 1). London: John Wiley & Sons.

Spence, S. H., & Marzillier, J. S. (1979). Social skills training with adolescent male offenders: I. Short-term effects. *Behaviour Research and Therapy, 17,* 7–16.

Spence, S. H., & Marzillier, J. S. (1981). Social skills training with adolescent male offenders—II: Short-term, long-term and generalized effects. *Behaviour Research and Therapy, 19,* 349–368.

Stanley, S. (1976). *A curriculum to affect the moral atmosphere of the family and the moral development of adolescents.* Unpublished doctoral dissertation, Boston University.

Stein, M., & Davis, J. K. (1982). *Therapies for adolescents: Current treatment for problem behaviors.* San Francisco: Jossey-Bass.

Stein, N., & Bogin, D. (1978). Individual child psychotherapy. In A. P. Goldstein (Ed.), *Prescriptions for child mental health and education.* Elmsford, NY: Pergamon.

Stephens, T. M. (1976). *Social skills in the classroom.* Columbus, OH: Cedars Press.

Strasburg, P. A. (1984). Recent national trends in serious juvenile crime. In R. A. Mathias, P. DeMuro, & R. S. Allensen (Eds.), *Violent juvenile offenders.* San Francisco: National Council on Crime and Delinquency.

Straughan, R. R. (1975). Hypothetical moral situations. *Journal of Moral Education, 4,* 183–189.

Stuart, R. B. (1967). Decentration in the development of children's concepts of moral and causal judgment. *The Journal of Genetic Psychology, 3,* 59–68.

Sturm, D. (1980). *Therapist aggression tolerance and dependence tolerance under standardized conditions of hostility and dependency.* Unpublished master's thesis, Syracuse University, NY.

Sullivan, E. V. (1980). Can values be taught? In M. Wendmiller, N. Lambert, & E. Turiel (Eds.), *Moral development and socialization.* Boston: Allyn & Bacon.

Sullivan, E. V., & Beck, C. (1975). Moral education in a Canadian setting. *Phi Delta Kappan, 56,* 697–701.

Sutton-Simon, K. (1973). *The effects of two types of modeling and rehearsal procedures upon the adequacy of social behavior of hospitalized schizophrenics.* Unpublished doctoral dissertation, Syracuse University, NY.

Swanstrom, C. R. (1974). *An examination of structured learning therapy and the helper therapy principle in teaching a self-control strategy in school children with conduct problems.* Unpublished doctoral dissertation, Syracuse University, NY.

Tharp, R. G., & Wetzel, R. J. (1969). *Behavior modification in the natural environment.* New York: Academic.

Thelen, M. H., Fry, R. A., Dollinger, S. J., & Paul, S. C. (1976). Use of videotaped models to improve the interpersonal adjustment of delinquents. *Journal of Consulting and Clinical Psychology, 44,* 492.

Thorndike, E. L., & Woodworth, R. S. (1901). The influence of improvement in one mental function upon the efficiency of other functions (I.). *Psychological Review, 8,* 247–261.

Tracy, J. J., & Cross, H. J. (1973). Antecedents of shift in moral judgment. *Journal of Personality and Social Psychology, 26,* 238–244.

Trevitt, V. (1964). *The American heritage: Design for national character.* Santa Barbara, CA: McNally & Loftin.

Trief, P. (1976). *The reduction of egocentrism in acting-out adolescents by structured learning therapy.* Unpublished doctoral dissertation, Syracuse University, NY.

Truax, C. B., Wargo, D. G., & Silber, L. D. (1966). Effects of group psychotherapy with high accurate empathy and nonpossessive warmth upon female institutionalized delinquents. *Journal of Abnormal Psychology, 71,* 267–274.

Turiel, E. (1966). An experimental test of the sequentiality of developmental stages in the child's moral judgments. *Journal of Personality and Social Psychology, 3,* 611–618.

Turiel, E. (1974). Conflict and transition in adolescent moral development. *Child Development, 45,* 14–29.

Turiel, E. (1980). The development of social-conventional and moral concepts. In M. Wendmiller, N. Lambert, & E. Turiel (Eds.), *Moral development and socialization.* Boston: Allyn & Bacon.

Turiel, E., Edwards, C. P., & Kohlberg, L. (1977). *Moral development in Turkish children, adolescents, and young adults.* Cambridge, MA: Center for Moral Development, Harvard University.

Turiel, E., & Rothman, G. R. (1972). The influence of reasoning on behavioral choices at different stages of moral development. *Child Development, 43,* 741–756.

Turk, D. (1976). *An expanded skills training approach for the treatment of experimentally induced pain.* Unpublished doctoral dissertation, University of Waterloo.

Ugurel-Semin, R. (1952). Moral behavior and moral judgment of children. *Journal of Abnormal and Social Psychology, 47,* 463–475.

Urbain, E. S., & Kendall, P. C. (1981). *Interpersonal problem-solving, social perspective-taking and behavioral contingencies: A comparison of group approaches with impulsive-aggressive children.* Unpublished manuscript, University of Minnesota, Minneapolis.

Vorrath, H., & Brendtro, L. K. (1974). *Positive peer culture.* Chicago: Aldine.

Vygotsky, L. S. (1962). *Thought and language.* Cambridge, MA: MIT Press.

Walker, H. M. (1979). *The acting-out child: Coping with classroom disruption.* Boston: Allyn & Bacon.

Walther, R. (1975). *The measurement of work relevant attitudes.* Manpower Research Projects, George Washington University, Washington, DC.

Waring, E. B. (1927). *The relation between early language habits and early habits of conduct control.* New York: Teachers College, Columbia University.

Warren, M. Q. (1974). *Classification for treatment.* Paper presented at the Seminar on the Classification of Criminal Behavior, National Institute of Law Enforcement and Criminal Justice.

Weinreich, R. J. (1975). *Inducing reflective thinking in impulsive, emotionally disturbed children.* Unpublished master's thesis, Virginia Commonwealth University, Richmond.

Werner, J. S., Minkin, N., Minkin, B. L., Fixsen, D. L., Phillips, E. L., & Wolf, M. M. (1975). Intervention package: An analysis to prepare juvenile delinquents for encounters with police officers. *Criminal Justice and Behavior, 2,* 55–84.

Whiteman, P. H., & Kosier, K. P. (1964). Development of children's moralistic judgments: Age, sex, IQ and certain personal-experiential variables. *Child Development, 35,* 843–850.

Williams, D. Y., & Akamatsu, T. J. (1978). Cognitive self-guidance training with juvenile delinquents: Applicability and generalization. *Cognitive Therapy and Research, 2,* 285–288.

Williams, J. R., & Gold, M. (1972). From delinquent behavior to official delinquency. *Social Problems, 20,* 209–229.

Wilson, J. (1973). *The assessment of morality.* Windsor, England: National Foundation of Educational Research.

Woodcock, R. W. (1978). *Development and standardization of the Woodcock-Johnson Psychoeducational Battery.* Boston: Teaching Resources Corporation.

Wright, W. E., & Dixon, M. C. (1977). Community prevention and treatment of juvenile delinquency: A review of evaluation studies. *Journal of Research in Crime and Delinquency, 14,* 35–67.

Zimmerman, D. (1983). Moral education. In Center for Research on Aggression (Ed.), *Prevention and control of aggression.* Elmsford, NY: Pergamon.

Zimmerman, D. (1986). *The enhancement of perspective-taking and moral reasoning via structured learning therapy and moral education.* Unpublished doctoral dissertation, Syracuse University, NY.

Index

About the Authors

Arnold P. Goldstein, Ph.D. (Pennsylvania State University, 1959), joined the clinical psychology section of Syracuse University's Psychology Department in 1963 and both taught there and directed its Psychotherapy Center until 1980. In 1981, he founded the Center for Research on Aggression, which he currently directs. He joined Syracuse University's Division of Special Education in 1985. Professor Goldstein has a career-long interest, as both researcher and practitioner, in difficult-to-reach clients. Since 1980, his main research and psychoeducational focus has been incarcerated juvenile offenders and child-abusing parents. He is the developer of Structured Learning, a psychoeducational program and curriculum designed to teach prosocial behaviors to chronically antisocial persons. Professor Goldstein's books include *Structured Learning Therapy: Toward a Psychotherapy for the Poor, Skill Training for Community Living, Skillstreaming the Adolescent, School Violence, Aggress-Less, Police Crisis Intervention, Hostage, Prevention and Control of Aggression, Aggression in Global Perspective, In Response to Aggression,* and *Youth Violence.*

Barry Glick received his Ph.D. from Syracuse University in 1972. Trained as a counseling psychologist, Dr. Glick has devoted his professional career to the development of policies, programs, and services for adolescents. His specialization is in juvenile delinquency as well as the emotionally disturbed adolescent. Dr. Glick has worked both in private child care agencies and in state government. He has held positions as a child care worker, a psychologist, an administrator, and a manager. He currently is Associate Deputy Director for Local Services, New York State Division for Youth. Dr. Glick is certified by the National Board of Certified Counselors and holds membership in a number of professional organizations.

Scott Reiner is a graduate student in clinical psychology with an M.A. from Syracuse University (1985).

Deborah Zimmerman is a graduate student in clinical psychology with an M.A. from Syracuse University (1986).

Thomas M. Coultry, MSW (Syracuse University, 1975), is trained as both an elementary school teacher and a social worker. Mr. Coultry has held a series of teaching and counseling positions working with incarcerated, delinquent youth. He is currently Facility Director, Annsville Youth Center, New York State Division for Youth.